The European Metropolis
Paris and Nineteenth-Century Irish Women Novelists

MATTHEW L. REZNICEK

The European Metropolis
Paris and Nineteenth-Century Irish Women Novelists

MATTHEW L.
REZNICEK

© 2019 Clemson University
All rights reserved

First Hardcover Edition, 2017

ISBN: 978-1-949979-20-6 (paperback)

Published by Clemson University Press
in association with Liverpool University Press

Chapter One is based on an essay published in
New Critical Perspectives on Franco-Irish Relations,
edited by Anne Goarzin (New York: Peter Lang, 2015).

For information about Clemson University Press,
please visit our website at www.clemson.edu/press.

Typeset in Minion Pro by Carnegie Book Production.

Contents

Acknowledgments	vii
Parvenir: An Introduction	1
The Novice in the City: Sydney Owenson and the *Bildung* of Metropolitan Economics	25
Much More than Only *Le Bel Irlandois*: Metropolitan Socioeconomics and Parisian *Bildung* in Maria Edgeworth's *Ormond*	63
The New Jerusalem and the Rue Vavin: Urban Space, Economic Exchange, and Gendered Modernity in *French Leave*	103
First Life—and then Fame: Gendered *Fin-de-Siècle* Cityscapes in *Max*	139
A City She Must Postpone: A Conclusion	181
Notes	189
Works Cited	211
Index	221

Acknowledgments

This book and my gratitude belong to many people in many different places. The book began as a PhD thesis at the Queen's University Belfast under the supervision of Sinéad Sturgeon and Eamonn Hughes. I owe them a great deal for their support throughout the many stages involved in developing this argument. I am grateful for Sinéad's constant support, her critical evaluations of each chapter, and her encouragement to remember the big picture and to realize the significance whenever I got lost along the way. I could not have found a more patient, more engaged, more reassuring supervisor than Sinéad. Eamonn's wisdom is renowned throughout the global Irish Studies community; his seemingly inexhaustible bibliography provided countless new paths of inquiry, new connections between Irish literature and its European counterparts. In addition to Eamonn and Sinéad, I would like to thank many other colleagues from Queen's, including Philip McGowan, Catherine Gander, Adrian Streete, and Ed Larrissy for their friendship and guidance.

Two key voices in shaping this project were Moyra Haslett from Queen's and Claire Connolly from University College, Cork. Their critical, probing, and exhaustive examination of this material demonstrated the way forward from a thesis to a book. Ever since their readings, I have returned to them for guidance on structural, thematic, and theoretical issues. They have been gracious and patient guides. This work stands in their shadows because they have been inexhaustible advocates for the recovery, study, and inclusion of Irish women's literature in the dominant conversation regarding Irish literature.

For their support, their critical readings, and their encouragement I owe a great deal of thanks to Moynagh Sullivan, Ellen McWilliams, Susan Cahill, Sonja Lawrenson, Ellen Scheible, Anna Teekell, Derek Gladwin, Jennifer Orr, Daniel Cook, Sean Farrell, Tim McMahon, Kathleen Costello-Sullivan, Clíona Ó Gallchoir, Eamon Maher, Tina Moran, Margaret Kelleher, Anna Pilz, Katie Conrad, and countless others. From conversations in pubs to questions on panels, to email exchanges, to serious and not-so-serious proposals of scholarly projects, you have all helped to shape this book. I hope I have done justice to your influence.

Creighton University has kindly supported this research through grants, guidance, good will, and great colleagues. Specifically, I would like to thank the Graduate School and the College of Arts and Science for their financial support. Bridget Keegan's wisdom and willingness to help understand readers' comments was invaluable. In the final stages of this book, I could not have relied on greater colleagues than Lydia Cooper, Faith Kurtyka, Surbhi Malik, and Tierney S. Powell. Your friendship, your copyediting, and your enthusiasm have made this book a reality. I cannot repay you.

Lastly, this book belongs to the many families that have shaped it. To Cat, Paul, Adam, Emily, Claire, Ríonnagh, Méabh, Megan, you all were born to run. To John, Kelly, Michael, Matt, Anne, Paul, Stephanie, Susan, John, Sheila, and John, you have been there from the beginning. To Megan and Emily, you two continue to challenge me every day. Anna, you make every adventure worth it. Finally, to my parents, Joe and Lynn, thank you for reading to me, for taking me to amazing places, and for encouraging me to pursue this dream.

"Old Paris is no more (the form of a city
Changes more quickly, alas! than the human heart)"

—Charles Baudelaire, "Le Cygne"

Parvenir: An Introduction

As the body of Jean-Joachim Goriot, better known as Old Goriot, is lowered to its resting place in Père Lachaise in the twentieth *arrondissement* of Paris, Eugène Rastignac stares despondently into the grave. Instead of attending their father's funeral, Goriot's daughters send two empty carriages and, when the gravediggers demand their tip, Rastignac must borrow five francs to oblige them. These final moments of indifference overwhelm Balzac's protagonist as "a wave of desperate depression" sweeps over him.¹ Then, defiantly, he climbs "to the higher part of the cemetery, and [sees] Paris spread out along the winding banks of the Seine" and here he declares war between himself and the city; eying "almost hungrily" that area "between the column in the place Vendôme and the dome of the Invalides, home to that fashionable society to which he had sought to gain admission," he declares "the epic challenge: 'It's between the two of us now.'"² This proclamation of war between Rastignac and the French capital sets the stage for a great deal of nineteenth-century writing about Paris; it highlights the city's indifference to the individual, the role of economics in determining one's position within the city, and, ultimately, the frustrating attempts to achieve and to articulate a specific sense of selfhood in the urban landscape of the French capital of the nineteenth century.

Balzac's *Père Goriot*, along with the rest of his *Comédie humaine*, demonstrates the centrality of Paris to nineteenth-century literature and presages the French capital's centrality in the development of urban studies. To say that the nineteenth-century novel could not exist without Paris is not hyperbole. From the dawn of the nineteenth century and Burke's *Reflections on the Revolution in France*, in which Paris occupies center stage, to mid-century and Balzac's attempts to place "modernity under the microscope" in the *Comédie humaine*, the influence of Paris is omnipresent in the literature of the long nineteenth century, whether that literature is celebrating or castigating the city. The French capital created the protagonist who would dominate the nineteenth-century novel.[3] Scholars like Walter Benjamin, David Harvey, and Franco Moretti all recognize Paris as "the capital of modernity" and the "capital of the nineteenth century,"[4] rejecting the centrality of London, in Moretti's words, "the 'workshop of the world', and of the Empire."[5] Moretti contends that without Paris, and especially the Latin Quarter,

> we wouldn't have the wonder of the French *Bildungsroman*, nor that image of youth—hungry, dreamy, ambitious—that has been its greatest invention. Think of the rival traditions, in Germany, Britain, Russia: all great literatures, without question; but they all lack a symbolic equivalent of the *rive gauche*—and so, they fall short of the intensity of Paris. Think of Pip's London, or David Copperfield's, or Pendennis': all of them caught in the gray universe of Inns of Court, so that the city can never become an object of desire. He who does not know the left bank of the Seine between the rue Saint-Jacques and the rue des Saints-Pères doesn't know life, says Balzac in *Old Goriot*, and he is right.[6]

For Moretti, as for others, the nineteenth-century literary canon depends entirely upon the centrality of Paris precisely because it creates the nineteenth-century individual through the complex relationships of metropolis, capitalism, and *Bildung*, the "process of becoming," as Bakhtin describes it.[7] One need hardly think of the characters who live, or who yearn to live, in Paris to recognize the impact the French capital has imposed upon other national literatures. Perhaps most famously, Stephen Dedalus, in Joyce's *Portrait of the Artist as a Young Man* (1916), declares his intention to go to Paris to complete his self-actualization as an artist, suggesting that the formation of an individuated selfhood is not only unachievable in Ireland, but that it is most achievable only in the capital of the nineteenth century. *The European Metropolis* builds upon Moretti's important work that recognizes the role of capitalism and Paris in the creation of selfhood, but extends his arguments in two directions by looking at novels written by women and by looking exclusively at Irish-authored novels. By foregrounding Irish women novelists' use of Paris, this study argues that the persistent ambivalence toward the metropolitan landscape stems from the tension between the overdetermined spaces that Irish women's literature has traditionally occupied, on the one hand, and, on the other, the commodifying tendency of the modern metropolis.

Though Paris is already seen as central to the nineteenth-century novel, *The European Metropolis* breaks new ground because this centrality has not yet been extended to the study of Irish literature. In Irish literature, as Fintan O'Toole has argued, there persists an internal "dominance of the rural over the urban, a dominance based on a false opposition of the country to the city."[8] Against the foreign "territory of modernity," as Seamus Deane describes France, Irish literature has established "the territory of tradition," a landscape that O'Toole characterizes as depending upon "the sacredness of the land, a mystical sense of place [...] postulating an immanent and 'natural' link between the peasantry and the land."[9] This combination of an anti-urban, anti-modern definition of Irish literature in opposition to English literature, on the one hand, and an Irish identity based solely on territorial and geographic traits, on the other, necessarily limits the engagement of Irish literature beyond its own borders; it establishes clear distinctions between what constitutes Irish literature and what does not.

While O'Toole's argument focuses largely on the literature of the Irish Literary Revival, the tropes of elegiac rurality dominated Irish literature long before the Abbey. Beginning with Maria Edgeworth's *Castle Rackrent, An Hibernian Tale: Taken from Facts and from the Manners of the Irish Squires, before the Year 1782* (1800), Claire Norris has argued that what makes "Irish fiction stand out as being 'Irish'" is the role of place, claiming that Irish literary tradition "is still 'different' because of place and space."[10] These spaces and places are routinely identified as rural because they are Irish and Irish because they are rural, separate from a metropolitan modernity associated with a foreign elsewhere. This has constructed a largely anti-modern identity for and understanding of Irish literature.

Indeed, as Seamus Deane has noted, the focus on the land in Irish history and in Irish studies has led to the formation of "a characteristically 'romantic' culture," in contradistinction to the "increasingly […] urban, 'mechanical,' or utilitarian, culture" of England.[11] This dominant characteristic of Irish literature stems, according to Julia Wright, from "Herderian or romantic nationalism" and ties the people of Ireland to the land in "organic" terms that are "rooted in the hills, rivers, and fields of the homeland."[12] Daniel Corkery, one of the foremost critics in the early years of an independent Ireland, celebrated the fact that "[m]uch of the literature produced in Ireland of late years has been about the peasant […] for we are in the main a nation of peasants."[13] For Corkery, the emphasis on a peasant-based literature extends from a distinction between Irish literature, which is "the literature written in the Irish language and that alone," on the one hand, and, on the other, Anglo-Irish literature, which is "literature written in English by Irishmen."[14] This latter does not constitute a "national literature" in part because it largely "cannot be distinguished from those of contemporary English literature," and, when it can, "we may speak of [it] as Colonial moulds."[15] Into this colonial tradition, Corkery places several of the writers discussed within this book, including Edgeworth and Somerville and Ross, associating them only with the Big House tradition. This early attempt to distinguish between Irish and

Anglo-Irish literature reflects what Deane has described as a "carefully constructed 'Other,'" a sociopolitical and cultural project that left Ireland "embalmed in the premodern formaldehyde of endearing backwardness."[16] The distinction between a backward and nostalgic Ireland and a modern England, based on ideas of Irish space and place, has dominated the definition of Irish texts. This has left little room for novels that take place on the Continent, beyond the colonial and imperial framework of London and the exilic framework of America and Australia. Ultimately, the general introduction to *The Field Day Anthology* (1991), a seminal collection on the history of Irish writing, sets out to "re-present a series of representations concerning the island of Ireland—its history, geography, political experience, social forms and economy—over a period of 1,500 years"—the "island of Ireland," but nowhere else, as though Irish literature only occurs in one space and one place.[17]

The rejection of elsewhere, while framed in terms of a rejection of English traits, ultimately stems, as Seamus Deane makes plain, from an early nineteenth-century rejection of the space of France and the place of Paris. France, at the beginning of the nineteenth century, becomes at once the embodiment *par excellence* of modernity and, as a result, foreignness in Irish literature.[18] For Deane, France occupies the vanguard of modernity in Irish literature thanks to the central position he grants to Edmund Burke's *Reflections on the Revolution in France* (1790). In its revolution, France "had destroyed all the foundations of traditional civilization and had gone so far as to produce an alteration in human nature itself [...] it had raised theory to an unprecedented position of power in European politics and social thought."[19] Underlying Burke's and Deane's response to France in the nineteenth century is an anxiety regarding the modernity that the French Revolution was perceived to have instantiated: a modernity that is characteristically described in the socioeconomic terms of capitalism in which traditional images and emblems lose their "fixed value" and, as a result, become "vulnerable to risk."[20] This fear that results from the modern act of speculation brings to the fore the central concerns that dominate the representations of Paris throughout this study: the ability or inability to read and evaluate the cityscape, the inability to maintain or understand values within a system of metropolitan exchange, and, most importantly, the fear of the loss of a fixed sense of self in a metropolitan and capitalist environment wherein everything is negotiable and commodified. All of these anxieties can be reduced to an anxiety over the inability to read the cityscape.

The anxiety that results from being incapable of reading the cityscape properly demands a redefinition of terms, or at least a shift in the focus of the dominant terminology used in studies that focus on urban literature. Texts like Kevin Lynch's *The Image of the City* (1960) and de Certeau's *The Practice of Everyday Life* (1984) focus on the concept of urban legibility, the ability of the city to be read. But I want to distinguish the term "urban literacy" from the term "urban legibility," which is more widely used in architectural and urban studies. The problem with the concept of "urban legibility" is that its focus is on the cityscape itself, rather than on the individual's ability to read that urban space. Prendergast explains that, thanks to "endless reports and proliferating nomenclatures of the urban bureaucracies [...], not to mention the cataloguing descriptions and ordering plots of the novelists," nineteenth-century thought understood that the "city is there to be 'read', often in the form of reading essences, fixed identities."[21] And yet, an equally popular and contradictory view of the city persisted throughout the nineteenth century, one that claimed "that the city is unmappable, defies understanding [...] the city is too complex to be understood or known."[22] The city as text, either legible or illegible, fundamentally misses the degree to which certain populations—police and criminals in Balzac, or bankers and capitalists in Zola—were able to read the city, while other populations were unable to decipher the urban text.

Of course, urban critics like Moretti, Deane, Prendergast, Benjamin, and Georg Simmel, all focus primarily, if not exclusively, on texts written by and about men; they all privilege male urban citizens over and above their female counterparts because they presume that, in the words of Baudelaire, the perfect metropolitan citizen is a "prince who everywhere rejoices in his incognito."[23] The ideal citizen of the modern metropolis is almost always figured as a man because of the insistence upon access to public space and participation within the marketplace, both of which, and the threat of the crowd, are anathema to the dominant construction of femininity in the nineteenth century. As such, this study's focus on women writers reveals the experience of modernity to be an unequal relationship between women and the urban sphere and, as a result, offers a much-needed corrective to both Irish literary studies and urban studies. The argument that this book makes is twofold: Paris functions in nineteenth-century Irish women's novels as a central site for debates and anxieties over the emergence of a capitalist modernity; additionally, these women's novels ultimately reveal the continued experience of inequality on which this capitalist modernity depends. These two arguments, of course, are naturally bound up with the types of concerns that characterize Rastignac's final confrontation with Paris in *Père Goriot*: the struggle of navigating the city; the struggle with metropolitan economics; and the struggle of the articulation of selfhood. Each of these struggles highlights a significant element of the experience of the modern metropolis, but, taken collectively, they point toward the difficult tension of socialization-formation and self-articulation in the urban cityscape. Thus, the best way to understand this nexus of concerns and anxieties is through the framework of the urban economic *Bildungsroman*.

Traditional definitions of the *Bildungsroman* characterize the *Bildung* process as one that "is spiritual rather than professional," achieving a selfhood oriented toward "the making of a gentleman."[24] For a study that focuses on Irish women writers' economic *Bildungsromane* that are themselves broadly concerned with the development of female characters' selfhood, it is important to recognize that the very concept of a female *Bildungsroman* is complicated and often contested. Susan Fraiman claims that a heroine's "progress toward masterful selfhood is by no means assured, even in apparently comic texts," in part, at least, because the "apprentice for womanhood" is consistently "divided among several routes, so that she lives her gender as a continuous movement in contradictory directions."[25] Similarly, Annis Pratt has argued that a woman-centered form of *Bildung* is an oxymoron, based on "a choice between auxiliary or secondary personhood, sacrificial victimization, madness, or death."[26] As these critics suggest, the very concept of development is defined "in emphatically masculine terms—for the contemporaneous heroine's relation to choice, mentors, and mastery is rather different."[27] This difference lies in the shifting recognition of "compromise and even coercion [being] more strongly thematized than choice."[28] Fraiman's argument regarding the lack of choice[29] available to women in the *Bildungsroman* tradition becomes more complicated over the long course of the nineteenth century, finding common ground with both William Gallois's and Moretti's claims regarding the socialization-formation process. Gallois, writing about capitalism in Zola's *Rougon-Macquart* cycle, asserts that "modernity is a place of increased choices, but that there are important qualitative differences between the kinds of choices one can make which are connected to one's relations to institutional and financial power."[30] In Zola more than in Balzac, women emerge as metropolitan practitioners, able to command and navigate the socioeconomic landscape of the marketplace.[31] But women's position within modern capitalism remains problematic.

Women's relationship to *Bildung*, contested as it is, would seem to become even more debatable as soon as it is bound up within the masculine sphere of the capitalist marketplace. The relationship between women and an economic process of *Bildung* is contestable not because women were barred from an economic role; as Edward Copeland has demonstrated, women's fiction from as early as 1790 is obsessively concerned with money. The end of the eighteenth century saw women enjoying "significant, if limited, economic responsibility."[32] But a woman engaged in economic exchange, especially any form that involved lending or speculating, invariably threatened notions of femininity since "the only 'real' property she had to risk was her body."[33] While men, including Edgeworth's M. de Connal and Sir Ulick

O'Shane in *Ormond* (1817), had recourse to duels to resolve crises of debt, women who were seriously in debt "became nonpersons, exiled to the continent, or, that worst of penalties for a woman of the town, rusticated."[34] Beginning in the early years of the nineteenth century, women's fiction slowly abandons "its narrative of economic victimization to embrace a narrative of economic empowerment."[35] Yet, despite Copeland's claims of increased autonomy and economic activity, their position within the economy remains problematic and dependent upon those relations that govern Gallois's reading of Zola's modernity. A woman's economic security and identity remain almost exclusively bound to her relationship to the heteronormative structures of marriage. Timothy Foley characterizes the whole nineteenth-century debate about women's economic roles as "fraught with contradictions," since the progressive case "was made in terms of what was increasingly seen as the reactionary doctrine of *laissez-faire*, a policy seen to militate structurally against the interests of the lower classes, including, of course, the women members of those classes."[36] These concerns present a fractured form of identity politics, complicated by class status, marital status, and religion. Rather than negating the viability of an economic *Bildungsroman* for women, the problematic relationship between women and the modern marketplace points toward the increasing difficulties of the socialization-formation process.

Instead of viewing the *Bildungsroman* in the binary terms of a male and, arguably an unsuccessful, female tradition, re-examining the genre through the lens of economics recognizes the intersection of social, economic, cultural, and institutional pressures on the process of becoming for both men and women in the metropolis. As Fraiman's critique of the *Bildungsroman* tradition suggests, however, compromise and coercion threaten the fundamental process of *Bildung*, obscuring the freedom of choice that Goethe's framework works so hard to maintain. This creates what Moretti has identified as "the crisis of the European *Bildungsroman*."[37] The economic *Bildungsroman* throws into relief the power relations that undergird the capitalist marketplace and social relationships within the metropolis. In the words of Simmel, this construction of the *Bildungsroman* interrogates "the deepest problems of modern life [which] flow from the attempt of the individual to maintain the independence and individuality of his existence against the sovereign powers of society."[38] Even though Simmel, like Moretti, remains exclusively focused on male subjects within the metropolis, the economic *Bildungsroman* enables an analysis of the tradition in terms of class, nationality, and gender. These diverse routes are aspects in the broader socialization-formation process under the system of modern capitalism, providing the means for a more inclusive version of Moretti's history of the European *Bildungsroman*. A novel that focuses on the ways in which an individual struggles with these pressures to achieve individuality within the metropolitan marketplace provides evidence for an examination of the process of a modern and economic *Bildung*. Because of its concentration of individuals and its economic system, the metropolis and its crowds threaten the necessarily fixed narrative sociology of the classical *Bildungsroman*. Such a framework enables a sustained discussion of an Irish women's economic *Bildungsroman* tradition that opens debates regarding the status of Irish men and women in the metropolitan landscape of a foreign and modern capital city.

The *Bildungsroman*, whether male- or female-focused, does not produce an isolated individual, completely severed from society. Bakhtin's narrative of the *"man in the process of becoming"* elides two significant questions that are fundamental to novels by Irish women set in the city.[39] First, there is the question of what does the *Bildungsheld*, the protagonist of the *Bildungsroman*, become? Second, what are the cultural, economic, political, social, and personal forces that shape the protagonist of the *Bildungsroman* to become whatever it is that she becomes? The classical *Bildungsroman* is premised upon the peaceful integration of the individual into society, convincing the *Bildungsheld* to curb her "tendency towards *individuality*" and adopt instead "the opposing tendency to *normality*."[40] This process of socialization-formation occurs, at least in the Goethean form of the *Bildungsroman*, when the individual "agree[s] to be determined from without."[41] The classical *Bildungsroman* achieves the balance of maturity by means of a symbiotic relationship between the *Bildungsheld* and the socializing institutions. In the final stages of *Wilhelm Meister*, Wilhelm is made aware of the machinations of the Society of the Tower, a secretive group of individuals who "have been taking a guiding interest in Wilhelm's educative experiences," demonstrating the "machinery [...] seeking to give him guidance."[42] Wilhelm acquires maturity and legitimation when he submits to the "plot patiently weaved 'around [him]' by the Society of the Tower."[43] The same society has "the right to devise and weave plots only in order to satisfy their novice."[44] This perfect harmony between governing institutions and governed individuals overlays an extremely organized and hierarchical society in which individuals have and also accept recognizable, fixed social positions into which they neatly and calmly fit. That the protagonists of these *Bildungsromane*, male and female, ultimately end in marriage demonstrates a gendered politics: the male *Bildungshelden* are able to become many things, but the female protagonists look forward only to becoming the wife in this perfect harmony.

Echoing the clear deference to social authority prevalent in the *ancien régime*, these fixed social positions depend upon "closed social forms," which are available only in "those ideal places—the holdings of the Tower, the Pemberley estate of *Pride and Prejudice*—where everything is 'well-being, transparency, and concreteness.'"[45] Goethe's Tower and Austen's Pemberley bolster, and remain dependent upon, the dominant system of social hierarchy, providing a remarkably limited and overdetermined array of existential opportunities. Insisting upon fixed social positions and forms, they function in order to suppress the threat of rebellion against the established social system, usually by fixing women in marriage. While Simmel never specifically addresses women, he presents another way of understanding this process of socialization-formation that again presumes masculinity. Simmel explains that "the smaller the circle which forms our environment and the more limited the relationships which have the possibility of transcending the boundaries, the more anxiously the community watches over the deeds, the conduct of life and the attitudes of the individual."[46] This recognizes an *inverse* relationship between the freedom of the individual and the size of the community because the smaller community is more easily policed and dependent upon, in Moretti's words, "the definitive stabilization of the individual."[47]

Both Simmel and Moretti contrast the rural and smaller world of Pemberley and the Society of the Tower with the European metropolis. The citizen of the metropolis is "free," writes Simmel, "in contrast with the trivialities and prejudices which bind the small town person" because of two fundamental characteristics of the modern cityscape: first, "[i]n the measure that the group grows numerically, spatially, [...] its immediate inner unity and the definiteness of its original demarcation against others are weakened"; second, the individual "gains a freedom of movement" and also "a peculiarity and individuality to which the division of labor in groups, which have become larger, gives both occasion and necessity."[48] This tension between the world of the capitalist metropolis and the world of the classical *Bildungsroman* provides the governing framework for the narrative of *Bildung* written in the early years of Ernest Mandel's first long wave of capitalism, which he identifies as "the long period from the end of the 18th century up to the crisis of 1847."[49] Unlike Balzac's metropolitan and fashionable construction of the *Bildungsroman*, money and the capitalist individual "cannot generate *Bildung*" in Goethe's formulation of the genre.[50] This inability to spur an individual toward maturity occurs because the "purely quantitative nature [of money], and the competition it is subject to" means "[i]t must grow, and change form, and *never stop*: as Adam Smith observed in *The Wealth of Nations*, the merchant is a citizen of no country in particular."[51] The social forms that capitalism brings to the metropolis diametrically oppose the fixity that is the hallmark of Goethean *Bildung*.

When the *Bildungsroman* is relocated to the metropolitan Paris of Balzac, Zola, Owenson, Edgeworth, Somerville and Ross, and Thurston, new anxieties and thematic stresses emerge. This means that the influence of metropolitan capitalism and fashion challenges, and ultimately entirely replaces, the influence of Goethe's strong socializing institutions. This shift is part of a broader sea change associated with the nineteenth century. In the eighteenth century, man "may have called for liberation [...] in order to permit the original natural virtue of man, which is equal in everyone, to develop without inhibition," but, in the nineteenth century, the demand became "to promote, in addition to man's freedom, his individuality (which is connected with the division of labor) and his achievements which make him unique and indispensable."[52] The connection Simmel makes between the rise of individuality and the expansion of the division of labor located within the rapidly expanding capitalist metropolis explains the threat which this socioeconomic system poses to the earlier *Bildungsroman*. In his Goethean form, the *Bildungsheld* achieves that social integration precisely because he possesses "a *pliant* character [...] the well-cut prism in which the countless nuances of the social context blend together in a harmonious 'personality.'"[53] To borrow from Edgeworth's *Ormond*, the Goethean *Bildungsheld* "is [...] what you call [a] cipher, but has no value in société at all" until the socializing institution declares his value and he takes his place within the preordained order at the end of his apprenticeship.[54] As Jarno, the head of the Society of the Tower, explains to Wilhelm, the role of the society is not to "guard from error [...] but to lead the erring pupil; nay, to let him quaff his error in deep satiating drafts."[55] It is society that determines both the worth and the worthiness of an individual, a concept that commodity capitalism will alter as it is integrated into its narrative of fashionable *Bildung*. But, with the collapse of the structures of the *ancien régime*, new forces of socialization emerge and, as a result, the *Bildungsroman* requires a new narrative of socialization.[56]

As with Simmel's philosophy of metropolitan selfhood, Moretti's understanding of the European *Bildungsroman* is intimately tied to the long waves of capitalism. Both produce a framework for the consideration of the tradition of an economic *Bildungsroman*. The radical political and socioeconomic changes of the years following the French Revolution and leading to the Congress of Vienna demand a new narrative of socialization that has decidedly moved from the "little world" to the "great world."⁵⁷ The great world is depicted most specifically in Paris, a site that, David Harvey argues, contains in embryo "the social forces omnipresent within the womb of bourgeois society."⁵⁸ This geographic relocation entails a narratological and existential reconfiguration. If it does not yet entirely shape the interiority of the protagonist, the metropolis clearly informs the new *Bildungsheld*. As the *Bildungsroman* begins to adapt to the capitalist landscape of the city, the ability to achieve a fixed sense of self begins to fracture and disappear. Instead, the narrative of becoming in the metropolis reflects the fact that the city is the modern embodiment of alienation:

> [The city] is supplied almost exclusively by production for the market, that is, for entirely unknown purchasers who never appear in the actual field of vision of the producers themselves. Thereby, the interests of each party acquire a relentless matter-of-factness, and its rationally calculated economic egoism need not fear any divergence from its set path because of the imponderability of personal relationships. That is all the more the case in the money economy which dominates the metropolis in which the last remnants of domestic production and direct barter of goods have been eradicated and in which the amount of production on direct personal order is reduced daily.⁵⁹

In a personal application of the most basic Marxist terms, the division of labor drives the weakening of personal bonds, according to Simmel, so that the metropolitan individual is no longer subject to the policing of strong social institutions like the Society of the Tower, nor is he subject to the limited outcomes available in the world of "closed social forms."

In the metropolitan *Bildungsroman*, growth has become instead a function of the socioeconomic principles of the capitalist marketplace; the diversification that results from the division of labor leads, ultimately, to a breakdown of fixed social forms. The new Society of the Tower is the fashionable metropolitan crowd. It is "society" itself that "scrutinizes," "discusses," and determines the new protagonist.[60] Under this new regime, the measure of success is not his ability to achieve a fixed and stable definition, but the protagonist's ability to become and to remain fashionable. If, as Baudelaire claims, modernity itself is "the ephemeral, the fugitive, the contingent," the Balzacian *Bildungsroman*, and its incorporation of fashion and capitalism, demands and proffers a necessarily ephemeral and contingent selfhood.[61] According to both Moretti and Harvey, Balzac's sprawling *Comédie humaine* provides the new literary paradigm for a capitalist *Bildungsroman*. Central to the socialization-formation process of Sydney Owenson's *The Novice of Saint Dominick* (1806), Maria Edgeworth's *Ormond* (1817), Edith Somerville and Martin Ross's *French Leave* (1929), and Katherine Cecil Thurston's *Max* (1910), a fashionable and modern selfhood is premised upon the belief that it "will vanish as rapidly as it came."[62] Even though it is fleeting and meteoric, its role is "not to change existing taste, but to satisfy and confirm it."[63] In this way, successful *Bildung* confirms rather than threatens or overturns the dominant sociocultural system. The novels that make up *The European Metropolis* recognize the fact that, in the modern metropolis, it is the crowd that has taken the position of the Society of the Tower as the socializing institution. In the realm of fashion, the urban individual is "determined by a 'collective other,' by a group of people whose behavior and appearance determine his own."[64] The combination of metropolitan fashion and the urban phenomenon of the crowd seeks to determine the *Bildungsheld* "from without" as the Society of the Tower did previously. Where the Goethean or Edgeworthian model of *Bildung* insisted upon the lifelong integration of the individual into the social network, this fashionable process of becoming is as fickle as the fashionable trends governing it.

Recent critical attention to the material manifestation of the economy and money contributes to the exploration of the relationship between the money form, the commodity, and the formation of selfhood in these novels. Alongside the emerging critical awareness of the physical forms of the economy, this book attempts to build upon recent work that has taken place in eighteenth- and nineteenth-century English literature. Matthew Rowlinson's *Real Money and Romanticism* (2010), Mary Poovey's *Genres of the Credit Economy* (2008), Gail Turley Houston's *From Dickens to Dracula: Gothic, Economics, and Victorian Fiction* (2007), Eleanor Courtemanche's *The Invisible Hand and British Fiction, 1818–1860* (2011), and Deborah Valenze's *The Social Life of Money in the English Past* (2006) all ground critical discussions of money in literature with a useful focus on the changing physical manifestation of the money form. Such attention to the physical form that money takes in literature enables a more thorough discussion of commodification, the exchange process, and speculation as capitalist practices become more complex and more abstracting. This book explores these economic processes in an Irish literary context, while also recognizing the impact they have upon the increasingly commodified selfhood of the protagonists within Irish women's writing

The formation of selfhood in the metropolitan and fashionable *Bildungsroman* assumes the socioeconomic characteristics of the fashionable commodity and is subject to the same pressures of taste, evaluation, and exchange. Individually and collectively, these novels interrogate the commodity-influenced *Bildung* in terms that express an anxiety about the socioeconomic landscape of the metropolitan marketplace. Moretti's earlier claim about the need of capital to "grow, and change form, and *never stop*" provides a useful lens through which these novels appear to understand the development of selfhood within the metropolis.[65] In Edgeworth's *Ormond*, this sort of hyperbolic activity embodies the concept of metropolitan identity. At his first dinner in the Black Islands, the cipher-like M. de Connal dominates the conversation, talking incessantly "of battles, of princes, plays, operas, wine, women, cardinals, religion, politics, poetry, and turkeys stuffed with truffles—and Paris for ever!—Dash on! at everything."[66] The tempo of Connal's speech, as well as its celebration of the ephemeral, designates him almost immediately as the herald of a modern and metropolitan selfhood.[67] As the second chapter will demonstrate,

Connal's intention mirrors the process of commodification and, more specifically, the increasing abstraction of the commodity form that occurs through the process of speculation. The commodity form, Marx writes, has "absolutely no connection with the physical nature of the commodity and the material [*dinglich*] relations arising out of this. It is nothing but the definite social relation between men themselves."[68] Marx's explanation of the commodity form provides a key insight into the successful achievement of metropolitan *Bildung*, especially as seen in the person of Connal. The metropolitan *Bildungsheld* depends upon the outward determination of the crowd and subsequently experiences a process of abstraction similar to that of Marx's commodity.

This process of abstraction produces one of the key anxieties that underlies this study. The character of the metropolitan individual, like the fashionable commodity, depends entirely upon the exchange process for the realization of its value. Modern capitalism and its alienating process of becoming creates unequal pressures for men and for women, which, in part, is a function of the unequal expectation of and access to capital that Sydney Owenson's *The Novice of Saint Dominick* (1806), Maria Edgeworth's *Ormond* (1817), Edith Somerville and Martin Ross's *French Leave* (1929), and Katherine Cecil Thurston's *Max* (1910) will all demonstrate. For Thurston, the uneven development of capitalism results in the need for a division of selfhood: a masculine figure who engages the modern metropolis and a feminine self who remains safely ensconced within the domestic sphere. For Edgeworth and Thurston, this increased abstraction of selfhood produces a crisis that replicates the increasingly abstracting process of the speculative exchange. For the novels in this study, commodification creates an even more tenuous link to the fixed forms of selfhood that characterized maturity in earlier formulations of the genre. Within the capitalist landscape of the metropolis, the *Bildungsheld* struggles to achieve and to maintain a concrete sense of self. No longer is the individual measured against even a seemingly, and apparently always fleetingly, fixed commodity; his selfhood now appears to depend simply upon the empty signifier of money.

Irish women's novels set in Paris register this socioeconomic shift at a textual level in two manners: first, through the increasing prominence of social mobility; and, second, through a gradual emergence of money as a governing principle for the process of *Bildung*, a new sort of "social bond" across the long waves of Irish women's literature.[69] Social mobility is intimately related to the fashionable, or Balzacian, *Bildungsroman*. Just like the money form and the commodity, fashionable society is consumed by social mobility because of "its boundlessness [...] the possibility to become 'anything.'"[70] Social mobility enchants metropolitan society and the metropolitan *Bildungsroman* because it "enables people to *conceive*" new material and existential desires, which expand exponentially as commodities flood the marketplace.[71] Social mobility provides the individual with the illusion that he can divorce himself from his material essence and become anything, since money seemingly makes anything available. The parallels to Edgeworth's Monsieur de Connal are striking, but the reaction, as my second chapter will seek to demonstrate, could not be more different from Balzac's decision to make Lucien the embodiment of metropolitan selfhood. Similarly, in *The Novice of Saint Dominick*, *French Leave*, and *Max*, the Irish woman's Parisian novel remains significantly ambivalent regarding the phenomenon of social mobility.

The metropolis and its increased opportunity for social mobility provide a tantalizing alternative to those afforded by the confining spaces of the Irish narratological landscape, especially for the female protagonists of these novels. As feminist literary critics and feminist geographers have shown, these canonical spaces are coterminous with patriarchal "[i]deas of antiurbanism, nationalism, and concern about the body, health, and physique [that] were projected onto the woman's body, and against England as urban, industrial and debased," carrying "the cultural weight of the idealization of traditional rural family life and its fixed morality and gender roles."[72] Intimately bound to these mythologized spaces, the tradition of the Irish national tale, the genre with which Edgeworth and Owenson are most often associated, sublimates "the founding violence of the proposed union"[73] between both individuals and the nation, transforming it "from a national or colonial conflict into a family secret" in an attempt to neutralize or to manage "the wild Irish girls."[74] The national tale, which Ina Ferris describes as "the most important literary form emerging out of the debate on Ireland," must be situated within the context of the late eighteenth-century discourse surrounding Ireland's relationship with Great Britain and more general concerns over the international landscape.[75] Just as the national tale "require[s] the domestication/ subjugation of the woman," the Act of Union simultaneously sought to contain "Napoleonic aggression and Irish republicanism," both of which posed a serious threat to the stability of Great Britain.[76] The spaces and the tradition of the national tale repeatedly reinforce limits upon the autonomy of the female characters, insisting upon "the values of motherhood, tradition, and stability," denying "women an autonomous sexuality in their idealized asexual motherhood."[77] The National Tale, like the Goethean and classical *Bildungsroman*, concludes more often than not with a marriage and the reinauguration of a stable and patriarchal order.[78]

As a literary and socioeconomic landscape, the city remains complex, providing alternately increased autonomy and increased pressures on selfhood. On one hand, Patsey Kirwen, George Lester, Owenson's Imogen St. Dorval, and Thurston's masculine performance of Max all achieve a selfhood within the metropolitan landscape that would have been unavailable within the traditional literary geography of the Irish National Tale; on the other hand, however, each of these novels appears to recognize, to varying degrees, Simmel's claim that "it is by no means necessary that the freedom of man reflect itself in his emotional life only as a pleasant experience."[79] These novels seem to do more than simply recognize the fact that metropolitan independence is not necessarily a pleasant experience. In Somerville and Ross's *French Leave*, as in so many of these novels, the representation of Paris demonstrates that "the kinds of choices one can make" within the capitalist metropolis "are connected to one's relations to institutional and financial power."[80] Both Harry Ormond and George Lester arrive in

Paris with the ability to command capital, while Dora, Ormond's childhood friend, and Patsey have little recourse to an income independent of either marriage or family. Once relocated in the cityscape of Paris, novels by these Irish women reveal the gendered power dynamics that undergird the modern capitalist metropolis.

As this introduction has sought to explain, the primary texts examined in *The European Metropolis*, Owenson's *The Novice of Saint Dominick* and *The O'Briens and the O'Flahertys* (1827), Edgeworth's *Ormond*, Somerville and Ross's *French Leave*, and Thurston's *Max* all share a set of important and common traits: each is a *Bildungsroman*, set to a significant degree in Paris, each incorporates money into the process of *Bildung*, is written by an Irish woman, and is, to some degree, an historical novel.[81] The historical nature of each of these novels proves fundamental to their ability to understand and to chart the changes within fashion and society, echoing the structural argument behind Mandel's long waves of capitalist development. Since fashion and capitalism, by definition, depend upon change, a novel that does not allow itself to look across a certain length of time cannot register the changes that dominate commodity-based capitalism. These four novels are certainly not the only examples that fit such criteria in the ever-expanding history of Irish women's writing, but these four provide significant ballasts in the long waves of Irish women's writing.[82]

Beginning with Owenson's little-known *The Novice of Saint Dominick*, this analysis certainly does not begin with the earliest forms of Irish literature, even Irish literature in English, as recent and valuable recovery work by Ian Campbell Ross, Aileen Douglas, and Moyra Haslett has illustrated in the Early Irish Fiction series, as well as the Loebers' *Guide to Irish Fiction* and Margaret Kelleher's recently launched digitalization of the Loebers' *Guide*. Nor does *The Novice* begin with the "pivotal position in any history of the Irish novel" occupied by the "national tale—that curious genre which emerged forcefully in the margins of the British-Irish state in the first quarter of the nineteenth century."[83] Instead, *The Novice* clears the way for a new conversation about the history of Irish women's writing, attempting to uncouple the tradition from the space of Ireland with which the national tale is, by definition, concerned.

Chapter 1 focuses on two Sydney Owenson novels: *The Novice of Saint Dominick*, which has remained in the shadows of the much more popular and more anthologized *The Wild Irish Girl*, published in the same year, and *The O'Briens and the O'Flahertys*. Coming from very different stages of Owenson's literary career, these two novels demonstrate two remarkably different representations of Paris, suggesting a reevaluation of the French capital. The first, *The Novice of Saint Dominick*, is set during the French Wars of Religion at the end of the sixteenth century; this novel has received scant attention and suffers from what Weekes describes as "excessive romanticism and sentimentalism."[84] This relatively unknown Sydney Owenson novel charts the development of the protagonist, the foundling Imogen (later of the St. Dorval family), alongside her ability to navigate the socioeconomic landscape of the metropolis, her economic practitionership. Moving from the pre-capitalist and autocratic space of the Order of Saint Dominick and the related Château de Montmorell by means of a pivotal moment of exchange, Owenson humanizes the Kantian concept of cosmopolitanism as an economic foundation for social relations. Owenson's novel involves an ever-expanding geographic and social scope, embodying narratologically the expansive and inclusionary model that underpins Kant's notion of capitalism. Imogen's reckless participation in the aristocratic life of the metropolis will demonstrate her inability to develop the skills of economic practitionership successfully, forcing her to return to the masculine protection of her guardian, the *chevalier* de Sorville. *The Novice* ultimately presents an ambivalent modern capitalism that Owenson cannot condemn outright nor can she present her protagonist conquering its marketplace.

The O'Briens and the O'Flahertys, a novel that has received much more critical attention, provides a starkly different representation of the French capital and the opportunities available in its marketplace. Although both novels occupy largely the same socio-geographic area of Paris, the Faubourg Saint-Germain, *The O'Briens* takes place after the French Revolution and during the reign of Napoleon. In contrast to the earlier instability of the Wars of Religion, Paris functions as a site not only of refuge from the instability of an Ireland caught up in its own insurrections but also as a site of social mobility. This novel, instead of condemning the socioeconomic opportunities of Paris, suggests that the marketplace and its mobility is, ultimately, better able to recognize social value than the ante-modern spaces of Ireland. Following the trials and tribulations of Murrogh O'Brien after he is unceremoniously expelled from Trinity College Dublin and Dublin high society, *The O'Briens and the O'Flahertys* ends with his ascension through the French military and social ranks, appearing with Napoleon at the Paris Opera. Thus, over the course of her career, Owenson's representation of Paris shifts dramatically, ultimately viewing the French capital as a site of opportunity and liberation.

Maria Edgeworth's *Ormond*, on the other hand, completely rejects the elements of a Balzacian *Bildung* and insists upon a Goethean form of socialization-formation. The development of the eponymous protagonist leads ultimately toward his assumption of the role of a responsible and reforming landlord, similar to that of Edgeworth's other Irish Tales. However, Ormond's *Bildung* depends upon his experiences within the cosmopolitan landscape of the French capital. Surprisingly, Edgeworth's rejection of the Balzacian and fashion-based *Bildung* does not immediately result in a rejection of the metropolis; in fact, the socializing institution similar to the Goethean Society of the Tower believes it to be its constitutive mission to "not let him leave Paris, as so many do, having seen only the worst part of our society."[85] While W. J. McCormack has referred to the Parisian scenes as "the Paris interlude," Chapter 2 argues that the brief scenes in the French capital function as a microcosm for socioeconomic debates.[86] These debates frame the tensions throughout the novel as between an irresponsible form of capitalism, embodied in gambling and speculation, and a socially responsible form, figured in the homes of the Enlightened literati. The two competing forms of *Bildung* reflect debates and anxieties over competing experiences of economic modernity and their impact upon the development of selfhood. This economic reconsideration of the novel shows a nuanced engagement with the socioeconomic marketplace in Edgeworth's writing, indicating a deep-seated wariness regarding the rapidly expanding phenomenon of fashionable commodities and presenting a much more reactionary view of the economy than Owenson.

In their novel *French Leave*, Somerville and Ross return to similar issues that characterized Owenson's earlier representation of Paris: the privileged relationship between men and the metropolitan marketplace. This novel relates the story of two young aspiring Irish artists, Patricia Kirwen and George Lester. By focusing on how they achieve their escape from the Irish socioeconomic system, *French Leave* proves Gallois's words quoted above, highlighting the unequal nature of modern capitalism, especially within the urban sphere.[87] The very fact that Patricia's lack of access to liquid capital forces her to return to Ireland and to abandon her dreams of Paris, while her male counterpart is able, from the moment of his arrival in the French capital, to inhabit Marx's "three *dramatis personae*" of the exchange process reveals the gendered power dynamic that structures the *fin-de-siècle* marketplace.[88] As a result, Somerville and Ross, in *French Leave*, begin to demonstrate the social and financial underpinnings of Moretti's crisis of the European *Bildungsroman*, wherein the social and economic institutions that previously directed seemingly natural and organic socialization-formation process are now recognized as social mechanisms with little regard for the individual's *Bildung*.

In certain ways that are similar to Somerville and Ross's *French Leave*, Katherine Cecil Thurston's novel *Max* traces the struggles of a young artist to achieve fame and success in Paris. However, as an Irish New Woman novelist, Thurston's *Max* proves much more complicated than a simple *Künstlerroman*. Arriving in Paris from Russia, the young protagonist, Max, befriends an Irish citizen of the world who finds something enchantingly odd with this young Russian émigré. As their friendship develops, it becomes clear that Max is more than another New Woman or Decadent embodiment of the "boy," a figure Tina

O'Toole describes as allowing New Woman novelists to "access male privilege" and to illustrate "the ways in which gender is constructed and performed."[89] As it becomes clear that Max is the masculine performance perpetuated by a young woman named Maxine, the novel ultimately reveals two competing modes of reading and accessing the city. Chapter 4 focuses on the ways in which *fin-de-siècle* Paris remains very much a gendered and unequal cityscape, particularly through the split experiences of the novel's protagonist. For Max, Paris takes on the traits of the masculine adventure narratives of the *fin de siècle*; for Maxine, the cityscape becomes romanticized, intimately associated with the inability to read the city properly. In both versions, the city remains dominated by the omnipresence of the masculine gaze, suggesting that even in the waning years of the nineteenth century, the French metropolis remains a site of anxiety surrounding the emergence of an unequal experience of modernity.

While Eugène Rastignac inaugurates modern representations of Paris with a combative challenge to the city, a declaration of war between an individual and the metropolis, Irish women's novels set in Paris never declare war on the French capital, but that is not to suggest that the relationship is not fraught. Indeed, this book demonstrates that Irish women's novels constitute a threat not to the city itself, but to the dominant understanding of literature about Paris. It might be that Vautrin and Saccard achieve a fleeting dominance over the city, through crime and knowledge and capital; but in Owenson's *The Novice of Saint Dominick* and *The O'Briens and the O'Flahertys*, Edgeworth's *Ormond*, Somerville and Ross's *French Leave*, and Thurston's *Max*, Irish women's literature declares that it too belongs to the French metropolis. These four writers and the novels considered within this study begin to open a space and a debate about the broader engagement of Irish literature written by women with the European and capitalist marketplace. Ultimately, *The European Metropolis* issues a declaration, not of war with the city, but of citizenship, declaring that these Irish women's novels, like Rastignac, have come to the city and have found that one word that unlocks Paris for the nineteenth-century novel—*parvenir!*

CHAPTER ONE

The Novice in the City
Sydney Owenson and the *Bildung* of Metropolitan Economics

In the atlas of Irish women's writing and of Irish literature more broadly, Sydney Owenson (Lady Morgan) (c. 1783–1859) remains exceptional for the geographic expansiveness of her *œuvre*. A brief mapping of Owenson's literary career highlights what Ian Campbell Ross, Aileen Douglas, and Moyra Haslett are beginning to recognize as an historically global trend in Irish writing.[1] *Woman; or, Ida of Athens* (1809), *The Missionary* (1811), *O'Donnell: A National Tale* (1814), *Florence Macarthy* (1818), *The O'Briens and the O'Flahertys* (1827), and *The Princess; or, The Beguine* (1835) refuse to accept a singular geographical category other than simply that of the global. These novels range from Greece in *Woman* to Portugal and Goa in *The Missionary*, Vienna and the Austro-Hungarian Empire in *O'Donnell*, New Granada and Columbia in *Florence Macarthy*, and Paris and Rome in *The O'Briens and the O'Flahertys*. This brief geographical sketch stretches from the Indian subcontinent to Paris, Dublin, and South America. Such a scope demonstrates the necessity of including Owenson in the broad project of mapping prose fiction, a project most clearly associated with Franco Moretti's attempts "to make the literary field longer, larger, and deeper," even though Moretti's *Atlas of the European Novel* recognizes Ireland only to dismiss it.[2] A critical mapping of

Owenson's novels challenges the paradigmatic concept that one of the definitive characteristics of Irish literature is the privileged narrative locus of Ireland.

To suggest that the central location of Owenson's fiction is not Ireland but France, and more specifically Paris, is to reassert the exceptionally broad geographic range of her *œuvre* and to reject a "pattern [...] of exclusion" that seems to dominate in Irish literary criticism.[3] While Moretti associates this exclusionary pattern with Jane Austen's novels, he conceives it in opposition to the historical and national tales of Walter Scott, which he relegates to the "Celtic Fringe."[4] This exclusionary pattern applies equally to the critical understanding of Sydney Owenson's novels, which has focused more on the Celtic space than on the role of the metropolis, especially Paris, in her novels. This chapter seeks to rectify this critical gap by focusing on two novels, one which has been neglected by criticism since its 1806 publication, *The Novice of Saint Dominick*, and another which is more commonly considered a National Tale, *The O'Briens and the O'Flahertys*. In her earlier and largely ignored *The Novice of Saint Dominick* from 1806, Owenson presents a Paris in the midst of a civil war, following the Saint Bartholomew's Day Massacre (1572). This is a Gothic and antimodern Paris. Conversely, in *The O'Briens and the O'Flahertys* of 1827, a novel that crosses the years of the Revolution, Napoleonic Paris becomes a site of refuge, social advancement, and cultural mobility that was unavailable in Ireland, providing a much-needed oasis for the type of development that reflects Moretti's "recognition-inheritance pattern," which appears to be unavailable, or at least disrupted, in the geo-social space of Ireland.[5] For Owenson, these two embodiments of Paris are centered on the competing geo-social spaces of the Faubourg Saint-Germain on the Left Bank and the Opera, providing an alternative cultural geography of post-Revolutionary Paris.

The Novice of Saint Dominick, published the same year as *The Wild Irish Girl*, has received none of the latter's critical or popular attention. While it has been the subject of scant critical attention since its publication, it also seems to have received scant attention in the press when it first appeared. In a one-page review, *The Monthly Review; or Literary Journal* said of *The Novice* that "the interest of the narrative improves with its progress; [...] it exhibits unity of design, and consistency and appropriation of character; it abounds in trying incidents; and all its tendencies are strictly moral."[6] The reviewer proclaims a "very favourable opinion of her [Owenson's] performance."[7] However, the review devotes most of its appraisal to the complaint that "it would have lost none of its effect by a little compression"[8]—*The Novice of Saint Dominick* is a novel in four volumes, each approaching if not exceeding 400 pages.

Even with its excessive length and relative obscurity, *The Novice of Saint Dominick* provides a clear and early instance of what will become a long-running tradition in Irish women's writing: the economic *Bildungsroman*. *The Novice* proves an important point of contact between the metropolitan and financial fictions of Johann Wolfgang von Goethe and Honoré de Balzac, a tradition that includes Charles Dickens, Émile Zola, Maria Edgeworth, and Somerville and Ross. This critical analysis of *The Novice* not only responds to Moretti's plea for criticism to broaden the literary field, but also exhibits traits of the two dominant iterations of the *Bildungsroman* he identifies, the Goethean and the Balzacian, a distinction to which I will return presently. Building upon Moretti's sharp awareness of the critical interplay between the *Bildungsroman* tradition and modern capitalism as experienced in the metropolis, this chapter will argue that, through its representation of the young female protagonist's individual development, *The Novice* demonstrates the Simmelian ambivalent relationship that exists between women and the emerging metropolitan commodity economy. By presenting capitalism as a conservative socializing system, this novel establishes a tension between the increased freedom of economic autonomy and the continued presence of the forces of socialization. Although Owenson clearly recognizes the potential opportunities for increased autonomy and self-determination specifically for women embedded within the complex cosmopolitan division of labor, *The Novice* ultimately cannot provide its female protagonist with unbounded independence because both capitalism and the *Bildungsroman* tradition necessarily reify the status quo. Conversely, *The O'Briens and the O'Flahertys* demonstrates a more liberal vision of the city that promises the type of social mobility that will characterize Balzac's Paris.

An historical tale set during the waning years of the French Wars of Religion and at the beginning of Henry IV's reign, *The Novice of Saint Dominick* traces the development of its protagonist, a young foundling named Imogen (later recognized as a member of the St. Dorval family), from her early days as a novice in the Order of Saint Dominick to her apprenticeship as an amanuensis for Lady Magdelaine de Montmorell, a member of the local nobility. When a minstrel from Provençe seeks shelter at the Château de Montmorell in Champagne, Imogen, who is working as amanuensis on a manuscript for the lady, falls in love with him before the resident friar imprisons him for tempting the young novice away from her sacred office. After the minstrel, who claims to be called Orlando, escapes, Imogen begins to devise her own escape to forge her own future beyond the overdetermined strictures of the cloister, to which she is expected to return upon the completion of Lady de Montmorell's manuscript. Imogen finds herself lost and ultimately captured by the army of the League, the ultra-Catholic force that opposes Henry IV and the Huguenots. During the battle, she meets a man whom Owenson eventually reveals to be the novice's father, the Count de St. Dorval. The Count introduces Imogen to the *chevalier* de Sorville, the Count's close friend and advisor who will become Imogen's guardian and presumptive husband. In a subsequent battle, the Count is severely wounded and yet saved by the Baron de Montargis, who is the minstrel who appeared at the Château.

After her father dies from a battle wound, the *chevalier* becomes young Imogen's guardian by *fiat* of her father's will. In this document, the Count hoped that his daughter would marry the *chevalier*, making her inheritance conditional upon this plan; he also hoped that she would agree to spend no more than three months in Paris. Pursuant to her father's wishes, the young Countess de St. Dorval and the *chevalier* agree to visit Paris; despite the relatively short amount of time they spend in French capital, she contracts such a heavy burden of debt while enjoying the lifestyle of the metropolitan aristocracy that the *chevalier* abandons her in remonstrance. She is forced to sell everything to a pawnbroker in order to repay these debts and returns in shame to her family's estate in Provençe. Once free of her debt, the *chevalier* embraces her for having learned the lesson of economy and self-retraint; she is also reunited with her love interest, the minstrel / Baron de Montargis (now called Duke de Beauvilliers), in marriage. They return to Paris for the celebration of Henry IV's wedding with Marie de Medicis, before settling into a life largely based in their Provençal estates.

The Female *Bildungsroman* in the Order of St. Dominick

Throughout *The Novice of Saint Dominick*, Owenson charts Imogen's narrative development along two complementary and perhaps indivisible paths: the personal and the economic. The personal or existential struggle for development is one for self-determination against the preordained path on which she is set as a novice as she declares: "If I am to be a saint [...] I will be the foundress of my own sect."[9] This desire for differentiation and personal distinction has clear echoes in contemporary *Bildungsromane* like Goethe's *Wilhelm Meister* (1795–96) and Jane Austen's *Northanger Abbey* (1817), as well as in the long tradition of what I have termed the Irish women's economic *Bildungsroman*. Yet, as Lorna Ellis has articulated, the typical trajectory of a young woman's *Bildung* proves problematic: "the protagonists begin as self-assured young women who question their subordinate place in society, but the endings find them less active, less assertive, and reintegrated into society."[10] In this process of "learning to understand and work within the limits of society," the protagonist of the female *Bildungsroman* is "able to gain a qualified power," Ellis argues, but ultimately "the options for continued adult growth at the end of *Bildungsromane* are more limited for female protagonists" than for their male counterparts.[11]

Implicit in the imperative to understand and work within the system is a command to accede to the laws of the marketplace, as Ellis demonstrates in her analysis of Austen's *Pride and Prejudice*. By conforming to the social expectations required in her marriage to Mr. Darcy, Elizabeth Bennet not only "obtains the social and economic advantage of mistress of Pemberley" but, more materially, "her ability 'frequently' to send money to Lydia and Wickham [...] shows that she gains some financial autonomy."[12] Ellis's analysis notes the potential for a paradoxically subversive trend in a conservative genre. Owenson interrogates a similar dynamic through the personal and economic development of Imogen de St. Dorval. Imogen's use and misuse of money corresponds to the development of a metropolitan mentality, which is predicated upon the successful navigation of the metropolitan marketplace. This process enables, contributes to, and reinforces the broader process of socialization of the *Bildungsroman*.

Imogen's *Bildung* is predicated upon an initial inability to order and structure her life according to her own desires and wishes. In Owenson's novel, this fundamental premise is routinely subverted, most obviously by the conservative figures of the Catholic Church and, subsequently, by the modern economy. Ever since a nun found her, her destiny has been determined, if not overdetermined. Providence ordaining one's place in society is central to what Moretti describes as the classical *Bildungsroman* because it points to the role of legitimation. In Moretti's first formulation of the genre, the social order "must appear *symbolically legitimate*," which is to say that, in the case of Goethe, "Wilhelm's formation is achieved only by subordinating himself to the Tower—the Tower's legitimation only by making Wilhelm happy."[13] With this in mind, the representation of the Church becomes markedly critical. The confusion that seems to authorize the Order's attempts to devise the overarching structure of Imogen's life renders that supposed authority illegitimate.

This illegitimacy becomes more problematic because of the historical context of *The Novice of Saint Dominick*. Set against the backdrop of the final years of France's Wars of Religion, the entire sociocultural environment fails to achieve this legitimacy. With France officially at war "for most of the time during 1562–63, 1567–70 and 1572–77," the social cohesion and legitimacy that undergird the classical *Bildungsroman* are almost entirely absent.[14] This is especially true *vis-à-vis* religion, in part because the Wars of Religion are largely figured as a conflict between the Catholic Valois dynasty and the Huguenot-allied Henry of Navarre (later Henry IV of France). But these wars evolve to include Henry III's later alliance with Henry of Navarre against the ultra-Catholic force of the League, governed by the Guise family. Ultimately, Henry IV legitimates his reign with his conversion to Catholicism in the Abbey of Saint-Denis. Religion cannot but be politicized in this context, losing its ability to legitimate. The recognition of social institutions as such separates *The Novice*'s process of *Bildung* from Moretti's definition of its classical form, in which the coterminous relationship of "[s]elf-development and integration" is the defining characteristic.[15]

But if the Tower is represented as a social institution and not as natural "relations among individuals," then it is unable to convince "the subject that what he must do is also symbolically right" and "[i]f this does not happen, and shared values are replaced by sheer coercion [...], the individual will hardly feel at home in his world, and socialization will not be fully accomplished."[16] This rupture is the "crisis of the European *Bildungsroman*," which Moretti sees as originating largely with Thomas Mann.[17] Yet this crisis is present in Irish women's *Bildungsromane* from a much earlier date. Owenson delegitimizes the Church and lays the groundwork for anointing capitalism as the dominant and socializing force of Imogen's *Bildung*. Such a shift in the governing system of the socialization-formation process necessarily involves relocating the narrative to the French capital.

Owenson contrasts this Gothicized representation of the Catholic Church with the liberative alternative of a cosmopolitan environment that ultimately occurs in the metropolitan center of Paris, but begins with the initial representations of a capitalistic and impersonal exchange.

Their Chief Market is at Soissons: Inclusionary Cosmopolitanism, Commerce, and Developing Urban Literacy

The illegitimate regime of the Order of Saint Dominick and the Château de Montmorell contrasts with what will become the alternative conception of society in *The Novice of Saint Dominick*, which is modern capitalism and its potential for increased self-determination. With the introduction of payment and, by extension, capitalism, the novel introduces the means by which Imogen will not only escape the overdetermined realm of the *château* and the Church but also begin to understand the expansive and inclusionary socioeconomic framework that underpins cosmopolitan society. The emotional and romantic connection Imogen places onto the objects of her now-imprisoned lover drives her first excursion into the world of commerce. "With affected indifference," she asks the page if he would part with the harp.[18] The performative quality of Imogen's initial query is significant because it lays bare the fundamental tripartite structure of fashion, what David Bell identifies as "the triangular structure of desire."[19] Building upon René Girard's *Deceit, Desire, and the Novel*, Bell explains that "desire never reaches out for the object in a direct and uncomplicated way, but always passes through a mediator/model/rival who must first designate the object as desirable."[20] Imogen is here demonstrating two complicated and nuanced economic performances. Firstly, by affecting indifference, she undercuts Girard's process of triangulation, potentially lowering the price of the harp because she refuses to grant it the status of a fashionable commodity, that is, a desired commodity. Imogen's affected indifference surely also reflects an appropriate maidenly modesty, a refusal to admit publicly her affection for the minstrel. The point is not to characterize the young novice as a cunning swindler, but to highlight the way in which Owenson's text expresses an understanding of this underlying psychological aspect of economic exchange. To this end, Imogen's performative act of indifference showcases the potential for her to develop and to practice urban literacy.[21]

Embedded within this broad skill is the capacity to function within the socioeconomic landscape of the modern metropolis. The long course of Irish women's European metropolitan writings can be seen as a struggle for the individual to learn and employ successfully the skills of urban literacy.

The second economic concept Imogen displays is perhaps more foundational than Girard's triangulation of desire or even than economic and urban literacy. The metaphorical substitution of the exchange process creates an intellectual framework in which the economic practice takes on a broader resonance. This mental capacity for substitution is of course fundamental to the use of money, as Marx demonstrates when he explains that "in order to equate [the commodity] with itself as an exchange value, it is exchanged for a symbol which represents it as exchange value as such."[22] Moreover, as Dipesh Chakrabarty makes clear, "there had to be a way of finding a common measure so that what was not equal could be equalized" because exchange "was central to the formation of a community."[23] For Chakrabarty, money provides this leveling function that distinguishes the value of like and unlike objects. Imogen evidences an understanding of the necessity of equivalency, objecting that she "must not take advantage of [Theodore's] gallantry" when he offers a kiss as a fair value for the harp and the minstrel's clothes, and instead offers "some valuable coins presented to her by the minor canoness."[24] Here, again, Owenson demonstrates Imogen's ability to navigate the economic principles of the exchange process. By offering valuable coins, Imogen recognizes the value of the harp and attempts to enact a fair and equal exchange. It is her personal and intimate relationship with Theodore that determines this interaction. Imogen's emphasis on maintaining the equality in this process reflects a form of social contract that is rooted in power. Imogen insists that she must not "take advantage" of Theodore, explicitly conveying the power embedded within the symbolic exchange.

These two economic acts, when considered at first glance, seem contradictory. How can Imogen affect indifference and yet insist upon a fair and equal exchange? Surely the more successful capitalists in the literature of the late eighteenth and early nineteenth century would have veered toward the more predatory style of cunning affectation; it is not difficult to see Balzac's Vautrin, Dickens's Ralph Nickleby, or even Goethe's Werner employ a similar sleight of hand in order to achieve their economic ends. For Owenson, however, the only true practitioner of this cold and calculating self-interested form of capitalism remains the Marquis de Sancy, a nobleman to whom Imogen becomes severely indebted. Instead, these contradictions undergird, and perhaps problematize, Owenson's attempt to represent what Margot Finn has called "a proper moral economy of exchange."[25] Owenson insistently humanizes the cosmopolitan economy in an attempt to insert the moral and the personal in the process of exchange. The insistence upon a fair exchange embodies an Owensonian humanist representation of capitalism that echoes Kant's cosmopolitanism. Just because she is capable of lowering the price does not mean that Imogen feels she ought to. Despite the anonymity and atomizing tendencies of the metropolis, Imogen encounters a similar humanized exchange process in the Parisian marketplace.

For Owenson and Imogen, commerce provides the unmoved mover that drives both the narrative of *The Novice of Saint Dominick* and the individual *Bildung* of its protagonist. In the sale of the harp, the novice's insistence upon a just rate of exchange recalls Cheah's explanation of the economic underpinnings of Kant's cosmopolitical writings: "commerce is a form of sociability that brings states and individuals into relation, collecting us into a larger whole."[26] The social relationship between Imogen and Theodore, then, is one based on justice and what Kant identified as "the cosmopolitan right."[27] Owenson explains that heretofore Imogen's and Theodore's "only intercourse [...] had been a repeated offer of little services, or oblique encomiums on his side, and of grateful refusals or modest rejections on her's [sic]."[28] This underscores the degree to which the exchange of goods, the harp for a silver reliquary and a kiss, has provided the foundation for an ongoing social relationship.

In an act based upon the mutual beneficence established in this earlier moment of just exchange, commerce's ability to bring us "into a larger whole" provides the narratological and socioeconomic means for Imogen's final rejection of the overdetermined sphere of the Château de Montmorell and of her preordained future within the Church. Imogen's "first and favourite plan of eloping in the disguise of the minstrel again recurred to her mind, as the only one she could adopt."[29] This escape depends almost entirely upon the goods she has procured through commercial exchange, a fact that reinforces both capitalism's liberative potential and its opposition to the overdetermined realm of pre-capitalist societies. Despite the fact that she declares she "must now [...] depend on [herself] alone," Imogen quickly realizes that "it was requisite to have some assistance; and there was but one person to whom she could apply: that person was Theodore the page."[30] The mirror return of both the objects and the page reminds Imogen and the reader of the underlying claims regarding commerce as the foundation for society, especially in so far as it contributes to the formation of social relations between individuals.

The plan itself reinforces the development of hospitable relations between individuals through the means of capitalism. After mentioning "her determination of avoiding a mode of life, to which she had objections, which neither her reason or her conscience could get over," Imogen explains to Theodore that she has an "expectation of an asylum with madame de Rosemont," a close friend of the minor canoness.[31] Theodore, learning that the Château de Rosemont "lay on the skirts of Picardy, and within three leagues of the city of Soissons," declares:

> Nothing can be more à-propos. You must know, mademoiselle, there lives about two leagues from the chateau, a widow and two sons, who deal largely in the frieze cloths for which this province is so famous; their chief market is at Soissons, and since this part of the country has been so disturbed, they carry their merchandize by water, and coast along the Aisne. [...] The poor people think me skilful; and having had the good fortune to cure one of the widow's sons of a disorder in his

> leg, they fancy themselves beholden to serve me to the utmost extent of their power. Sunday is the day appointed for you to enter your holy profession; Saturday is the market of Soissons; these good people will set out with their merchandize early on Friday morning: I will recommend you to their protection as a younger relation of my own, going into the service of a lady in Picardy; when you are once at Soissons, they will easily find a mode of conveyance for you to the chateau at Rosemont.[32]

This passage provides several significant socioeconomic principles that, together, demonstrate the way in which Owenson's text understands the relationship of individuals to both regional and national marketplaces. The repetition of relationships and interconnectedness undergirds both the economic and the broader social system. Theodore's relationship with the widow and her sons exhibits economic characteristics: the use of "beholden" indicates a debt, which ideally functions upon the premise of equivalent exchange. Sociability, here, also provides a narratological benefit that Moretti associates with urban novels, specifically those of Balzac and Dickens. The expansive inclusionary framework in which *The Novice* operates depends upon an increasing number of participants and characters. With the exception of the minstrel, this merchant family is the first group of characters Owenson introduces outside of the broadly ecclesiastical framework that has previously dominated the text. Describing this increased number as "qualitative [and] morphological," Moretti explains that "with five characters [...] the plot is usually confined within one social group, and slides between two opposite but equally stable arrangements: idyllic peace [...] or unbearable despotism," but with the addition of other individuals, "the narrative system becomes complicated, unstable."[33]

There is a concentricity between the expansion in the social circle and an expansive economic marketplace that stretches across regions. In the passage above, Owenson provides the first specific geography that fixes the location of the narrative, beyond merely the region of

Champagne, placing the Château de Montmorell within a day's journey by water from the market town of Soissons. It is not simply the relationship of the Château to the market, but also that of Soissons to the Château de Rosemont, which lies in the region of Picardy, that comes into focus as the map of the novel broadens. The broadening of the map produces a similar destabilizing effect on the autocratic rule of the Order of St. Dominick and Lady Magdelaine. More specifically, this relational model of economic geography provides a telling window into the uneven development of capitalism that expresses itself in a narratological division of labor between the provinces and the metropole. Moretti explains this phenomenon in terms of Balzac's *Illusions perdues* (1837–43) when he explains that "to the provinces [falls] the endless, heavy task of physically producing paper; to the capital, the privilege of covering those beautiful white sheets with fascinating ideas."[34] Instead of the paper that proves so pivotal to Lucien de Rubempré's meteoric rise and fall, the trade in "the frieze cloths for which this province is so famous" marks an increase in the luxurious commodity trade that characterizes France under Henry IV.[35]

Imogen's and Theodore's plan begins to exhibit the novice's development of what Georg Simmel would define as a metropolitan mentality. Owenson pairs Imogen's *Bildung*, the development of her character, with the development of urban literacy, which is the ability to learn, navigate, and employ the laws of metropolitan capitalism. In a moment of confusion and trepidation, the young novice wonders aloud, "Suppose [...] I were to disguise myself as a minstrel; might not a man's garb be some protection."[36] Here Imogen reveals two fundamental and perhaps paradoxical qualities of the metropolis that will continue to inform Irish women's European novels for the next 200 years: firstly, she exhibits the Simmelian claim of "a type and degree of personal freedom" available within the cityscape; secondly, she demonstrates the problematically gendered relationship of individuals to the city.[37] Imogen's ability to adopt this disguise demonstrates Simmel's claim insofar as it is predicated upon the anonymity that characterizes the "depersonalized" culture of the city, especially in contrast to the "supervision of the citizen" that is fundamental to the Simmelian small town.[38] The depersonalization of the urban sphere is attributable to the division of labor that already undergirds Owenson's narrative.

Of course, one of the critiques of Simmel's writings on the city is that, as the French literary critic William Gallois has pointed out, "there are important qualitative differences between the kinds of choices one can make which are connected to one's relations to institutional and financial power."[39] Throughout the history of Irish women's Parisian novels, the primary determining factors of an individual's ability to navigate the metropolis are his or her gender and class status. Both enact limitations upon the individual in terms of access to capital and the necessity of adhering to closely policed mores. This is especially true once commerce is understood as the fundamental experience of sociability. Theodore goes on to elaborate and to substantiate Imogen's concerns, explaining that "neither your sex, face, or form [sic], are much calculated to insure your safety in an adventure such as you are now on the point of entering; and a minstrel's garb is a passport everywhere."[40] That a man's garb and identity provide access and freedom cannot be ignored. Significantly, Theodore's explanation characterizes this gendered imbalance of access as a uniquely urban reality. He tells Imogen he sees "no necessity" for her to disguise herself "until you arrive at Soissons," making a clear distinction between the rural and the urban realms, even that of a provincial town.[41] And if this power dynamic is true in a provincial town, it becomes even more evident when Imogen arrives in Paris.

Despite this gendered nature of the marketplace, Owenson's frieze merchant, Dame Marguerette, is clearly able to navigate the economic landscape of Soissons's marketplace, providing a fascinating contrast to the sort of economic agent Imogen will attempt to become. A "middle-aged woman, habited in the peasant dress of the country, and who welcomed her in a patois dialect so broad and unintelligible," this merchant from Champagne seems to be entirely self-sufficient and self-reliant.[42] There is neither mention of a husband nor any suggestion that her two sons contribute in any meaningful way to the economic stability of the family. Owenson's characterization emphasizes her capability to function as an independent economic agent so that the potential autonomy of the urban economic system becomes clear. She is the vehicle by which the young novice truly escapes forever the *ancien régime* of the Order of Saint Dominick and the Château de Montmorell. While Imogen is lost in the new-found freedom of the river, the frieze merchant "seemed lost in silent calculation of her expected profits."[43] This contrast emphasizes Imogen's novice status within the economic realm and depicts one of the key aspects of urban literacy: the ability to calculate and to forecast income in order to budget. Budgeting demonstrates one's ability to understand the proper value of objects, while ensuring the ability to continue to participate within "the endless chain of what Marx called the 'three *dramatis personae*' of the exchange process" where he or she swiftly transitions from a producer to a consumer by means of the money received for the goods he or she brought to the market.[44] Dame Marguerette reveals the independence that the interrelationship of individuals in a complex commodity exchange affords. If this is true in the provincial town of Soissons, how much more complex and endless will this exchange of goods and identities prove in Paris? As Owenson's representation of the Parisian marketplace will demonstrate, this phenomenon remains gendered.

Society's Great and Powerful Claims: Revolutions of Fashion and the Problems of Debt in Metropolitan *Bildung*

As with the provincial market of Soissons, there is a complex and often-times contradictory relationship between women and the capitalist marketplace. While the metropolis holds the promise of Simmelian independence and autonomy, the ability to achieve that autonomy depends upon an individual's relationship to institutional and financial powers. Indeed, Owenson has already declared that Imogen's continued access to capital and to the city hinges upon fulfilling her father's wishes as legislated in his will and, subsequently, in maintaining the proper relationship with the *chevalier* de Sorville. Even before she arrives in Paris, Imogen's experience of the city is already restricted on account of her gender and as such remains mediated by the Virgilian guide de Sorville. Since the Count de St. Dorval appointed him "guardian to his daughter, until that title should be superseded by a husband's claim," the authority of both father and husband resides in the person of de Sorville.[45] In this way, *The Novice of Saint Dominick* reveals the problematics of gender and class in Moretti's socio-geographical conception of the European *Bildungsroman*. Claiming that "[i]n the great city, [...] the heroes of the *Bildungsroman* change overnight from 'sons' into 'young men,'" Moretti grants to young men the privilege of autonomy and the opportunity of formation outside of the well-policed circle of the family.[46] This transformation privileges men when we consider Lucien de Rubempré or Nicholas Nickleby, both of whom are able to shed their familial identities through changing their names in different towns in order to move more freely; Imogen, on the other hand, has become only more enmeshed within the familial unit through the change in her identity. Even though she has gained access to capital and to a social legitimacy that would have been denied a foundling, it results in a more permanent fixing of her position within the social whole.

This is the fundamental contradiction within *The Novice of Saint Dominick*: Imogen rejects the ordained future of the convent in order to choose her own life, but the life she finds as the daughter of Count de St. Dorval is arguably just as overdetermined as that within the walls of the Church. The difference, however, is that Imogen never feels coerced and in fact feels as though she is absolutely free to learn and to develop within the city of Paris. This distinction between the world of the convent and that of Paris is one of recognizing the socializing forces as such and this is the foundation of the economic *Bildungsroman*. Throughout Imogen's novitiate in Paris, then, her continued failure to learn urban literacy and to become an economic practitioner forces her to rely more and more upon the male-dominated structures that determine the limits of her existence, leading ultimately to her acceptance of the plan her father's will ordained. Moreover, Owenson's representation of this process of *Bildung* both legitimizes the capitalist social structure and points out women's problematic existence within that system.

When Imogen enters the gates of Paris, the narrator emphasizes a contrast between her "pleasures of fancy and expectation" and the "narrow, dirty, and gloomy streets" that constitute "her first view of that great and populous city."[47] This opening description of Paris clearly undermines the young novice's romantic expectations; the city's medieval geography belies its grandeur. It need hardly be said that this is not the Paris of Haussmann and the *grands boulevards*. Instead, the city is less associated with a Seamus Deane-like modernity than with "a vast and ancient structure," as the narrator describes the *hôtel* de St. Dorval.[48] Indeed, the very architecture of the house and its accoutrements are measured in historical terms: the "old coachman [...] had served two generations of her family" and the carriages under his command "had not been drawn out since the coronation of Charles the Ninth," which dates their last journey to 1560, nearly forty years before Owenson's novel.[49] Exacerbating both this historical character and the monarchical connections embedded in this ancestral house is the fact that the narrator locates it in the Faubourg Saint-Germain, which lies on the Left Bank and is bordered on one side by the Seine and today by the Rue de Sèvres and the Boulevard de Grenelle. As Anna-Louise Milne has noted, the Faubourg Saint-Germain rose to prominence and "[b]y the end of the seventeenth century, this district had become the hub of fashionable life."[50] This area assumes its central role as the "locus of power and refinement" in Paris because of "two royal residences, in particular the huge domain chosen by the Reine Margot, Henry IV's first wife," the *Hôtel de la Reine Margeuritte*.[51] However, this development occurs largely after the end of the novel, which is dated from Henry IV's 1600 marriage to Marie de Medici. The palace built for Marie after Henry's assassination largely extended the Faubourg Saint-Germain toward the Montagne Sainte-Geneviève.[52] As Jones demonstrates, the expansion of the Faubourg Saint-Germain from the late sixteenth century through the mid-seventeenth century highlights "a gradual but clear-cut drift of the city's centre of gravity to the west" toward the Faubourg Saint-Honoré and the Faubourg Saint-Germain.[53]

Thus, the Paris of *The Novice* seems to contradict slightly the historical reality of its late sixteenth- and early seventeenth-century setting. Instead, the sociocultural geography that dominates Paris in *The Novice* is largely bipolar, oscillating from the Hôtel de St. Dorval "in the Fauxbourg St. Germaine [sic]," and "the gay and voluptuous court of Paris," then located at the Louvre.[54] This division across the Seine seems to omit the urban reformations instituted by Henry, specifically the Pont Neuf and the Place Dauphine; according to Colin Jones, these became "the springboard for a broader urban development on the Left Bank, now more tightly conjoined with the Louvre neighbourhood" thanks to the construction of the Rue Dauphine that continues the "line of the Pont Neuf on the Left Bank."[55] While *The Novice* does not explicitly recognize the impact of the social division of labor upon the urban landscape, the mosaic of Paris nevertheless informs the narrative. As the historian Collin Jones explains, the relocation of the court to the Louvre "stimulated growth along the Rue Saint-Honoré," as well as "provid[ing] a fillip to sectors of the city economy which supplied a growing demand for luxury commodities."[56] This developing luxury commodity exchange registers within and in fact governs the plot of the novel through Imogen's extraordinary expenditure; as she arrives in Paris, the narrator explains that she "looked on her riches as inexhaustible, and expended them as if they were so," accruing debts to "tradesmen, artisans, and mechanics [...] that] exceeded the large sums she had brought from Provence."[57] Distinguishing between the ancient and the modern reinforces the binary structure of Owenson's map of Paris and obscures the socioeconomic reality of the French metropolis; it presents a Gothicized Faubourg Saint-Germain that ignores Henry IV's urban and economic renovations and allows its society to orbit largely around the Marais and the Hôtel de Guise, the authoritarian space of the illegitimated ultra-Catholic League.

This distinction, more importantly, provides the first instance of Imogen's attempt at a metropolitan *Bildung*, which ultimately adds to the sense of an anti-modern, luxury-economy-driven Paris, through the novel's very condemnation of her luxurious expenditure. As is typical of the youthful *Bildungsheld*, Imogen seeks to remake the "ancient" in the face of the "gay and voluptuous" new.[58] The Gothic Hôtel de St. Dorval provides the young novice "boundless scope to taste and fancy in the *revolutions she began to plan* and the improvements she meditated."[59] The syntax Owenson deploys in this description of Imogen's attempts at interior decoration provides a key insight into the complex workings of both the urban spectacle of metropolitan capitalism and the novel's relationship to the sociological function of the *Bildungsroman* in the wake of the French Revolution.

The specific word "revolution" has grave connotations, especially for an early nineteenth-century left-leaning Irish writer following the revolution in France and the abortive Irish uprisings of 1798 and 1803. Moreover, the application of the word "revolution" to the realm and phenomenon of fashion demonstrates the unsettling potential of a commodity-based capitalism. Marc-Alain Descamps has described fashion as:

> [A] series of uninterrupted, sudden, unjustified and ephemeral diffusions, fashion corresponds to the need for change for the sake of change [...] it essentially reflects social mobility [...] it is in harmony with the fundamental machinery of modern societies and reproduces at a staggering rate that which constitutes the essence of their system [...] It is a question of innovating ceaselessly. Now, the risk inherent to progress—its quickening, the uncertain future—generates uneasiness [...] Fashion is the training ground for a symbolization whose function it is to accustom us to the new and to discredit the old.[60]

The discrediting of the old, change for its own sake, and social mobility all essentially point the way toward the revolutionary process, whether it be political, social, or commercial. Imogen participates in this uncanny echoing of sociopolitical revolution when she declares her intention to "dispossess the usurper *Gothic Inelegance* of her throne, and restore *Taste* to her rightful empire."⁶¹ Although these comments can be seen as softening the more radical aspects of Descamps's definition through its insistence on the restoration of rightful rule, the *chevalier*'s response seeks to contain and to restrain this revolutionary impulse.

Demonstrating again his narratological function as a member of the cognoscenti, the *chevalier* warns his ward that she is "not aware of the danger of sudden innovation in every system; and that even the efficient cause of the best change in antiquated error frequently becomes itself the first victim of revolutionary influence."⁶² The echoes of late eighteenth- and early nineteenth-century conservative horror at the recent bloody events in France are impossible to miss. The use of "victim" recalls Edmund Burke's indictment of the French revolutionaries as "gross, stupid, ferocious, [...] poor and sordid barbarians" and "a swinish multitude."⁶³ While Imogen seemingly participates in this rebellious chaos of renovation, the *chevalier* defends instead the home, the ancient home of her family. The echoes of Burke's metaphor of the little platoon, with its structural relationship between the home and the nation-state, are clear. Kissing Imogen's hand, de Sorville declares that he is "too anxious to agree with [Imogen] on every point to oppose [her] arguments on this; only remember this, that in every scheme, whether public or private, trivial or important, prudence forms the firmest basis of success," attempting to convince Imogen to exist within the established social order.⁶⁴

This potential revolution demonstrates the way in which Imogen is adapting to and adopting the mentality of the socioeconomic landscape of the metropolitan marketplace. The unifying principle behind Descamps's extensive definition of fashion is the concept of change, which is fundamental to the mode of *Bildung* that Moretti sees as arising within the cosmopolitan environment of Balzac's Paris. It is telling that Descamps attributes so many iterations of change to fashionable commodities because, by definition, this sort of consumable good "will vanish as rapidly as it came."[65] The velocity with which goods identified as fashionable change underlies the increasing rate of exchange within commodity-based capitalism. Moreover, this has a significant impact upon the consciousness of metropolitan individuals because that term "fashionable" is transposable or transferable from the items an individual owns to the individual's person. If the definition of fashionable goods is forever changing, so too must the identity of the individuals who chase that horizon-like label. Figures like Balzac's Lucien de Rubempré and Edgeworth's Lady Clonbrony both demonstrate this fundamental relationship between the mutability of metropolitan fashion and metropolitan selfhood. In *The Absentee*, Edgeworth ridicules the Irish Lady Clonbrony, whose Sisyphean pursuit of the fashionable not only forces her to change her "strong Hibernian accent [...] into an English tone," but who, for a party, transforms her London apartments variously into a "*Turkish tent,*" "*the Alhambra,*" and "a Chinese pagoda."[66] The metropolitan Londoners who mediate fashion for this Irishwoman unsurprisingly recognize Lady Clonbrony's person and her home as a "Fool's Paradise."[67]

Yet before Balzac, and even before Edgeworth in *The Absentee*, Owenson captures this socioeconomic phenomenon and its impact upon the individual. She telegraphs this materialist correlation between the self and commodities through an exchange between Imogen and de Sorville at the same moment of her fashionable revolution. When the *chevalier* finds her in "the midst of that delightful flurry of spirits which new and pleasing objects and sensations ever awaken," she affably exclaims, "how busy you find me, but I am now only busy in speculation."[68] While *The Novice of Saint Dominick* is singular in this study for the fact that it alone does not provide any concrete representation of banking, this term "speculation" should not be uncoupled from its economic connotations. As Bell explains, speculation depends upon an economic process that strips the commodity "of all its material properties, of all its use value" and "in which this origin of value [the commodity as expressed in terms of real human labor] is obscured and can be ignored."⁶⁹ While critics⁷⁰ have pointed out how Balzac and Zola replicated this speculative process in the transformations of their characters, this same process occurs in the metropolitan struggles of *The Novice of Saint Dominick*, indicating that Owenson provides a complex socioeconomic lens through which she views and understands the forces of the modern marketplace.

The first embodiment of this sort of transformation is the Hôtel de St. Dorval, the site of Imogen's speculative revolution. The representation of Imogen's refashioning provides a unique moment of revelation into the ongoing changes occurring within the young novice, since a dwelling "bears the impression of its occupant."⁷¹ For this reason, it is easy to confuse the results of her renovations within the house as Owenson revealing and commenting upon the novice's internal development. At the end of her efforts, "magnificence was every where chastened by simplicity and splendour by taste, and all that could allure to pleasurable enjoyment or tasteful and intellectual gratification, added to the social comforts of convenience and accommodation" of the de St. Dorval residence.⁷² Reading the interior of the hôtel as an expression of the novice's identity suggests that she has, at this point, maintained a balance, effecting a modernization without too bloody a revolution against the previously entrenched Gothic rule. All of this interior renovation is less of a radical departure from or effacement of Imogen's selfhood and more accurately a liberal modernization of Parisian society.

Only once Owenson situates Imogen's transformation of the Hôtel de St. Dorval within the broader socioeconomic landscape of the French capital does the degree to which she lacks the skills of economic practitionership become apparent. "Hitherto a stranger almost to the use and entirely to the possession of money," Owenson explains of her young novice, "she looked on her riches as inexhaustible, and expended them as if they were so."⁷³ The hourly presentation of accounts and bills demonstrates Imogen's lack of economic practitionership. The debts she owes to "tradesmen, artisans, and mechanics [...] exceeded the large sums she had brought from Provence, and which she supposed would have nearly carried her through the winter's campaign."[74] These tradesmen, artisans, and mechanics embody both the growing demand for and the resultant boom in the Parisian industry of luxury commodities.[75] By the beginning of the seventeenth century, Paris is estimated to have around 300 goldsmiths, 200 tennis courts, as well as artisans "working with precious stones, ivory, glass and fancy metals."[76] By remaining completely anonymous and yet still exacting heavy demands from her, these depersonalized capitalists inaugurate Imogen's participation within the metropolitan landscape of capitalism, echoing the type of disinterest that characterizes Simmel's metropolis. Owenson provides her young novice the means of enjoying the independence enabled by the metropolitan division of labor's weakening of personal bonds. With the revolution of fashion, Owenson depicts the beginning of Imogen's dynamic process of metropolitan *Bildung*.

The economic *Bildungsroman* of Owenson's novice, then, is grounded firmly in the world of the aristocracy and in the expanding world of the luxury commodity exchange. The development of the luxury economy is part of a much broader project of urban renewal that took place under the reign of Henry IV, who "wanted to draw to the capital the high nobility" and to "shape the city so that it could match the grandeur to which he aspired for the nation and for his dynasty."[77] The Reine Margot pulled the Faubourg Saint-Germain toward the Seine, while the redevelopment of the Luxembourg Palace helped push the Faubourg eastward toward the Montagne Sainte-Geneviève and the Sorbonne.[78] These urban developments spurred the building of aristocratic homes, inaugurating the "golden age of the private hôtel," drawing from aristocratic, established families as well as the "financial, legal and administrative cadres of the Bourbon state."[79] Situating Owenson's representation of the flourishing economics of early seventeenth-century Paris in this historical context, it becomes clear that debts and tradesmen signal a recognizably modern Parisian landscape. This geography, again, is implicitly connected to the spaces of the monarchy by the focus on the social realm of the Hôtel de Guise and the Louvre across the Seine as well as the fact that the

Faubourg Saint-Germain's development depends upon the connection to the Reine Margot. These spaces must be read via this connection in terms of an autocratic determination of selfhood: historically, Henry's attempts to reform the cityscape function as attempts to surveil the nobility; narratologically, Imogen's time in Paris is dictated by her father's will. She depends upon her appointed guardian for access to wealth; she ultimately receives the condemnation of that same guardian for her economic expenditure. This royal and social geography perfectly encapsulates the complicated and contradictory impulses of the classical *Bildungsroman*, which seeks to conceal the mechanism of socialization through convincing its subject to accede to its sociocultural demands.

In fact, Imogen explains that her initial streak of consumption in renovating the Hôtel de St. Dorval was a prerequisite for her entry into the fashionable world of Paris's upper class. Only once the renovation is complete does she intend to "send her father's letter to the duchess de Guise" because only "*now*, should she deign to visit me, I shall not be afraid […] I am armed at all points for the critical review of Parisian taste and judgment."[80] There is an undeniable need on Imogen's part to impress, a fear of not surviving the evaluating gaze of the Parisian nobility, embodied in the person of the Duchess de Guise. The fear of appearing out of fashion not only reveals the degree to which fashion is fleeting and constantly changing but, more importantly, signals the function of the crowd in metropolitan fashion. As Bell explains, the modern economy of the fashion commodity exchange "is a domain in which the freedom of the individual subject is effectively negated […] his desires and needs are determined by a 'collective other,' by a group of people whose behavior and appearance dictate his own."[81] Fashion has become the dominant mode of socialization within this capitalist metropolis. By learning to yearn for the latest fashionable commodity, the system convinces Imogen to participate in the single activity that constantly reifies the broader structure of capitalism.

Fashion, just like the Society of the Tower in *Wilhelm Meister*, convinces the individual that his or her happiness lies in the recognition and reaffirmation of the dominant social structures. When Owenson explains that "a week only had elapsed from the period of Imogen's introduction at court, and that notoriety which even the secret ambition of the novice of St. Dominick had panted to possess was now all her own," she is demonstrating both the alacrity with which the young novice has adopted the laws of fashion and capitalism that govern the metropolis and, moreover, the reward for the proper submission to those laws.[82] The reward for that submission is the acknowledgement of success, just as it was for Wilhelm and Elizabeth Bennet. Because fashion enacts a different system than that of Goethe or Austen, that success is fleeting; as Moretti explains, "it is only a moment, and no use asking it to stop, because the time of individual life and that of the social system have gone definitely out of step."[83] Echoing these claims of a lack of sympathy between fashion and the individual, Owenson clearly points out that Imogen's success does not carry "the magic influence" that would have acted as guarantor of happiness in the classical *Bildungsroman*.[84] Instead, Imogen is decidedly "indebted for its possession to a whimsical coincidence of circumstances, or to the self-love of those in whose hands the power of bestowing it was vested."[85]

This form of "success" is a metropolitan alternative that employs the language of commerce and, more specifically, that of credit and debt, explicitly recognizing capitalism as a socializing system and, subsequently, the power structures that instantiate the larger system. Imogen's success belongs just as much to chance and the self-indulgent whims of the arbiters of fashion. Similarly, her ability to be "armed at all points for the critical review of Parisian taste and judgment" is attributable to the credit of Parisian bankers.[86] She is now doubly invested in the metropolitan system of credit: with the renovations of the Château de St. Dorval, she is involved in credit and lending; in the fashionable world of court and the aristocracy, she is indebted by means of a form of the gift. In a way that recalls both Richardson and Burney, Imogen's debt functions as a fulcrum of the plot that results in her condemnation and exile from the city; furthermore, this economic subplot also reveals the problematic relationships of power between individuals, especially women, in this metropolitan and credit-based economy.[87] The relationship between debt, moral censure, and a recognizably economic system reinforces the novel's association with an *ancien régime* Paris.

So much of Imogen's success depends upon flattery. The Marquis de Sancy, "flattered by the pleasure she hung upon his brilliant conversation, [...] cried her up every where as a wit of the first order" and the Duke de Montmorency "found in her that novelty which alone had now the power to awaken a thrill on its languid pulse, [and] established every where the fame of her beauty."[88] Both of these men respond to what can be seen as actions that promote their own grandeur, or at least their own pleasure. Their description of Imogen as fashionable functions as a form of reciprocity or repayment. The Duchess de Guise enacts a different form of credit when she, "in the kind policy of her friendship, [repeats] many of those enthusiastic and rapturous expressions of admiration with which Imogen had dwelt on the character [...] of her accomplished sovereign" to the king himself.[89] All of these relationships, however, exhibit unequal power structures in that Imogen's continued recognition depends upon her constant obsequiousness. As Bourdieu explains, this "is the very essence of social alchemy through which an interested relationship is transmuted into a disinterested, gratuitous relationship, overt domination into [...] *legitimate authority*."[90] In this way, the language of commercial credit understandably applies to social relationships, since these relationships are another form of socialization that teach the individual to whom he or she should be submissive. In this case, the individual learns to recognize the authority of the bankers and the aristocracy.

The combination of bankers and aristocrats as lenders of credit returns creates a dynamic parallel between the two different manifestations of debt. Owenson employs both forms in a way that participates within a broader eighteenth- and nineteenth-century discourse on the moral character of the emerging economic landscape. Similar to such novels as Samuel Richardson's *Pamela; Or, Virtue Rewarded* (1740–41) and, later, Fanny Burney's *The Wanderer; Or, Female Difficulties*

(1814), Imogen's debt functions as a fulcrum of the plot, while also revealing the problematic relationships of power between individuals, especially women, in this metropolitan and credit-based economy.[91] In the first instance, Imogen's contracts with the tradesmen, artisans, and mechanics who carry out her fashionable revolution in the Hôtel de St. Dorval seem relatively benign, even if they are expensive. Once she repays them, their commercial relationship will have reached its end. This transaction ostensibly repositions her "in the impersonal world of the market" where "her market exchanges with tradesmen are liberated from onerous personal obligations by their contractual form" because it relieves her of the gendered imbalance of power that these debts have established.[92] However, it is not that simple because Imogen's debts surpass the liquid capital she brought with her from Provençe. In order to "satisfy even the present demands she was therefore obliged to draw on a Parisian banker for a sum deposited in his hands by the late count."[93] Owenson deftly presents the conundrum that underlies and is fundamental to the development of credit-based capitalism and the modern economic system. That this initial drawing upon her father's credit is an attempt to "satisfy even the present demands" crystallizes the fact that this will not be a one-off, but rather is the beginning of a long and eventually destructive relationship between the indebted Imogen and various creditors.[94]

Owenson makes this dangerous transactional relationship abundantly clear by returning to the representation of gambling as a form of aristocratic leisure. Gambling is inextricably bound up with debates about and representations of the city throughout nineteenth-century literature, recurring in Balzac, in Zola, as well as in Pushkin's *The Queen of Spades* (1834) and in Edgeworth, most often in the form of the roulette table. Gambling, as Richard Sennett explains, functions as a totalizing metaphor for the nineteenth-century economy since "the businessmen and bureaucrats of the last century had little sense of participating in an orderly system" and, as such, workers "used to picture their activities in terms of the gamble, the game of chance—and the appropriate scene was the stock exchange."[95] Moretti expands upon this metaphorical relationship, arguing that gambling, especially roulette, "best reflects the potential rapidity of urban social change" that is part and parcel of playing the stock market.[96]

During a party at the Hôtel de Guise, the Marquis de Sancy challenges the young novice to a game of primero, urging her to "throw the gauntlet [and] I will pick it up, and think myself honoured in the challenge."[97] The imagery resembles that of a duel, registering the danger latent in this leisurely activity and the underlying adversarial contest between individuals in the game of chance and of social power. In poker and in social relationships, "[t]here are two sides: one wins, the other loses; one wins *because* the other loses."[98] "The marquis de Sancy was one of the best primero-players in France," Owenson explains, and "Imogen perhaps the very worst," a discrepancy that enhances the predatory quality of the entire exchange.[99] Recalling Sennett's parallel between gambling and the metropolitan economy, it is not a surprise if the young novice is also "perhaps the worst" player of the broader metropolitan game. Owenson's representation of the card game itself is worth quoting at length:

> [S]he played with so little attention, with so little skill, and in the exhilaration of her spirits staked so high, that in a short time she lost all the ready money she was mistress of, and found herself the marquis's debtor for a sum treble what she had ever before contracted to anyone. The marquis insisted on considering the debt as cancelled, except she gave him an opportunity of allowing her a chance of winning back some of her own money. Imogen by the instances of De Servin, who leaned at the back of her chair, was prevailed on. The game was begun with fresh spirit; fortune at first seemed to smile on Imogen, but before it was finished she had doubled her debt.[100]

In this scene, Owenson demonstrates what Finn and Bourdieu have described as the creation of legitimate authority by means of the socioeconomic phenomenon of the gift.[101] This constructs a double bind for Imogen: she is indebted to the marquis for the actual sum of his winnings and for the grace he has displayed. When she "begged to be considered the debtor of the marquis de Sancy till the following day, [...] De Sancy begged she would not limit his enviable privilege to a day."[102] The term "privilege" functions in two distinct senses: firstly, in the most surface reading, it is the chivalrous act of not demanding immediate payment and, thus, preserving the young woman's respectability in public. "Privilege" also reminds Imogen of a hierarchical relationship that exists between higher and lower members of society, replicating the binary of debtor and creditor.

Owenson expresses a similar understanding of the "symbolic violence" of credit that recognizes the power structures that undergird the broader socioeconomic system.[103] Because Imogen is a woman, the violence enacted is greater, reasserting the problematically gendered nature of the metropolitan economic landscape. The *chevalier* half warns the young novice that, "though the marquis de Sancy is what the world calls a man of honour, [...] yet is he not the man to whom a young, a beautiful unguarded woman; on too but—," before pausing abruptly.[104] The assumption is that the marquis is not a man to whom a woman should be indebted. The use of "unguarded" reinforces this sense of predation and the threat of violence against the female body. Owenson's implication that women are secondary citizens in the cosmopolitan economic landscape demonstrates a complicated understanding of the social relationships that result from commodity capitalism and the modern metropolis.

Imogen's debts to the Marquis de Sancy represent merely one debit on her accounts, albeit a rather serious one; the vast amount of debt she has accumulated reveals the novel's relationship between debt, moral censure, and a recognizably capitalist economic system reinforces this novel's characterization of Paris as a masculine space. The morning after the *chevalier* quits Paris for London, a woman seeks an audience with the countess because her "husband is the person who furnished the silk hangings for your house; when he received [the] order, he was but just recovering from some heavy losses in trade; the silk [...] he got on credit."[105] When seeking his payment, he was "always denied; at last he was arrested for the money himself. For six weeks he has lingered in prison under a slow fever; while [her] children call for bread."[106] As Imogen comes face to face with the individual whose sufferings result from her own inability to manage her finances, Simmel's claims of "entirely unknown purchasers who never appear in the actual field of vision" is utterly turned on its head.[107] This scene of despair results from a "chain of unpaid debts that place[s] the onus of obligation upon precisely those creditors least able to sustain their debtors' refusal to make repayment."[108] In response to the presentation of suffering, Imogen retrieves a purse that was meant to repay her debt to de Sancy. In repaying this woman's bill from the debt owed to the marquis, Imogen renders herself unable to fulfil the debt to the marquis, incorporating the novice in an ever-increasing cycle of debt.

Imogen is utterly enmeshed within the credit system and unable to extricate herself from the obligations enjoined by debt, to the point that the *chevalier* must "plead the claims of the indigent, the oppressed, the defrauded, of those whom [her] blind extravagance has rendered poor," listing the account of "a mercer in the city, who, impoverished by the ill payment of the countess de St. Dorval and other ladies of distinction, has become a bankrupt," and an "unfortunate jeweller [who] is now languishing in a prison.—Here is the account of a poor tradesman."[109] Replicating the same humanizing embodiment of the economy, the *chevalier*'s litany of Imogen's debts recounts the degree to which she has been unable to negotiate the landscape of the metropolis. Her debts emphasize the immorality of excessive consumption and the number of times she has relied upon credit, deepening her debt and thus the entitlement afforded to her creditors as Owenson depicts the metropolitan marketplace in commercial and moral terms.

While these expenditures imprison Imogen in the never-ending cycle of consumption and debt, they ironically also provide her the means of fulfilling her social and moral obligations. They have heretofore functioned as a symbol of her inability to negotiate the rules of the metropolitan marketplace. Yet, by employing these economic signs in the repayment of her debts, Imogen exhibits a remarkable understanding of the socioeconomic principles that undergird cosmopolitan capitalism. The bills that tabulate her debts "convinced her of the great value" of her possessions, but the problem of how to "transmit these rich possessions into specie" remains.[110] In these commodities she perceives her own ability to participate doubly in the exchange process. Beforehand, she had only ever ventured into the marketplace as a consumer, but now she understands that she must take up the other side of Marx's *dramatis personae*; she must sell her possessions. In a serendipitous moment, a stranger emerges who offers to buy all of Imogen's property and possessions for a sum equal to her debt. This stranger claims he is there "to serve you, young lady; [...] I have enriched myself by relieving the necessities of those who, by their own unguarded and careless liberality, by the vilany [sic] of others, or unavoidable misfortunes have been plunged into pecuniary difficulties."[111] This secretive individual reiterates the broad condemnation of the modern metropolitan economy. As we have seen with the threat the marquis poses to Imogen, the association of consumption with villainy, misfortunes, and simple difficulties highlights the sexualized and threatening nature of the capitalist cityscape.

The next morning, before an assembly of all her creditors, Imogen "had at last the pleasure of holding in her hands the receipts in full for every thing she owed them."[112] Appearing before this collection of creditors, the young novice outlined "that conduct by which they had been so much injured, and endeavoured to palliate its errors, by pleading the inexperience of youth."[113] This phrase "inexperience of youth" emphasizes the fact that this narrative functions as an economic *Bildungsroman*. In accepting "the humility of the debtor" and making reparations for the "conduct by which [the lenders] had been so much injured," Imogen recognizes and performs the fiduciary arrangement that exists between economic agents.[114] She takes her place as an economic practitioner within, and resigns herself from, the metropolitan credit economy.

As a result, she must also retire from the urban landscape itself. In a scene that bookends Imogen's initial view of Paris, she:

> cast back one longing lingering glance, beheld the rising smoke, the lofty towers and pointing spires of Paris [...]; and if one tear of youthful regret fell to the recollection of those festive gaieties, those brilliant pleasures, and splendid triumphs, she had once enjoyed, and now for ever relinquished, many drops of anguish stained her cheek at the goading recollection, that she who had entered Paris a few months back, rich in circumstances, spotless in fame, without one self-reproach rankling at her heart, supported by friendship, and proud in her own consciousness, was now leaving it with a fortune injured by her own imprudence, a character calumniated by that malice her own unguarded levity had sanctioned.[115]

The "youthful regret" ties the space of fashionable Paris to the immature revolutions of her first entry into the capital, while the combination of "regret," "anguish," "self-reproach," and "imprudence" all convey the condemnation of consumption and frivolity that characterize Edgeworth's *Tales of Fashionable Life*.[116] That this novel achieves its narratological end thanks to the hallmarks of the classical *Bildungsroman* should not be surprising; in fact, it is clearly linked to its metropolitan and urban setting, especially the spaces of the Hôtel de Guise and the Louvre on the Right Bank, and the Reine Margot's Faubourg Saint-Germain on the Left Bank. It is, lastly, important to note the repetition of "unguarded," which was used to caution Imogen against her initial foray into aristocratic gambling at the Hôtel de Guise. Again, it seems to characterize the urban landscape as inherently threatening to women, a trait that Irish women's representation of Paris will exhibit throughout this study.

Once her debts are paid, there is nothing left for Imogen but to return to her ancestral estates in Provençe, where Owenson demonstrates the ultimate achievement of the socializing project of the

Bildungsroman. While this succinct recounting of her time in Paris ignores the metropolitan development that has taken place, it characterizes the urban sphere as one associated with youth, inexperience, and loss. Imogen's maturation is based upon an anxious desire "to commence a new era of existence" paired with the renunciation of the urban, which "she was, she believed, for ever quitting."[117] In quitting the metropolis, Imogen returns and submits to the stipulations of her father's will, which commanded "that her residence in Paris should never exceed three [months], and that she would chiefly reside at the chateau de St. Dorval."[118] Her *Bildung* is predicated upon her rejection of the cosmopolitan world of fashion, and, more conventionally, it is accompanied by the completion of her ordained social role.

Thus it is difficult to read *The Novice* as providing a clear path for aristocratic women's emergence into the metropolitan marketplace and, additionally, their enjoyment of the liberties that later theorists of the city assign to that *mise-en-scène*. The fact of the *chevalier* posing as the usurer further complicates any broad claim for Imogen's metropolitan practitionership, since her economic engagement exists largely within the patriarchal sphere of the family. Undeniably, Imogen has successfully repaid her debts, taking on the socioeconomic identities of consumer and merchant. She looked "over the amount of her debts, and then counted the gold which the usurer had spread on the table, *for the first time felt the value of money.*"[119] This recognition completes Imogen's urban novitiate. In this way, then, Owenson is not suggesting that upper-class women are categorically incapable of successfully operating within the capitalist marketplace. Instead, she sets a precedent for Irish women writers by representing economic practitionership as a vital skill that registers the complex interrelationships of an individual's class, gender, and relationship to institutional power.

But Owenson's sociocultural representation of Paris shifts in her later novel *The O'Briens and the O'Flahertys* from the same Faubourg Saint-Germain and moves across the Seine to the Théâtre de la République, after the novel returns to the French capital from Ireland. This later novel, widely regarded as Owenson's best, is often discussed in terms of its representation of the United Irishmen's 1798 uprising and the concomitant debate surrounding forms of nationalism; however, this novel equally demonstrates an important interest in the role of the city broadly, and the French capital more specifically, in providing an alternative space to the overdetermined and over-historicized space of Ireland.[120] *The O'Briens and the O'Flahertys* opens with a series of letters between the General Count Sir Malachi O'Fflaherty at his "Hôtel, Rue de l'Université, F. St Germain, à Paris" and Major O'Gara at "St. Grellan, Barony of Tar Connaught, Co. Galway."[121] These letters begin in "1 April 177—," which means that Owenson's two novels are set in same geographic location nearly 200 years apart. In the eighteenth century, the Rue de l'Université, along with the rest of the Faubourg Saint-Germain, remained "the haunt of the older nobility."[122] A mid-eighteenth-century memorandum describes this neighborhood and the Faubourg Saint-Honoré as the only ones "appropriate for building big houses which would be the residence of distinction."[123] Again, however, Owenson's representation of the Faubourg focuses less on its modernity and more on the "older" nature of its nobility as a connection to the past. The university from which the street derives its name dates back to the twelfth century, although in the mid-seventeenth century it would sell its land in the Pré-aux-Clercs area and relocate its focus to the eastern fifth *arrondissement*.[124] Instead of repeating the anti-modern representation of Paris that we saw in *The Novice*, *The O'Briens and the O'Flahertys* ultimately positions Paris as a site of social mobility in a way that becomes all too familiar over the course of the nineteenth-century novel, especially the Parisian *Bildungsromane* of Balzac's *Comédie humaine* and Zola's *Rougon-Macquart* cycle. And, unsurprisingly, Owenson's late-1820s novel registers this social mobility most clearly in the representation of the Opéra.[125]

After the majority of the novel takes place in the western counties of Ireland, *The O'Briens and the O'Flahertys* shifts, rather suddenly, to post-revolutionary Paris after the protagonists' escape from Ireland in the novel's concluding chapters. The narrator explains that on this particular evening Napoleon "and the ladies of his family, with the

Generals Rapp, Bessières, Lannes, and Lebrun" accepted "a proposal, made by Madame Murat, to go to the Opera to hear the grand oratorio of Haydn, which was the rage of the day."[126] As Julia Wright notes, this follows "the details of 24 December 1800 (including names of historical figures) when Napoleon escaped an assassination attempt as he was on his way to a performance of Josef Haydn's new oratorio, *The Creation*."[127] Musical historian James Johnson notes that "Bonaparte had made a point of appearing regularly at the Opéra" ever since his Italian campaign. But, in typical Parisian fashion, Napoleon always arrived late.[128] And this late arrival, both in the novel and historically, allows the space of the Opéra to function as a space of social observation and urban legibility. By 1800, the Paris Opéra had relocated to the Théâtre National near the Bibliothèque National on the Rue de la Loi, now the Rue de Richelieu,[129] whose interior:

> boasted an opulence far from republican simplicity. Citizens and sansculottes seated themselves in boxes swathed in fabrics of red and gold. A new system of lighting placed lamps behind diaphanous clouds on the walls, bathing the hall in warm, diffuse light, an effect observers described as more magical and enchanting than in any previous hall.[130]

This description of the hall emphasizes the very modernity of the space, a modernity that places the Opéra in marked distinction to Owenson's earlier Gothicized spaces. This modern interior, however, mirrored the Revolution in another, more important, manner that exacerbates the social mobility that dominates Owenson's representation of the Opéra. As Johnson explains, the Opéra "was much less an institution of elites after 1789," in large part because the Revolution "severed any remaining connections between visibility and social status, at least as the pattern had developed in the middle decades of the [eighteenth] century."[131] In this post-Revolution theater, the seating "now seemed more random than ever" and often produced rather unlikely neighbors.[132] This commingling of audience members in the Opéra, based on a reconfiguration, if not an outright rejection, of class structures leads to one of the primary difficulties that occupies nineteenth-century French novels: the difficulty of reading the urban scene, what might be termed urban literacy.

Owenson uses this confusion in order to promote a sense of meritocratic social mobility thanks to the very end of the novel. Here, among "the wife of the Austrian Plenipotentiary [...] a true German Princess" and "[t]he Austrian Minister," emerges "a general officer, attended by his two aides-de-camp [... who] was rendered conspicuous by being the only General present who did not wear the new decoration of the Legion of Honour."[133] The person, the text continues, "was in the prime of his life, of lofty stature, and commanding air; and so distinguished by personal advantages [...] that [he] is, or would be, a personage, a modern Alcibiades: like the Athenian General."[134] This celebrated figure is, of course, General O'Brien, "a fellow like that, that no one would speak to in Ireland—he a General in the French service."[135] The disbelief at the deserved social recognition of the general not only highlights a recognizable critique that Owenson levels against the Gothicized space of Ireland, but demonstrates the emerging notion of social mobility and urban literacy that will come to dominate the urban novels of Balzac's *Comédie humaine*, as well as the rest of the novels within this study.

In the end, Owenson's Parisian novels reject the simple return to the pre-capitalist world that largely characterizes the classical *Bildungsroman* tradition. Instead, they present a complicated point of departure for later Irish women writers who would seek to explore the relationship of the individual and society. This point cannot be isolated entirely within the metropolis, nor divorced completely from the country estates of the aristocracy. *The Novice of Saint Dominick* cannot provide Imogen the unfettered freedom of later protagonists, continually reinscribing her within the limits of patriarchal authority. Yet this early economic *Bildungsroman* reveals a complicated and nuanced understanding of, and engagement with, socioeconomic conditions, especially the ambivalent struggle to achieve self-realization under modern capitalism. *The O'Briens and the O'Flahertys*, on the other hand, presents a Paris that is recognizably more modern, more liberal. In this later novel, the space of the city becomes not only a refuge for an outlawed Irishman, but a space that recognizes his worth. Ultimately, however, these competing attitudes leave us with a certain ambivalence about the formation of modern metropolitan selfhood and toward Paris as the primary location for the interrogation of the effects of capitalism on the process of *Bildung*.

CHAPTER TWO

Much More than Only *Le Bel Irlandois*
Metropolitan Socioeconomics and Parisian *Bildung* in Maria Edgeworth's *Ormond*

> Paris was not then as fine a city as it now is. Ormond, in his secret soul, preferred the bay of Dublin to all he saw on the banks of the Seine.
>
> —Maria Edgeworth, *Ormond*

One productive way of reading Maria Edgeworth's Irish Tales, claims Marilyn Butler, is "in some sense [as] explicitly a sequel to or re-working" of her earliest and most well-known Irish Tale, *Castle Rackrent* (1800).[1] When considered as a response to the first of her Irish Tales, *Ennui* (1809), *The Absentee*, and *Ormond* all share at least one notable trait: they shift the focus of the narrative away from "the quaint, archaic" and Irish narrator, Thady M'Quirk, and instead privilege the person and position of the landlords who "had in reality a more significant part to play in Irish life."[2] With this shift in narratological emphasis, Edgeworth's later Irish Tales can be seen as participating in the sociocultural project of the classical or, as Franco Moretti describes it, the Goethean *Bildungsroman*. The primary aim of this formulation of the *Bildungsroman* is a socialization-formation process in which "the certainty of meaning lies here not in conflict, but in a *participation* in the Whole," in which the individual achieves meaningful selfhood only by taking up his socially ordained and socially required position.³ Whether we consider the former Lord Glenthorn, Lord Colambre, or Harry Ormond, each of these characters' narratives close with his having achieved a successful *Bildung*.

This is in no small part because each of them has accepted the necessity of participation "in the Whole" and rejected the self-centered alternative socioeconomic systems that they have encountered, which is consistently related to the modern metropolitan landscape of London and, especially, Paris. The tension between a self-centered socialization-formation and a responsible participation in the progressive and reformist mold, which Richard Lovell Edgeworth had fostered in his daughter, carries with it an economic and allegorical component that has been absent from criticism of *Ormond*. While Claire Connolly recognizes *Ormond* as "unusual in shaping such a distinct set of relations between Ireland and France," this focus highlights the degree to which France should be an object of study in Edgeworth criticism.⁴ More recently, Clíona Ó Gallchoir has argued that Edgeworth's *Madame de Fleury* (1809) and *Emilie de Coulanges* (1812), both anti-Jacobin tales, "frequently feature a strategic defence of France," while *Ormond*, more specifically, represents "another possible configuration of gender and national identity by using the French language to construct a masculine identity that is informed by traces of femininity."⁵ This points, as Ó Gallchoir claims, to the complex position that France occupies in Edgeworth's writings; throughout her *œuvre*, Edgeworth's representations of France "rhetorically assume the image of the home of Enlightenment, the cultural centre of Europe, a decadent regime run by and for an effeminate elite, a beacon of hope for equality and justice, or a tyrannical regime."⁶ As Ó Gallchoir's analysis reveals, France is an ambivalent space in the map of Edgeworth's fiction; however, *Ormond* is exemplary in its embodiment of both representations of the French capital, ultimately associating *Bildung* with the project of Enlightenment. This chapter's focus on "the Paris interlude" in *Ormond* recognizes an ambivalence toward the influence of emergent capitalism on the formation of the self in Edgeworth's final Irish Tale.

The responsible quality of an Edgeworthian *Bildung* becomes evident when we consider the sociocultural location that dominates the closing scenes of her other Irish Tales: the Big House of the Anglo-Irish demesne. While *Castle Rackrent* also concludes within the sociocultural sphere of the demesne, the social authority that invests the later Irish Tales is absent as a result of the Rackrents' reckless management of their estate. In the later novels, *Ennui* comes closest to repeating *Castle Rackrent*'s crisis of mismanagement: after the rightful heir to the Glenthorn estate, the young blacksmith Christy Donoghoe, takes his place in Castle Glenthorn, his family's overconsumption and disregard for their wealth results in the death of Christy's son and the ruin of the estate. But, in order to avoid a repetition of *Castle Rackrent*, the former Glenthorn, now Mr. Delamere, returns as inheritor by virtue of his wife being "the *hare* at law," concluding with the restoration of a now responsible and beneficent Anglo-Irish landlord, whose rule guarantees the perpetuation of the estate.[7] The same pattern of reformation and restoration is found in *The Absentee* and *Ormond*, the latter of which is the focus of this chapter. *Ormond* follows the moral development of its titular character as he moves from a passionate and impetuous ward in his uncle's country household in the west of Ireland to a denizen of Enlightenment Paris and, ultimately, to a responsible and moderate land-owner in Ireland, where he marries and settles into the improving ranks of the Anglo-Irish Ascendancy. Just as the concluding marriage between Ormond and the worthy daughter of Lady Annaly demonstrates, the ending of all three of Edgeworth's Irish Tales echoes "that pact between the individual and the world, that reciprocal 'consent' which finds in the double 'I do' of the wedding ritual an unsurpassed symbolic condensation," a hallmark of Moretti's Goethean *Bildungsroman*.[8] The symbolic locus of these endings, as Moretti claims, is one of the "conclusive places" like *Wilhelm Meister*'s Tower and *Pride and Prejudice*'s Pemberley, the world of "closed social forms," which are "fully possible *only in the precapitalist world* [...] far from the metropolis."⁹ Edgeworthian criticism has reinforced Moretti's literary geography; however, a reconsideration of the representation of Paris ultimately challenges this *ortgebunden* nature of *Bildung* in Edgeworth's novels.

If we were to create a map of the ending locations of Edgeworth's Irish Tales, it would largely resemble the map Moretti has constructed of Jane Austen's endings and reflect a similar pattern "of exclusion."¹⁰ The Edgeworthian map would, first of all, exclude Europe and England, but it would also exclude most of Ireland; centered largely in the western midlands around Longford, it would obviously exclude Dublin, Belfast, Cork, Limerick, and Galway. *Ormond*, like *Ennui* and *The Absentee*, largely ends where it began: in a world where the European capitalist metropolis seems to have little or no recognizable influence. W. J. McCormack's introduction to the novel bolsters the stark division between the world of closed social forms and that of the modern marketplace; he describes the admittedly small number of pages devoted to *Ormond*'s representation of Paris as "the Paris interlude," language that seems somehow dismissive of this European context.¹¹ If, however, *Ormond*'s Paris is taken not as an interlude, distracting from the more on-target Ireland-located narrative, but as the centralizing framework for the narrative tensions that govern the process of the protagonist's *Bildung*, then the novel takes its place within the emerging tradition of the Irish woman's economic *Bildungsroman*.

Such a reframing enables a critical reappraisal of Edgeworth's last Irish Tale that demonstrates a more nuanced engagement with the experiences of selfhood and socialization-formation under the emerging system of nineteenth-century capitalism. As Moretti's description of "the reciprocal consent" of marriage and the role of the Society of the Tower make clear, central to the completion of the *Bildungsroman* is a twinned experience of sympathy and distance: there must exist a mutual sympathy between the *Bildungsheld* and society (or the Society), but there is also a requisite distance so that the machinations of the Society are never felt to be dictated or imposed. This pairing of sympathy and distance is fundamental to understanding the intellectual project that undergirds Edgeworth's engagement with the social and economic context of the Enlightenment. While Seamus Deane has argued that this pairing of sentiment and distance was only available to Walter Scott and Scotland because of the aesthetic and philosophical influence of Adam Smith, it will become clear that *ancien régime* Paris provides the "Stoic distance of the 'impartial spectator' in moral manners" as well as "the polite distance of the historian from historical events, adapted in preference to a proximity that would not allow for the overview that enabled the history of society to be written."[12] Deane argues that this type of perspective "was not available to Burke or Edgeworth" precisely because "Irish economic and political realities made such a balance little more than a fictional convention."[13] This view, however, disregards the significance of Edgeworth's representation of Paris in favor of the critically dominant position that elevates the novel's representation of Ireland. In the geo-social landscape of the French metropolis, modernity becomes achievable precisely because France provides the "theory of society" that Deane argues was inimical to Irish literature in the wake of Burke's *Reflections on the Revolution in France*.[14] Edgeworth's contradictory representations of Paris as a seat of Enlightenment sociability, on the one hand, and spectacular consumption, on the other, enables *Ormond* to engage the modern type of selfhood that Deane considers to be lacking in Irish literature of the early nineteenth century.

In the Paris of *Ormond*, Edgeworth shifts the construction of this experience of *Bildung* away from the binary terms of a commodity-based modern socioeconomic system and a pre-capitalist alternative, the dominant paradigms which Deane elucidates in his analysis of Burke's writings. Instead, competing modes of socialization-formation become a function of the tension between an irresponsible commodity-based socioeconomic system, embodied in fashion and gambling, and a responsible form of investment in landed estates and in personal relationships, embodied in the "virtue and domestic life" of Enlightenment literary figures such as the Abbé Morellet and Jean-François

Marmontel, who function as the moral impetus for Ormond's reform and final achievement of *Bildung*.[15] Confronted with two competing socioeconomic systems in the Parisian metropolis, Harry Ormond rejects the fashionable world of the gambling table, which Deane and Burke associate with the Revolution and Jacobins, and its commodification of the self in order to complete his *Bildung* by reaffirming the proper value of "that 'pact' between the individual and the world," which is embodied in the Enlightenment of the *ancien régime*.[16] Ormond ultimately rejects the new capitalist-influenced formulation of the *Bildungsroman* and chooses instead to follow the type of *Bildung* enshrined in Goethe's paradigmatic *Wilhelm Meister*.

The Air of a French Coxcomb:
The Metropolitan *Bildung* and Fashion

That *Ormond* expresses, at the very least, an ambivalence, if not outright wariness, toward the emerging nineteenth-century system of capitalism is unsurprising because, as my analysis of Owenson's *The Novice of Saint Dominick* in Chapter 1 has demonstrated, the modern metropolitan marketplace can hardly be said to be the world of fixed social forms. In Moretti's formulation of the Goethean model of *Bildung*, this process of development cannot occur within the metropolis precisely because the modern city, as Georg Simmel has claimed, "has always been the seat of money economy."[17] Defined by its "many-sidedness and concentration of commercial activity," the metropolitan money economy fundamentally rejects the fixed maturity that is the classical *Bildungsroman*'s goal; instead, as the writers in this study and others such as Honoré de Balzac, Charles Dickens, and Émile Zola demonstrate, the forms of identity that the modern city and economy champion are those that mirror money's ability to "grow, and change form, and *never stop*."[18] This is the narrative sociology that dominates the first manifestation of Paris in *Ormond*, the Paris of the theater, boulevards, galleries, courts, and gambling tables, the Paris embodied in Monsieur and Madame de Connal.

Monsieur and Madame de Connal immediately challenge the notion of a fixed identity, since their own formulation of self seems to shift with the fickle winds of fashion throughout the novel. Also known as Black Connal and Dora O'Shane, these two figures deserve greater attention than they have received in recent criticism. The way in which Edgeworth continuously reshapes their identities acknowledges the impact of the commodity-based money economy on the individual in a way that anticipates the type of metropolitan selfhood that distinguishes the Goethean from the Balzacian *Bildungsroman* in Moretti's formulation.

Black Connal, the son of Old Connal and the younger brother of White Connal, emerges to take Dora O'Shane's hand in marriage only after the untimely death of his brother, to whom her father's drunken pledge had originally promised her. As the younger of old Connal's sons, Black Connal did not inherit the land or the cattle that made his older brother "a fat grazier" and, as a result, has been "abroad these great many years, ever since he was a boy [...] an officer he is in the Irish brigade [...] captain Connal now."[19] In this light, Connal immediately creates connections with a broad network of Irish fiction that has used the Continent as a place of economic opportunity for dispossessed Irish men, including Owenson's *O'Donnell* (1814) and *The O'Briens and the O'Flahertys*, Randal William McDonnell's *Kathleen Mavourneen: A Memory of the Great Rebellion, from the Record of Hugh Tallant, Rebel to King George of England in the Year of Grace One Thousand Seven Hundred and Ninety Eight* (1898), Stephen MacKenna's *Roddy the Rapp; or, the Whiskey Still of Glanvoe* (n.d.), and William Parnell's *Maurice and Berghetta; or, the Priest of Rahery. A Tale* (1819). Such a tradition would provide Edgeworth a literary and social context in which to place this continental captain, enabling a recognizable, almost stock identity. Owenson's O'Donnell, however, exhibits a fixed identity throughout the novel; only his social situation fluctuates as he is forced to return to the Continent after being dispossessed of his ancient territory. In this fixity, O'Donnell demonstrates less of a connection with Black Connal than with his older brother

White Connal, whose entire existence is determined "to get money," and who is described as being "not only industrious but rapacious."[20] White Connal's miserly fetishization of money contradicts the fluid construction of selfhood of modern capitalism because it prevents its circulation. The fact that his acquisition of wealth is entirely self-centered prevents him from achieving any of the closed social forms privileged by the Goethean *Bildungsroman*.

Edgeworth's younger Connal has more in common with the mysterious Abbess O'Faolain of Owenson's *The O'Briens and the O'Flahertys*, whose identity remains masked beneath a series of disguises for the majority of the novel.[21] Edgeworth similarly buries and disguises Connal's past beneath all the trappings of his continental identity. After seeing the younger Connal arriving in "a French cabriolet, and a French servant riding on to advertise" his approach to Corny Castle, Mademoiselle O'Faley immediately reproaches the servant Sheelah for recalling the fact that "sure Black Connal's Irish born" and insists "he is call [*sic*] M. de Connal. Now did I not hear him this minute announced by his own valet?—Monsieur de Connal presents his compliments."[22] Dismissing the Irish location of Connal's birth, Mademoiselle O'Faley, who is herself half-Irish and half-French, insists upon a social construction of identity that is largely dependent upon the material culture and commodities undergirding it. The moment of Connal's arrival is the first time she has addressed anyone by the title "monsieur," extrapolating from the French nature and quality of his carriage and footman that he merits the title. Edgeworth recognizes that an identity premised on the deployment of commodities destabilizes the fixed notion of selfhood, providing the emerging classes of consumers with the opportunity to perform wealth and status based entirely upon their access to surplus capital. This initial showcasing of wealth and commodities plays upon Mademoiselle O'Faley's understanding of social capital; she recognizes the symbols of wealth and assumes that the possessor of such symbols must be a possessor of wealth. Moreover, she assumes that such a possessor of wealth must be "a man of a certain quality, who knows the best people in Paris, who can talk, and tell every where."[23]

In Mlle. O'Faley's initial recognition of wealth, Edgeworth introduces and problematizes the concept of urban literacy, which is a skill that demonstrates the individual's ability to read and to comprehend the physical and social signs of the metropolis. Reading Connal's entrance, Mlle. O'Faley understandably arrives at the conclusion that he is "French, I told you [...] and quite the gentleman, depend upon it."[24] Connal seeks to buttress this conclusion with his initial face-to-face performance with Dora and her French guardian, since he is entirely aware of the impact his commodities have upon his audience. As the women accidentally meet Connal, Corny, and Ormond walking, the French captain consciously gives

> them full leisure to form their opinions as to his personal appearance. He had the air of a foreign officer—easy, fashionable, and upon uncommonly good terms with himself—conscious, but with no vulgar consciousness, of possessing a fine figure and a good face: his was the air of a French coxcomb, who in unconstrained delight was rather proud to display than [sic] anxious to conceal his perfect self-satisfaction.[25]

Connal consciously stages this introduction so that he might be adequately considered in a proud display of self-satisfaction. There is something of the eighteenth-century macaroni in Connal's self-conscious presentation of a French-fashioned identity. Throughout *Ormond*, Connal is repeatedly referred to as a "coxcomb,"[26] a word that conjures this eighteenth-century forerunner to the dandy.[27] He deploys his figure, his fashion, his overall appearance as an actor would use props to affect a certain character's air. He enhances this performance with a conversation that insists upon his association with Mademoiselle O'Faley's "best people in Paris" when he steers the conversation toward "Paris and Versailles, and various people of consequence and fashion at the court. The dauphiness!—she was then but just married—M. de Connal had seen all the fêtes and the fireworks."[28]

That these performances are strategically designed to play upon Mademoiselle O'Faley's and Dora's understanding of social capital is of little doubt. Connal functions as an empty signifier: he is, to paraphrase Mlle. O'Faley, "what you call cipher, but has no value in société at all, till [someone else] come[s] to give it the value."[29] Mlle. O'Faley addresses him with the politeness of French upper-class society because she perceives him to belong to that world. If Connal functions as a cipher receiving meaning and value from being made desirable by fashionable society, he functions similarly to the money form that dominated the English and then the Irish market from 1797 following the Restriction Act, which issued inconvertible paper money.[30] This form of money, unlike that backed by and convertible into bullion on demand, is "detached from any referent."[31] As Bell has claimed, this form of self-referential paper money "is emptied of any conceivable use value, and its exchange value is itself exchangeable."[32] What this means for Connal and for Edgeworth's understanding of selfhood under the socioeconomic system of emerging capitalism is that the self is, like money, detached from any referent: the self, as Edgeworth says of Connal, amounts to exactly what he appears to be.

This appearance is a function of performance, deploying the symbols of wealth and, more latently, the acquisition of enough capital to take one's place within the theatrical space of the metropolitan commodity economy. As *The Novice of Saint Dominick* made clear and as Somerville and Ross's *French Leave* will attest, an individual's access to capital fundamentally informs the nature of his/her relationship with the metropolis and, as a result, also informs the nature of his/her socialization-formation process. The way in which Connal acquires the necessary capital embodies this increasing importance of money, highlighting the influence of capitalism on the socialization-formation process. Edgeworth explains that he "might, perhaps, as he said, with his figure, and fashion, and connections, have made his fortune in Paris by marriage, had he had time to look about him—but a sudden run of ill fortune at play had obliged him to quit Paris for a season."[33] In this passage, Edgeworth reinforces the earlier conception of Connal as a fashionable commodity; the Parisian aristocracy evaluates him in terms of his "figure, and fashion, and connexions."[34] That the upper circles find this novelty valuable enables him to move into the socioeconomic marketplace with the expectation of a profitable exchange value. It is clear that he seeks to arrange a marriage for the social capital it would provide and as a mode of increased access to capital or, in his words, "his fortune." Calling attention to the fundamental process of exchange that underlies the Parisian marriage market, Connal points to what Marx would later term the fetishization of the commodity.[35] In the first volume of *Capital*, Marx explains that "it is only by being exchanged that the products of labour acquire a socially uniform objectivity as values."[36] As a commodity, Connal understands that this exchange value is potentially convertible into social capital in the form of a socially and economically advantageous marriage; his figure, fashion, and connections can be exchanged for their equivalent value in a marriage. Fundamental to the socioeconomic landscape of the French capital is an economic vision that treats the individual as a commodity with an exchange value that increases and decreases with the rise and fall of fashion, which leads to the commodification of social relationships.

Connal's understanding of marriage as an economic venture is not new. Frances Burney's *Camilla* (1796) and Samuel Richardson's *The History of Sir Charles Grandison* (1753), among countless others, including Sir Ulick O'Shane in *Ormond*, have recognized the economic underpinnings of marriage. As Ó Gallchoir notes, Richardson's *Grandison* provides a telling intertextual reference; Lady Annaly gives him a copy of the novel, hoping that it might better guide Ormond's *Bildung*.[37] The explicit nature of Connal's views, however, depicts the shift toward a capitalist understanding of the unmoored social relations because of the Paris from which they emanate. As a result of his bad fortune, it becomes "necessary to make his fortune by marriage in England or Ireland, and as expeditiously as possible. In this situation, Dora, with her own and her aunt's property, was [...] an offer not to be rashly slighted."[38] In addition to an economic evaluation of

Dora and her assets, which might themselves be exchanged for liquid capital, Connal expresses a sociological phenomenon that exerts a largely unrecognized influence on the representation of capitalism in the novel. Following from Trotsky's "universal law of unevenness" and "the law of *combined development*," Moretti constructs a narratological division of labor that views the provinces, or non-metropolitan spaces, as providing the materials that enable myriad metropolitan pursuits and consumption.[39] Employing Balzac's *Illusions perdues* as an exemplary text, Moretti attributes the provinces with "the endless, heavy task of physically producing paper; to the capital, the privilege of covering those beautiful white sheets with fascinating ideas (and glittering nonsense)."[40] Similar to the expectation that "an endless supply of funds [...] derived from the estate in Ireland" should furnish the fashionable expenditure of absentee landlords in London in *The Absentee*, Edgeworth re-enacts this same division of labor between the provinces and the metropole in Connal's mining of Ireland, by means of Dora and her property, for the wealth to return to the fashionable circles of Paris.[41] The provinces, the non-metropolitan areas, merely provide the means of acquiring liquid capital; as such, they seem to be left out of the development of modernity. This wealth is not to be left languishing in Ireland but is to be converted into "plays, operas, wine, women, cardinals, religion, politics, poetry, and turkeys stuffed with truffles—and Paris for ever."[42] A similarity between the attitude underlies Connal's economic understanding of Ireland and his commodification of social relationships, which is, at the most basic level, the triumph of money as the "universal signifier," the "universal equivalent."[43]

Before demonstrating the effect of this commodification of self and others on the process of *Bildung*, it is necessary to explore further the other aspect of Connal's method of accumulating capital: gambling. In the passage quoted above, Edgeworth reveals that "a sudden run of ill fortune at play" had forced Connal to seek his fortune by marriage in England or Ireland.[44] The linguistic exchange of gambling for capitalism represents a broader trend in late eighteenth- and early nineteenth-century fiction on both sides of the English Channel, as

Thomas Kavanagh and Jessica Richard have shown. In *The Romance of Gambling*, Richard convincingly argues that novels of this period, including Edgeworth's *Belinda* (1801), employ gaming as part of "an ongoing interrogation of the relationship between gambling and activities of finance capitalism, a relationship that itself is marked by dynamic tension between chance and control."[45] In *Ormond*, Edgeworth has already engaged in this intentional slippage through the figure of Ormond's original guardian, Sir Ulick O'Shane. Just as Connal sees Dora as a viable marriage partner because of the capital she will bring, the Anglo-Irish landowner "laid hold of the widow Scraggs [...] and her plum stocks" because Sir Ulick has lost "his place by the change of ministry, and one half of his fortune by the canal, in which it had been sunk."[46] This other "sudden run of ill fortune" comes not at the faro table but in the economic marketplace, since several of Ulick's speculative investments, including the canal and silver mines,[47] do not pay. The almost perfect parallel between Ulick's and Connal's economic evaluation of marriage reinforces Richard's claims of the intertwined nature of gambling and the emerging economic system, especially when we consider Ulick's investment in the silver mines.

In a conversation between the truly pre-capitalist Corny and the speculator Ulick, Edgeworth reveals a longer history of Ulick's investments, including the silver mines. Corny asks his cousin, "How do your silver mines go on, sir Ulick? I hear all the silver mines in Ireland turn out to be lead."[48] Ever with an eye toward profit, Ulick quickly retorts that he wished they had turned out to be lead, "for then we could turn all our lead to gold."[49]

The suggestion of the potential profit of converting lead into gold proves significant in the sociocultural history of money. It is important to remember that, as mentioned above, Edgeworth published *Ormond* during the period of the Restriction Act that shifted England and Ireland onto an inconvertible paper money system which, as Poovey argues, is "backed only by the dictate of a government."[50] During this period, gold and silver were "largely unobtainable; they remained, however, the only legal tender," enabling Ulick to amass great quantities of it in order to increase his value as a result of its scarcity.[51] Ulick's investment can be seen not only as a form of gambling, but, in some ways, as rigging the game. The potential for cheating the marketplace, especially by a counterfeit specie, has a significant purchase on economic debates in Ireland from at least the time of Swift's *Drapier's Letters* (1724–25), in which Swift accuses William Wood of forcing an inferior coin on the Irish marketplace, and of expecting enormous profit as a result. For Sean Moore, the *Drapier's Letters* demonstrate a belief that "words and coins were homologous signifiers of sovereignty," highlighting the very problem of forgery that undergirds Connal's attempt to achieve a greater social station through the acquisition of a false source of wealth.[52] Swift's *Drapier's Letters*, Burke's *Reflections*, and Edgeworth's *Ormond* all express deep-seated anxieties over "what constituted real money" precisely for this sense of cheating and trickery.[53]

The predatory acquisition of wealth, for Connal, cannot be separated from the emerging phenomenon of social mobility. Edgeworth has already revealed that Connal turns to Dora and her property because "it was necessary to make his fortune by marriage in England or Ireland, and as expeditiously as possible," treating Dora simply as a means of obtaining wealth.[54] It is only once a newly wealthy Ormond has arrived in Paris that Connal's predatory intentions, and subsequently the underlying predatory nature of metropolitan capitalism, emerge, highlighting again a dynamic of differentiation between the combined and uneven experience of capitalism. Edgeworth explains that "no man could feel better disposed towards another" as Connal now feels toward Ormond "except so far as the *arrangement* might, or might not, interfere with his own views," which are "to win all the young man's fortune at play. A cela près—excepting this, he was sincerely Ormond's friend, ready to do every thing possible—de faire l'impossible—to oblige and entertain him."[55] Connal conceals his intention to win Ormond's fortune beneath a veneer of friendship, replicating Connal's treatment of Dora as an economic opportunity. Yet the difference between his exploitation of Dora and his plan to exploit Ormond can best be explained in terms of a business takeover.

Where his marriage to Dora creates an ongoing relationship similar to that of an investor or board member who derives wealth from continuing involvement and, more importantly, an ongoing solvency, Connal's intention to swindle Ormond's fortunes is more exploitative and one-sided.

The representation of gambling captures the diversification of social relations that occurs with the development of capitalism within the metropolis. Connal "was, upon all occasions, careful to impress upon Ormond's mind that he left him wholly to himself" and "never even invited him to play, though it was his main object to draw him to his faro-table."[56] To accomplish this goal of separating Ormond from his money, he

> made use of some of his friends or confederates, who played for him: Connal occasionally coming to the table as an unconcerned spectator. Ormond played with so much freedom, and seemed to have so gentlemanlike an indifference whether he lost or won, that he was considered an easy dupe. Time only was necessary, M. de Connal thought, to lead him on gradually and without alarm, to let him warm to the passion for play.[57]

The theatrics that mask the identity of the true opponent or predator become commonplace in the writings of Balzac, especially in the omnipresent figure of Jacques Collins, or Vautrin, who haunts countless disguises throughout the *Comédie humaine*. As Damian Catani explains, both Lukács and Prendergast have, perhaps contradictorily, associated this mastermind criminal not only with "modern capitalism," but also with an "unstable" identity.[58] Prendergast takes this instability one step further, Catani claims, explaining that he functions as a symbol of modernity precisely because of his "multiple and shifting narrative viewpoints," which actually reflect "the very instability and indecipherability" of Balzac's Paris.[59] This urban modernity, due to its instability, reveals the increasing significance of "the act of *mediation*: you can ruin or be ruined by someone without ever having looked them in the face, even remaining unaware of their existence."⁶⁰ Moretti explains this urban and sociological phenomenon in terms of roulette, claiming that the game "is crude mutual looting, in which no one looks the other in the eye; rather, everyone automatically turns to an impeccably dressed intermediary who, in the blind-folded goddess's stead, never looks anyone in the face."⁶¹ Connal's use of intermediaries replicates this structure of sleight of hand, of combat without confrontation, as he attempts to loot Ormond's wealth. Like the Vautrin of Balzac's novels, Connal seems to remain unimpeachable and above the fray, only "occasionally coming to the table as an unconcerned spectator," obscuring his intentions.⁶²

Moretti has described this gaming principle as an "urban mechanism," a leisure activity and a narrative technique that replicates the broader experience of an individual within the metropolitan marketplace.⁶³ Connal's ability to mask his true identity as the enemy depends upon a primary characteristic of the new metropolis, which Simmel has defined as the "indifferent" relationships that distinguish the metropolitan individual from his small-town counterparts.⁶⁴ In this way, Connal's indifferent treatment of Ormond as an economic opportunity is indistinguishable from his treatment of Dora as a cipher for her property's exchange value. Edgeworth's characterization attests to this sense of indifference, especially insofar as she paradoxically insists both upon Connal being "sincerely Ormond's friend, ready to do every thing possible [...] to oblige and entertain him" and at the same moment scheming "only to win all the young man's fortune at play."⁶⁵ Simmel explains that this metropolitan indifference reduces human interactions and that relationships develop out of the influence money exerts on the cosmopolitan mentality. Just as money disregards "the unique element in events" and is "concerned only with what is common to all, i.e., with the exchange value," the metropolitan individual too reduces "all quality and individuality to a purely quantitative level," evaluating individuals like fashionable commodities in terms of their exchange value.⁶⁶ Just as Dora became important for the exchange value of her property, Ormond becomes important as a fashionable commodity on which Connal seeks to speculate and increase his own social capital. He "really wished that Ormond should *succeed* in French society," Edgeworth claims, because "he foresaw that he should gain credit by *producing* such a man."[67] Emphasizing Connal's role as producer positions Ormond as the commodity produced, while Connal takes up a position as one of Marx's "'three *dramatis personae*' of the exchange process" in the broader socioeconomic landscape of the metropolis, which enables him a greater degree of autonomy.[68] By characterizing this relationship in terms of production and the commodity exchange, Edgeworth's narrator recalls the predatory nature of the metropolis and the socioeconomic system that governs its relationship to its citizens.

Broadly, this mirrors the threat that Burke saw in this metropolitan modernity. According to Deane, the dominant condition of modernity for Burke was "a condition of control" that threatened to undermine the very concept of "character and tradition [...] by erasing rather than incorporating them."[69] Burke cuttingly asks whether lesser men "were to be tempered and restrained by other descriptions, of more sober minds, and more enlarged understandings," clearly suggesting that they were not to be controlled by this sense of authority, having succumbed instead to the rule of the mob and of uncontrollable passions.[70] It seems contradictory, but the lack of control accedes quite readily to a situation of "unbounded power" in which "[n]othing in heaven or upon earth can serve as a control."[71] In this situation of complete chaos, the lack of control becomes a controlling mechanism because of the dominance of ambition.[72] The disciplinary regime of modernity, by enforcing the plasticity of paper money and commodities on the very level of selfhood, threatens to undermine the conditions of individuality, a threat that Connal's refashioning of Ormond seems to echo. This occurs, not least, through the historical proximity of character and credit, as Margot Finn has persuasively shown. Finn distinguishes between early modern debt relations, which "had been predicated on conceptions of mutual trust," and modern consumer credit relations, which are shaped "decisively by notions of personal character," which is highly problematic because of its illegibility.[73] Character, Finn argues, reflects credit in so far as it functions "as the basis upon which lenders extended credit to borrowers," but, equally, credit constitutes character since perceptions of wealth "registered the successful use of goods and services obtained on credit to construct creditworthy characters."[74] This odd tautology doubly demonstrates the problematics of forgery and of self-creation in the development of metropolitan selfhood.

Edgeworth's description also emphasizes credit and, by extension, *Ormond* as a whole can be read as a commentary on forms of credit, as Kevin Barry has shown.[75] This late seventeenth-century economic development reveals and depends upon social relations.[76] Since "modern consumer credit was shaped most decisively by notions of personal character," the eventual collapse of Ulick's bank, precipitated by a run on its capital, is tantamount to an indictment of his "personal character" as well as his creditworthiness, all of which is based on a forged currency.[77] But Connal is using this socioeconomic phrase in a different manner and context, one that is decidedly more social than economic. Finn observes that nineteenth-century social thought "understood character to constitute an essential form of social capital" and it is precisely this form of credit that Connal seeks to accrue.[78] Connal speculates that he "should gain credit by *producing* such a man" as he believes Ormond can become in Paris, an investment that highlights the twinned fears of a forged and commodified identity.[79] Connal's socioeconomic investment in this newly arrived Irishman is intended to increase his own stock in the fashionable circles of Paris, attempting to counteract or erase the social and economic debt that originally drove him back to Ireland in search of a wife with capital.[80] In addition to implicating the emerging metropolitan system of capitalism in the—potentially fraudulent—formation of the individual, Connal's use of credit as a form of social capital also highlights the role social mobility plays in this modern landscape.

In the first description of Connal, Edgeworth emphasized the performative quality of his identity, bolstered by his deployment of fashionable commodities that reinforce his appearance of belonging to what Mademoiselle O'Faley calls "the best people in Paris."[81]

Edgeworth explains that this young man "had made his own way up in the world—a petit-maître, who had really lived in good company at Paris, and had made himself agreeable to women of rank and fortune."[82] Similar to "coxcomb," discussed above, "petit-maître" is connected to the same eighteenth-century construction of the dandy and masculinity.[83] Connal possesses a self-fashioning quality, an ability to make "himself agreeable," that echoes Mademoiselle O'Faley's use of the term "cipher," indicating an adept mastery of the laws of fashion. He has been able to remain in fashion despite Descamps's definition of fashion as "change for the sake of change."[84] This ability to appear and remain fashionable enables him to live "in good company at Paris," so much so that he appears to have gained access to its center by the time Ormond returns, signaling this Irish captain's continued navigation of social mobility through the ranks of Parisian society. In his first *petit souper* at the Hôtel de Connal, Ormond experiences the rapidity and degree of change that defines metropolitan social mobility through the transformation of Dora. Surrounded by "admirers, by adorers in embroidery, and blazing with crosses and stars," Ormond finds it "wonderful to see how quickly, how completely, the Irish country girl had been metamorphosed into a French woman of fashion."[85] The imagery of "embroidery, and blazing with crosses and stars" alerts us to the rank of the society in which Ormond finds Dora: the embroidery clearly signifies wealth and the consumption of luxury goods, while the crosses and stars recall Connal's military background, suggesting members of both the Church and distinguished orders. Dora and Mademoiselle O'Faley attest to the grandeur of their company when they receive and introduce Ormond to "M. de Jarillac [...] M. le comte [...] and another count and another came, and a baron, and a marquis, and a duke, and Mad. la comtesse de—, and Mad. la duchesse—."[86] That any daughter of the ridiculously anti-modern King Corny should be in the company of, let alone receiving "*les hommages* [...] *le succes*" from Parisian dukes, marquises, and duchesses, indicates the degree to which the Connals have infiltrated the metropolitan experience of social mobility.[87]

This phenomenon of social mobility exerted a profound impact upon the nature and experience of *Bildung* throughout the course of the nineteenth century. As Connal's treatment of Ormond demonstrates, social mobility is based upon social capital, a commodified and economic understanding of individual relationships. If the classical *Bildungsroman* is predicated upon the individual's meaning being bound up with his participation in the Whole, as Moretti claims, then a *Bildung* defined by fashion, commodities, and social mobility fundamentally lacks the permanence required by the Goethean iteration. The *Bildungsroman* of the metropolitan marketplace depends upon the exact opposite: it is a socioeconomic and narratological landscape "where values and meanings are always and only 'relative,' because they are based solely on [...] unstable, often enigmatic relationships."[88] The degree to which *Ormond* as a whole and, specifically, the Connals' Parisian world of fashion and high society exhibit these characteristics of relativity and instability is uncanny. Connal's use of intermediaries at the gambling table, his consideration of both Dora and Ormond as economic opportunities, and the ultimate radical transformation of Dora into a French woman of fashion all highlight the instability and negotiable nature of relationships in this metropolitan world of commodities.

That this environment remains only ever relative, negotiable, and enigmatic becomes apparent through a consideration of how it impacts on and is registered by Ormond himself. Connal's duplicity, although revealed to the reader, remains throughout the novel concealed from Ormond; he never even suspects Connal's predatory intentions, just as he never becomes convinced of Ulick's schemes to defraud him. Perhaps this is simple naïveté on the part of Ormond. In fact, among Connal's fashionable set, Ormond "was considered as an easy dupe" because of his perceived inability to recognize the treacherous economic practices Connal is performing.[89] Yet Ormond's understanding of the metropolis is far from unintelligent; in fact, it more accurately reflects Enlightenment principles of community.[90] As I have written elsewhere, this initial denunciation of theatricality places Ormond in the philosophical tradition of Denis Diderot, beginning to provide an alternative model for understanding the French metropolis.[91] This negotiable and relative nature of metropolitan relationships calls attention to two significant facts: firstly, the theatrical, false appearances that uniformly undergird the metropolitan world of commodity fashion and, secondly, Ormond's distinction from the indifferent and blasé mentality that defines Simmel's metropolitan individual, separating him from this landscape.

On his first night in Paris, Ormond insists to Connal that he must "go to the play, to accustom himself to the language. He must wear off his English or Irish awkwardness a little, before he should be presented to Mad. de Connal, or appear in French society."[92] Ormond first enters the world of the metropolis significantly and tellingly by means of the world of the theater, where he is confronted immediately with the performative nature of metropolitan society.[93] Whereas in Owenson's *The Novice*, Imogen's Virgilian guide, the *chevalier* de Sorville, is able to explain to her the snares and pitfalls of the metropolitan landscape without ever becoming implicated in their danger, Ormond's guides are entirely characteristic of the metropolis. In addition to Connal, a young *abbé* and a "pretty little French actress" join Ormond in order to initiate him into French society.[94] When Ormond surveys the audience and admits that "the French ladies did not strike him as handsome; they looked as he said like dolls, all eyes and rouge [...] without any pretence to the imitation of natural colour," his guides immediately explain to him that "women only of a certain rank have the privilege of wearing their rouge in that manner—your eye will soon grow accustomed to it, and you will like it as a sign of rank and fashion."[95] Ormond's critique of the Parisian scene is formulated in terms of an opposition between artifice and nature; the cosmopolitan corrective, Connal assures him, will occur over time. With enough time, Ormond will become entirely enmeshed in the metropolitan mode of existence, suggesting that there is no alternative to the dominance of an unnatural, fashionable existence in the modern metropolis.

The French Enlightenment figure Denis Diderot, according to Richard Sennett, argued that a social act can be expressive only if it is repeatable, transferrable and, as such, "put[s] a distance between [the individual's] own personality and the speech or bodily dress he shows to others."[96] This impersonal distance echoes the blasé attitude that distinguishes Simmel's metropolitan individual from his small town counterpart, demonstrating, as Sennett argues, the "superiority of artifice over nature in expressing an emotion."[97] The modern theater of personality that Ormond finds so distasteful signifies a broader social trend toward the public dissolution of selfhood under the guise of commodity fashion, which, in effect, functions as the control symbolic of modernity, according to Deane.[98] In this initial lesson in urban literacy, Edgeworth lays down the markers that separate the emerging world of fashion and commodity capitalism from what will emerge as the alternative the *ancien régime*. While she indicts the former precisely because its theatrics and fashion are artificial and indifferent to nature, the latter she associates with and justifies through a mimetic relationship with nature.

That Young Man Is Worth Something: Ormond, the *Abbé*, and Responsible *Bildung*

Artificiality and fashion characterize Edgeworth's representation of the metropolis, but these two dominant characteristics become the grounds on which *Ormond* critiques the world of the Connals and provides an alternative form of metropolitan *Bildung*. Ormond accompanies Mademoiselle O'Faley to a public gallery in order to see a painting of Marie Antoinette, "which was at this moment an object of fashionable curiosity in Paris."[99] Even before arriving at the gallery, the language Edgeworth uses to describe the picture situates it not only within the realm of fashion but, in specifically calling it an "object," emphasizes its role as a commodity intended for consumption. In the gallery, Ormond

> had now an opportunity of seeing a display of French sensibility, that eagerness to feel and to excite *a sensation*; that

desire to *produce an effect*, to have a scene; that half real, half theatric enthusiasm, by which the French character is particularly distinguished from the English. [...] It was real! and it was not real feeling!¹⁰⁰

Edgeworth's description equates the gallery and the theater from Ormond's first night in Paris. Just as the costumes and the make-up of the audience distracted Ormond, the public performance of the gallery's audience "bridged stage and street," confusing both the space and the identity of the actor.¹⁰¹ Ormond again emphasizes the artificiality of the spectacle, confusingly identifying it as both "real! and [...] not real."¹⁰² Yet, as the text demonstrates, this was the purpose with which the Parisians approached the gallery and the painting: "to excite *a sensation* [...] to *produce an effect*."¹⁰³ The creation and performance of an act that is entirely unnatural reflects what Sennett defines as Diderot's theory of drama as "divorced from ritual [...] an art form in and of itself, without reference to what was to be performed. The 'signs' of the performance were not for Diderot the 'signs of the text.'"¹⁰⁴ The Edgeworthian metropolis has become a stage full of sound and fury that signifies nothing other than the triumph of the modern and the artificial.

Again Ormond is excoriated for his inability or refusal to perform his role in the fashionable spectacle. This time Mademoiselle O'Faley commands a performance, demanding "where is your sensibilité then? [...] Ah! but what good all [*sic*] the sensibilité in the world do at the bottom of your heart, where nobody see it."¹⁰⁵ The worth of the metropolitan individual, according to the second-best urban practitioner in the novel, is based upon his performance of "sensibilité." This is tantamount to acceding to the control of character, which, as seen above, is already difficult to read and easy to forge. To put it another way, Sennett calls this "impersonality" because it is the elevation of the artificial and unnatural expression of fashion and the suppression of the individual and the natural. This artificiality, the desire to be seen as performing, contradicts the Enlightenment project of community that undergirds a larger aesthetic and urban project. While artificiality dominated the early part of eighteenth-century French drama, the Enlightenment insisted instead on an early form of realism that, according to Denis Diderot, enables the individual to "find those with whom they would live."[106] As I have shown elsewhere, this "should extend well beyond [the theater's] walls into the surrounding urban space," and this is precisely what occurs to Ormond.[107]

Ormond cannot bring himself to abandon his natural self to the artificially produced and commodified existence of fashion. He finds himself recoiling before the

> quantity of exclamations he heard at the sight of this picture; the lifting up of hands and eyes, the transports, the ecstasies, the tears—the actual tears that he saw streaming in despite [sic] of rouge. Of one thing he was clear—that this superfluity of feeling or exaggeration of expression completely silenced him, and made him cold indeed: like one unskilled or dumb he seemed to stand.[108]

While everyone around him participates in this cultish performance of ecstasy before the fashionable object of devotion, Ormond's stillness, his dumbness, and his coldness speak volumes precisely because they function as an external manifestation of what he feels internally. Finally establishing a correlation between metropolitan performance and an individual's nature, Ormond, in a tone of "determined resignation," insists to Mlle. O'Faley that he "must be content to seem and to be what I am."[109] There is, in this phrase, an ironic repetition of Edgeworth's claim that Connal "was exactly what he appeared to be."[110] Whereas Connal's essence is based in appearances, Ormond is determined that his appearance must be based upon what he is, must reflect an internal and natural identity. In this contrast, Edgeworth reiterates the division between the emerging world of fashionable society, on the one hand, in which identity has become another commodity by which individuals seek to speculate upon social credit, and a natural and organic identity, on the other, that does not belong to the world of the metropolitan marketplace, but exists despite the pressures the metropolis exerts upon the individual. Moreover, this debate about *réalisme* reinforces the threat of forgery that exists in Swift's and Burke's critiques of the metropolitan socioeconomic system.

This claim of naturalness, of an identity that is authentic instead of artificial, establishes a binary between the world of the Connals, the gallery, and the theaters on one hand, and, on the other, what other world? The answer to the question lies in the different iterations of the *Bildungsroman* with which this chapter began. If Edgeworth's criticism of metropolitan identity emanates from its dependence upon fashionable commodities, then this form of identity, just like fashion and money, can never achieve the fixity of the world of "closed social forms," meaning that the fashionable and metropolitan individual "must grow, and change form, and *never stop* [... and] never know the quiet happiness of 'belonging' to a fixed place."[111] The representation of fashionable Parisian society, the attendant emphasis on appearances and performativity, bolster the claim that the world of fashion, by its very nature, resists the permanency of selfhood and belonging. The rhetoric of movement parallels Deane's emphasis on the "form of energy that is in need of appropriation, external control" in order for modernity to exist.[112] This undermines the achievement of selfhood, the teleological aim of the classical and Goethean *Bildungsroman*. In order to assert and even to acquire a sense of self based upon fixed sense of meaning, Ormond must reject the possibilities of social mobility and fashion embodied in the modern world of the Connals.

And yet Paris is not altogether antithetical to the type of *Bildung* that Edgeworth's novel seeks to perform. There is another manifestation of Paris in which *Bildung* is possible, complicating the neat disregard for "the foreign country *par excellence*" that characterizes Deane's understanding of Paris in early nineteenth-century Irish literature: the world of the Enlightenment *philosophes*, which recalls the multifaceted roles France can occupy in Edgeworth's fiction, as Ó Gallchoir has demonstrated.[113] This world presents itself immediately after his declaration that he needs "to seem and to be what I am," when a disembodied voice rewards his proclamation of anti-theatricality with "Bon."[114] Even before Edgeworth reveals the identity of this speaker, she has already established him in a position that will be familiar to readers of *Ennui* and *Madame de Fleury*, which mirror a similar structure of socialization. After the protagonist rejects the possibility of a fashionable model of socialization, a figure emerges (in *Ennui* it is Lord Y and in *Madame de Fleury* it is the eponymous benefactor) who encourages the protagonist to follow an alternative path that leads to him or her ultimately achieving the socially ordained position that completes the arc of *Bildung*.[115] Such a system of external socialization, which leaves to a group of others the task of shaping the protagonist's life, is a hallmark of the classical *Bildungsroman*, precisely because it engages in a process of social legitimation that reinforces the contractual arrangement of belonging to a broader and stable society that is at the heart of this literary model—which, as I have noted, is precisely the type of socialization that Diderot sought to foster in his theater of the Enlightenment.

A brief outline of this concept will enable a better understanding of the way it functions in *Ormond*, as well as creating a dialogue between Edgeworth's novel and a broader range of European writers than has been usual.[116] The dominant literary expression for this form of external socialization is the Society of the Tower from Goethe's *Wilhelm Meister* (1795–96), even though Thomas Carlyle's English-language translation did not appear until 1824, seven years after the publication of *Ormond*.[117] There are structural similarities between the two and an understanding of how Goethe's Society functions can illuminate Ormond's experience of socialization-formation. The Society of the Tower, the secretive organization that "has been clandestinely guiding [Wilhelm's] development" selects the individuals who have navigated and responded to their guidance successfully, awarding to those biographies "that meet the Society's approval [...] a second scroll containing a *Lehrbrief*," or his certificate of apprenticeship, which effectively brings to an end the narrative and his process of *Bildung*.[118] Unlike the type of socialization that dominates Somerville and Ross's *French Leave*, such a system of socialization-formation, to re-emphasize an earlier argument, derives its legitimacy from the symbiotic relationship between the Tower and the protagonist: Wilhelm "can become an individual only by accepting the guardianship of the Tower" and the Tower has "the right to devise and weave plots only in order to satisfy their novice."[119] This is the same type of *Bildung* that *The Novice* attempted to legitimate, despite its apparent uneasiness. The society that constructs and emerges out of this form of *Bildung* is premised upon "that 'pact' between the individual and the world, that reciprocal 'consent,'" binding the individual to the broader social world.[120]

In the works of Goethe and Austen, as in Edgeworth, the traditional locations for such a form of socialization is the Big House, where everything is fixed and everything belongs to a proper, externally ordained position. Following Edgeworth's representation of the Connals' Paris, this would suggest that a classical *Bildungsroman* would have as little to do with the world of the metropolitan marketplace as possible, as Moretti has demonstrated. But, unlike Goethe, Austen, or even Edgeworth's other Irish Tales, *Ormond* clearly presents a form of the socialization-formation process redolent of the Society of the Tower within the metropolitan socioeconomic landscape of the French capital. It is in this process of *Bildung* that *Ormond* most clearly challenges the dominant understanding of Paris in nineteenth-century Irish literature broadly and, more specifically, in the works of Maria Edgeworth.

Emerging from the metropolitan crowd only after "Mademoiselle went off in impatience to find some better auditor," the disembodied speaker of the rewarding "Bon," the French *philosophe* Abbé André Morellet who was himself an historical figure associated with the Enlightenment and its dramatic criticism, separates himself both physically and ideologically from the mass of hysterical fashionable performers.[121] That Mademoiselle O'Faley does not hear Morellet's "Bon" is the first narratological act demarcating these two spheres. This effectively demonstrates the presence of varied manifestations of Paris and of Parisian metropolitan mentalities that do not fall into the Simmelian binary of the small-town and the metropolis; instead, following Ó Gallchoir's argument, Paris can function in a variety of ways within the same text, suggesting that there are multiple ways to inhabit and to experience the French capital, some of which the novel actually celebrates. After hearing this approval, Ormond turns and recognizes:

> a gentleman, whom he had often met at some of the first houses at Paris—the abbé Morellet, then respected as the most *reasonable* of all the wits of France, and who has since, through all the trying scenes of the revolution, through the varieties of unprincipled change, preserved unaltered the integrity and frankness of his character.[122]

There are, in this first introduction to the *abbé*, several hallmarks that position him in the realm of the Edgeworthian Society of the Tower. Simply recognizing the *abbé* as a "gentleman, whom he had often met at some of the first houses at Paris" creates an implicit contrast to the way in which Edgeworth introduced Connal, whom Mademoiselle O'Faley insisted must be "quite the gentleman" in large part because he "knows the best people in Paris."[123] Edgeworth has condemned Mademoiselle O'Faley's judgment, as a result of her metropolitan and fashionable proclivities; now, O'Faley is the one who is unable to read this manifestation of the metropolitan landscape properly, instead of Ormond. Following immediately after Ormond's rejection of Mademoiselle's metropolitan performance, the *abbé* repeats his praise. This repetition operates as a further rejection of that mentality. In so doing, it becomes clear that Edgeworth's and Ormond's valuation of character recognizes a true gentleman in both the literary and historical figure of the *abbé*.

It should not be surprising that Edgeworth chooses the Abbé Morellet as the paragon of responsible *Bildung* in the metropolis; she draws upon her own and her father's personal relationship with the French philosopher. In his memoirs, Richard Lovell Edgeworth praises Morellet for "the high character which [he] bore, not only for learning and sound judgment, but for the courage and uncommon consistency of his conduct through the whole of the Revolution."[124] After meeting Morellet, Maria Edgeworth wrote to Mary Sneyd, praising the French priest since "so many of his ideas [are] so like my Father's."[125] The parallel between father's and daughter's writings on the *abbé* are striking; each recognizes in him the same fundamental quality of constancy in a time of great upheaval and wild change, a trait that offers a balance to Burke's fears of a lack of control. Bearing a further relationship to *Ormond*, R. L. Edgeworth continues his praise of Morellet for his influence amongst "all that remained of the ancient men of letters, and of the most valuable of the nobility:—not of those who had accepted places from Buonaparte."[126] R. L. Edgeworth's division between the ancient men of letters and the valuable nobility, on the one hand, and those who had sided with the emergent Bonapartist regime, on the other, largely reflects the dominant framework that divides both *Ormond*'s Parisian society and its processes of metropolitan *Bildung*. Moreover, it reflects Edgeworth's own experience in Paris, during the family's 1802–03 trip. In contrast to "*les nouveaux riches*, who are not worth seeing or hearing," the Enlightened members of the *ancien régime* unsurprisingly prove fundamentally pivotal to the Edgeworth family's perceptions of Paris, seemingly rescuing the French capital from its present superfluity and obsession with fashion.[127] These letters not only echo the previous critique of *les nouveaux riches* like the Connals and Mlle. O'Faley, but also establish the cultural authority and legitimacy that the novel attributes to the society of the *philosophes*, separating the two along the line of pre- and post-Revolution.

Unlike Connal's claims to the title of gentleman, which were based entirely on the laws and deployment of metropolitan fashion, Maria Edgeworth reflects R. L. Edgeworth's praise by echoing the *abbé*'s claims in opposition to the fickle mechanisms of the emerging system of fashion and the attendant sociocultural phenomenon of social mobility. The omniscient third-person narrator praises the *abbé* for his reasonableness, made plain by the fact that, "through all the trying scenes of the revolution, through the varieties of *unprincipled change*, [he] preserved the *integrity and frankness* of his character."[128] Morellet's character, unlike that of a fashionable commodity or a fashionable individual, falls outside the realm of shifting and relative meanings that inform the socioeconomic landscape of the metropolis. As Maria Edgeworth's letters suggest, "the men of letters and *les anciens nobles*" are the only part of Parisian society worth seeing.[129] The emphasis on Morellet's ability to preserve "the integrity and frankness of his character" functions as a corrective to the ambiguities of the metropolitan landscape in two ways. Firstly, the tension between the "varieties of unprincipled change" of the Revolutionary and the Napoleonic eras and the *abbé*'s reported "integrity and frankness of character" function in order to present the priest as a fixed bulwark against what Edgeworth, in a markedly Burkean manner, considers "change for the sake of change."[130] Drawing the contrast in such a way presents the Revolution and the subsequent regime in line with the ideologies of fashion. There is a remarkable parallel of tone, if not of precise rhetoric, between Edgeworth's description of the French Revolution and Descamps's definition of metropolitan fashion. Surveying the scene in the gallery, the *abbé* condemns the fashionable metropolitan crowds as they parade and perform before the Dagote painting of the Dauphiness, prophesying that they "will lead [Marie Antoinette] wrong, and then will be the first to desert her."[131] Of course, Morellet's comments have the ironic gravity of having already come true. The danger this system of socialization poses, according to Edgeworth's *abbé*, is that it all "might change as quickly as the turn of a weathercock," leaving individuals unmoored from a fixed sense of identity, a society unmoored from tradition, and a politics unmoored from law.[132] This, unsurprisingly, echoes Burke's claims that post-Revolutionary France "is as void of solid wisdom, as it is destitute of all taste and elegance," that now "laws are to be supported only by their terrors, and by the concern, which each individual may find in them, from his own private speculations."[133] Burke's condemnation is that society is subject only to the private will, the fleeting and fickle nature of individual taste. Fashion's definitive trait is that it "will vanish as rapidly as it came," and Morellet recognizes this meaninglessness, for this lack of fixity unsettles the very foundations of the sociopolitical state as well as the very identity of the individual.[134]

Underlying the metropolitan laws of fashion, there is an indelible relationship between gambling and capitalism; Connal's use of gambling as a means of capital acquisition grants him access to the upper echelon of French society, where gambling becomes a metaphor for the socioeconomic relations that stretch across the metropolitan landscape. The *abbé* admits that he has seen Ormond "in the midst of the din of all the passions at the faro-table," where the young Irishman "play[ed] with astonishing coolness [...] the determination not to play at all," but the danger remains merely "in acquiring the taste."[135] In a moment that contradicts Connal's belief that he would be an easy prey, Ormond explains to the *abbé* that "there is no danger of my acquiring a taste for play, because I am determined to lose."[136] At the behest of his revered interlocutor, Ormond continues to explain that once he has lost a "certain sum—suppose five hundred guineas [...] I shall stop short. By this means I have acquired all the advantages of yielding to fashionable madness without risking my future happiness."[137] Borrowing from Deane, this demonstrates Ormond's adherence to Edgeworth's Enlightenment values, set in contrast to the "Frenchified frippery of high society."[138] However, Deane's definition proves too simple precisely because the opposition cannot be between Frenchified frippery and a "Protestant" thrift since the French philosopher commends the Irishman for this virtue.[139] That the *abbé* "was pleased with the idea" exemplifies the refusal of the Edgeworthian *Bildung* to reject completely metropolitan socioeconomics; instead it tempers the process of *Bildung* to assert a responsible engagement with the emerging system of fashion.[140] Both Ormond's and the *abbé*'s recognition of there being a certain advantage in gambling does not endorse the form of capitalism linked so closely to gambling, but, as Thomas Kavanagh has convincingly argued, reflects the eighteenth-century

French attitude toward a specific form of gambling. Whereas Connal gambles with "the primary intention of winning money," Ormond engages in a form of gambling that "demonstrate[s] his independence from money as money," reflecting what Kavanagh has identified as a gentlemanly social practice of gambling.[141] Indeed, this indifference to money reflects Ormond's submission to the social strictures—"that generous loyalty to rank and sex, that proud submission, that dignified obedience, that subordination of the heart"—that characterize Burke's understanding of a well-structured society.[142] In his complicated relationship with the system of fashionable gambling, the *abbé* recognizes that Ormond "is worth something: I thought he was only *le bel Irlandois*, but I find he is much more."[143] Here, again, Deane's too-neat distinction neglects the sociability and distance with which Morellet imbues this novel of metropolitan development.

The second way in which Edgeworth's representation of the Abbé Morellet complicates the emerging metropolitan landscape is in terms of the socioeconomics of the cityscape. If the world of fashion and the corresponding world of paper money are defined by their indifference "in relation to meanings" and their inability to retain value, then the *abbé*'s ability to preserve "unaltered the integrity and frankness of his character" presents not only an alternative form of socialization but also an alternative method of economic valuation.[144] In the eighteenth and nineteenth century, according to Finn, there was a fluid movement between economic and personal credit, mediated by the concept of character, in response to increased anxieties about national and personal debt crises.[145] These anxieties emerge from a difficulty that Mary Poovey identifies as being coterminous with the "exponential increase in the volume and variety of paper money": a tendency toward deflation, which is a "decrease in its value against the gold [or other substantive capital] it represents."[146] The form of money most closely associated with the fashionable metropolis is also the form with the least stable sense of value. The alternative economic form, the capital that retains its wealth while paper money loses its own, is not only gold but also land. When considered in the literary framework of the classical

Bildungsroman, this difficulty becomes the solution to successfully navigating *Bildung* even with the emergence of commodity-based capitalism. The individuals connected with a landed estate remain slightly apart from the world of liquid capital. This means that individuals who derive their wealth from land also derive a fixed sense of selfhood. In contrast to paper, the landed estate provides the possibility of closed social forms in a world where everything else is fluid, where value and identity remain stable. The Abbé Morellet proves pivotal in Ormond's return to a land-based capitalism and the ultimate successful completion of his *Bildung*. The *abbé*'s ability to resist the emergence of both sociopolitical and socioeconomic fashion trends casts him in a role of opposition to Connal, the paragon of metropolitan social mobility, signaling his function in the process of Ormond's *Bildung* as a member of the Society of the Tower.

The *abbé* differs in one major respect from Goethe's Society of the Tower in that Ormond begs for his services, while Wilhelm never requested similar intervention. But if the purpose of the Goethean *Bildungsroman* is to recognize the beneficial relationship of external socialization, then the fact that Ormond "beg[s] to be permitted to cultivate the acquaintance of M. l'abbé Morellet," whom he recognizes as "a safe, good guide at Paris," demonstrates the protagonist's willingness to submit to the guidance of an authority figure.[147] In revealing Ormond's use of a system of valuation that prioritizes social responsibility, authority, and worth, the French *abbé* initiates a process that might best be described as a corrective apprenticeship, a program of alternative metropolitan *Bildung* that is oriented toward the goals of a classical *Bildungsroman*. He invites Ormond "to name a day when he could do him the honour to breakfast with him" where "we must show you our men of letters" because these figures, including Jean-François Marmontel, Pierre de Marivaux, and Jean le Rond d'Alembert, embody the principle that governs Edgeworth's concept of a properly ordered society and *Bildung*.[148]

In the Paris of the 1780s, this group of writers, the *abbé* explains, "began to feel their own power and consequence, and had assumed a tone of independence, as yet tempered with due respect for rank."[149] Within this brief explication, Edgeworth reveals the fundamental structure of her *Bildungsroman*, which is both progressive and yet still wedded to the *ancien régime* through its respect for rank. Ormond's *Bildung* can be charted along several arcs, but the two dominant and interconnected ones remain a movement from being "ungovernable by most other people, and rude, even to insolence, where he felt tyranny or suspected meanness" to this proper recognition of "the value [...] of a safe, good guide."[150] Throughout the novel there has been a tension between authority and independence, which is part of a broader narrative of *Bildung* based on Ormond's need to learn the proper mode of valuation. This aspect of his socialization-formation process is best understood through the various and competing influences of Sir Ulick, King Corny, and Lady Annaly, who, like the *abbé*, is most redolent of the Goethean Society of the Tower. The other interrelated course of narrative development is Ormond's rejection of "all the dissipation that he had seen" in the fashionable Paris of the Connals "in favour of virtue and of domestic life," which he encounters at the Abbe Morellet's breakfast table, especially through the person of Marmontel.[151]

The scene in which Ormond's *Bildung* completes this second arc is not in some Irish or English estate, but in Paris with the *abbé*'s learned society at a private breakfast. While this scene has received relatively little critical attention in studies of *Ormond*, the *abbé*'s breakfast establishes the binary between Edgeworthian and fashionable socialization-formation, depicting Ormond's accession and submission to the external determination of this society. Even though "Voltaire was not then in France; and Rousseau, who was always quarrelling with somebody, and generally with every body, could not be prevailed upon to go to this breakfast," the Abbé Morellet introduces Ormond to a "great variety of different characters and talents."[152] Morellet instead forces Ormond to prove himself by demonstrating his knowledge of the French literary figures in order to introduce himself; he makes "his young friend guess who the people were, before he told their names."¹⁵³ Ormond guesses Marivaux because his "conversation was so like the style of his writings," discovers Marmontel by the fact that he is "the only man in the room who ha[s] not mentioned to him any of 'Les Contes Moraux,'" but confesses that he could not have guessed the identity of d'Alembert.¹⁵⁴ While this can surely be seen as a test of Ormond's knowledge, it more accurately demonstrates the process of narrative *Bildung* because it forces the young Irishman to recognize the benefit of submitting to Lady Annaly's education and her "well-chosen present of French books" that equipped him with enough knowledge to pass Morellet's friendly examination.¹⁵⁵ The culmination of diverse and seemingly separate experiences enables both Ormond and the reader to recognize the invisible hand that undergirds the process of the *Bildungsroman*, an external influence that directs the formation of the protagonist's experiences and his selfhood.

The recognition and legitimation of an external influence occurs only when the protagonist believes that authority is working for his benefit and when he recognizes a relationship between his own self and that authority. Morellet's breakfast exhibits this process of recognition through the development of a significant relationship between Ormond and Marmontel, a figure whose use of the French "philosophic tale" deeply influenced the literary style of Maria Edgeworth.¹⁵⁶ Edgeworth explains that Ormond finds d'Alembert and Marmontel "the two most agreeable men in the company" and emphasizes the fact that

> it was fortunate for our young hero that Marmontel was, at this time, no longer the dissipated man he had been during too great a period of his life. He had now returned to his early tastes for simple pleasures and domestic virtues—had formed that attachment which afterwards made the happiness of his life: he was just going to be married to the amiable Mdlle [*sic*] Montigny, a niece of the abbé Morellet. She, and her excellent mother, lived with him; and Ormond was most agreeably surprised and touched at the unexpected sight of an amiable,

united, happy family, when he had expected only a meeting of literati.[157]

Clearly Edgeworth intends to establish a parallel between Marmontel's narrative of reform and the *Bildung* of her protagonist. Not only does Marmontel reject fashionable Paris's life of dissipation from which Morellet intends to rescue Ormond, but he also sets the world of closed social forms, embodied in the real and metaphoric relationship of marriage, in opposition to the dissipated world of the *nouveaux riches*. This recalls countless eighteenth- and nineteenth-century works of literary fiction that straddle the public world of fashion and gaming, on the one hand, and the world of domestic felicity, on the other; more importantly, the manner in which Morellet constructs this encounter recalls the *réalisme* that undergirds Enlightenment theatrical criticism, better enabling Ormond to identify with the proper community that Diderot identified as the aim of the theater. Part of Enlightenment theatrical criticism is an emphasis on realistic details, which offers a "greater degree of truth."[158] The focus of these details was often on some element that prevents the protagonist "from being characterized as participating in the 'convention' of heroes, princes, or kings. He is a figure with whom a bourgeois spectator can identify."[159] Marmontel's reformation anticipates Ormond's own narratological maturation, ending the novel with the insistence that Lady Annaly witness "the perfect felicity that subsisted between her daughter and Ormond."[160] This dramatic device parallels the moral structure of *Wilhelm Meister*, when Jarno explains that the individual who "only tastes his error, will long dwell with it, will take delight in it as in a singular felicity: while he who drains it to the dregs will, if he be not crazy, find it out."[161] He who indulges his dissipation to the depths will recognize and regret his error more fully. Of course, a similar moment occurs in both *Ennui* and *The Absentee*. What is more significant for the *Bildungsroman* in this moment of parallel constructions is that Ormond, and the reader, recognizes himself in the mirror-image of Marmontel, both in the past life of frippery and in the current embodiment of domestic felicity.

The French historian's impending marriage and his subsequent happiness reminds the young Irishman of the Annalys, bringing "the image of Florence to his mind," inserting Ormond within the same process of reformation and, implicitly, the same progression toward "domestic happiness."[162]

This process of reintegrating Ormond into the scheme of domestic felicity and *Bildung* is the intentional and narratological aim of the breakfast. After Ormond has left, Morellet asks Marmontel if he did not see "how much [Ormond] was struck and *edified* by your reformation," evincing the claim that "his head and his heart are more in our favour, trust me, than his age and his figure are against us."[163] Morellet and Marmontel construct a binary between an "us" and a "them" that correspond to the two dominant modes of socialization-formation that Ormond has encountered throughout his visit to Paris, processes that he has described as "the real, natural course of things" and "contrast[ing] with all the dissipation he had seen."[164] Associating the domestic life with the "real, natural course of things" implicitly recalls all the "half real, half theatric" scenes of affectation and artifice that characterize the world of the Connals and of metropolitan fashion.[165] If the latter world embodies the fetishized commodity and the abstracting paper money, then the former emphasizes the physiocratic world of the *ancien régime* estate, a pre-revolutionary society that is both metropolitan and ante-modern.

While *Ormond* praises the Abbé Morellet for his unique ability to preserve his character in a way that recalls the consistent value of gold and land as capital, neither Marmontel nor Ormond can be praised for their constancy. Their system of valuation, unlike that of gold or land, fluctuates before ultimately returning to the land or gold standard. Does this translate into an economic model? For Ormond, who inherits "a prodigious fortune" following the death of his "mahogany-coloured stepmother and [his] Indian brother," the source of wealth is only ever identified as "the property, which, on the Indian mother and brother's demise, falls, by the will of the late captain Ormond, to his European son, Harry Ormond, esq."[166] This detail further imbricates the protagonist within the socioeconomic regime of the classical *Bildungsroman*. He does not enjoy an "endless supply of cash" and his participation within the world of liquid capital is limited because he draws his wealth from a landed estate, which is itself largely inconvertible and fixed.[167] This double engagement, participating within both the land-backed economy and the world of liquid capital, reflects the monetary position Burke advocates in his opposition to the French issue of *assignats*. In contradistinction to the French assignant, the "representative […] of credit but of power," English currency and credit "had its origin in cash actually deposited; and that it is convertible, at pleasure, in an instant, and without the smallest loss, into cash again."[168] Whereas the emergent French regime issues fiat money, as the British government began to do in 1798 under the Restriction Act, the Bank of England in Burke's consideration is backed entirely by real money, bullion. This dual existence of paper money and what Matthew Rowlinson has termed "real money" enables Ormond, like his approach to gambling, to enjoy "all the advantages of yielding to the fashionable madness, without risking [his] future happiness."[169] Ormond recognizes, if not necessarily the underlying economics, then the social aspect of the competing socioeconomic systems.

In Marmontel, Edgeworth explains, Ormond has met a man "who had had opportunities of seeing and feeling all that it could possibly afford at the period of the greatest luxury and dissipation ever known in France" and who has, in turn, chosen "simple pleasures and domestic virtues."[170] The contrast between the luxuries available to Marmontel, and by extension Ormond, in the world of fashion and dissipation and the simple pleasures of this other socioeconomic sphere registers the shift toward the proliferation of paper money. Marmontel's and Ormond's future happiness depends upon skepticism toward and, ultimately, the rejection of the socioeconomic regime of fashion and paper money, the world of "the greatest luxury […] ever known in France."[171] Instead, they must opt for the domestic felicity that has been proven to exist in Paris, despite its overwhelming association with Deane's "Frenchified frippery."[172]

Morellet's breakfast necessarily provides an alternative model of social relations. The alternative social relationship that dominates Enlightened Paris and concludes Ormond's process of *Bildung* depends not upon capital acquisition but upon progressive and reforming investment. As soon as Ormond has left his breakfast, Morellet comments to Marmontel that Ormond "is worth something: I thought he was only *le bel Irlandois*, but I find he is much more."[173] Edgeworth inserts economic language even in Morellet's appraisal of Ormond, suggesting that the social is not divorced entirely from the economic, a point central to Margot Finn's argument. Moreover, this contradicts the earlier representation of Connal and Ulick, who prove to be base metal; in contrast, Ormond's value only increases because of Morellet's earlier moral and personal investment in the Irishman. Because Morellet and Marmontel recognize something in Ormond, they feel they cannot "let him leave Paris, as so many do, having seen only the worst part of our society" and these "benevolent intentions [...] were of use to him all his life afterward."[174] While clearly exhibiting the double legitimation fundamental to the Goethean *Bildung*, Marmontel's efforts to recuperate the French metropolis for the young Irishman also demonstrate the sort of social investment that underlies Edgeworthian authority and patronage. The *abbé*'s commitment to his Irish companion's betterment reinforces his beneficence but also enables Ormond to assume a similar position of internalizing and reinvesting Morellet's interest, all while reaffirming the potential for Enlightened development in the metropolitan cityscape of Paris.

This double justification of the individual and society distinguishes Edgeworth and *Ormond* from the other writers and novels considered in this study. While Imogen and the Duc de Beauvilliers retire to a similar landed estate to rule in a similar fashion to Ormond's eventual rule, the fact that she leaves Paris as a result of her debts problematizes the seamless legitimacy that Ormond enjoys. Similarly, as the Irish woman's economic *Bildungsroman* moves through the nineteenth and into the twentieth century, the Society of the Tower loses its patina of naturalness and beneficence. With *Ormond*, Edgeworth remains committed not only to an economic but a social form of interaction that attempts to mitigate the emerging pressures of the modern and metropolitan marketplace. Of all the Irish women's economic *Bildungsromane* considered in this study, Edgeworth's is the most Goethean, and is the last to end with "the perfect felicity" of the protagonist.[175] And yet, despite what we might expect, *Ormond* insists that this type of felicity can be found in the heart of the French capital, even if momentarily. Paris remains, for Edgeworth, deeply engaged in the contest between an Enlightened past and a dissipated modernity; however, the fact that Ormond finds the secret to development in Paris means that the French capital remains much more than the "Frenchified frippery" that has characterized it in Irish criticism.

CHAPTER THREE

The New Jerusalem and the Rue Vavin
Urban Space, Economic Exchange, and Gendered Modernity in *French Leave*

Maria Edgeworth's and Sydney Owenson's work consistently engages with the European continent, with Paris functioning as an *omphalos* on the map of Irish women's literature. Following these earlier nineteenth-century Irish women writers, Edith Œ. Somerville (1858–1949) and Violet Martin Ross (1862–1915) continued the tradition of complex connections between Irish literature and continental spaces, especially Parisian spaces. As sociological studies of the city have long claimed, it is the city that renders legible economic development and the concomitant shifts in social practices, including civic and social institutions, gender relations, and class relations. In the space of the city in Irish women's literature, capitalism occupies an undeniable role. Somerville and Ross's *French Leave*, a novel which has rarely been the subject of critical analysis, participates in this relationship between Irish women's European metropolitan fictions and the experience of modernity as mediated by capitalism, attempting to create a literary map of Paris's economic spaces.[1] While Edgeworth and Owenson have also highlighted the economic spaces of the French metropolis, Somerville and Ross specifically call attention to the ways in which these spaces make legible the complex and gendered experience of *fin-de-siècle* Paris and its urban and economic realities.

The story of two young Irish artists, Patsey Kirwen and George Lester, who escape rural Ireland to pursue their careers in Paris, *French Leave* has attracted little critical attention, especially in comparison with Somerville and Ross's *The Real Charlotte* (1894), *Some Experiences of an Irish R. M.* (1899), and *Further Experiences of an Irish R. M.* (1908). *French Leave* has not been reissued since 1988. By and large, critical studies have heretofore considered it as an historical novel and focused on its biographical similarities with the authors, firmly locating it within the Anglo-Irish Big House estate. Hilary Robinson dedicates only six pages of critical attention to *French Leave* in her *Somerville & Ross: A Critical Appreciation* (1980). Robinson claims that the book is "partly an attempt at reviewing" the years before Somerville and Ross began their friendship and their creative partnership.² In these years before the two cousins met, Somerville "was one of the numerous female artists enjoying *la vie de Boheme* in the ateliers of Paris."³ Julie Anne Stevens and Síghle Bhreathnach-Lynch have sought to reintroduce aspects of Somerville's experiences in France into the critical discourse but, even in the case of Stevens, the critical focus has remained on how these European experiences influenced the representation of Ireland. Bhreathnach-Lynch emphasizes Somerville's "absorption of French peasant realism" in her visual art, which "reveal[s] Somerville's genuine interest and empathy with villagers of West Cork," while Stevens argues that her literary work reflects "the vibrant poster art of Paris in the 1890s."⁴

This Irish-focused evaluation is not a new phenomenon. Lady Violet Powell, Hilary Robinson reports, described *French Leave* as "an inferior *Mount Music*," a novel that "takes up the story of the Ascendancy where *The Real Charlotte* left off."⁵ Anne Oakman argues that Somerville and Ross's travel writing "adopt[s] the jarring position of both tourist and native," mirroring "their already anomalous Anglo-Irish identity."⁶ In her 1928 review of *French Leave*, Katherine Tynan praises the new issue of *The Irish R. M.* and declares that the writers have done "for their time what Maria Edgeworth did for hers," while she bemoans the fact that "*French Leave* is full of the old qualities but one feels sadly that it is a disillusioned Miss Somerville," who "realises that the old order has changed and that the new is not to her liking."⁷ The comparison to Maria Edgeworth, often remembered primarily as another "Big House novelist," reinforces the centripetal force Ireland exudes in critical assessments of these writers. Although the novel was published in 1928, years after Violet Martin Ross had passed away, Somerville set the novel in 1884, two years before she first met her cousin and future collaborator, during the early years of what we now know as the *fin de siècle*. Even though there is little decadent about the representation of Ireland in this novel, the writers clearly transpose the cultural politics of the time period onto a Cork landscape in *The Real Charlotte* when it is remarked that the eponymous character's bookshelves "held a large proportion of works of fiction of a startling advanced kind, 'and,' it was generally added in tones of mystery, 'many of them French.'"⁸ The "tones of mystery" that surround these French novels highlight the fraught position that French literature occupied in *fin-de-siècle* Ireland and Britain. While appraisals of Somerville and Ross's representation of late nineteenth-century Ireland are in themselves valuable, it is significant that this novel's decided engagement with Paris has received little comment, let alone any attempt to situate it within the broader tradition of Irish women writers whose novels take place on the European continent. This chapter argues that *French Leave* complicates the dominant critical analyses of Somerville and Ross's writings by providing both a decidedly European setting and, as is the case with the other novels in this study, connections with European literature.

As an economic *Bildungsroman*, *French Leave* emphasizes the fundamental role played by personal access to capital in an individual's struggle to establish an independent identity, a struggle that is mediated by the complex intersection of class and gender. The term "economic *Bildungsroman*" is meant to call attention to "the tensions between the development of the autonomy that characterizes traditional forms of the *Bildungsroman* and the socioeconomic pressures the characters face that result from modern capitalism."⁹ This economic literary tradition includes works by Balzac, Dickens, and Zola.[10] As the previous chapters have demonstrated, a comparable tradition exists within the Irish context. Somerville and Ross's novel finds its place alongside works by Owenson, Edgeworth, and, as the fourth chapter will demonstrate, Katherine Cecil Thurston's *Max*. In each of these works we read a variation on *French Leave*'s female protagonist Patricia—or Patsey—Kirwen's lamentation: "Oh, how disgusting was money—or the want of it! Such a miserable thing to have power to spoil a life."[11] Fundamental to the achievement of Patsey's selfhood, and equally fundamental to her failure to achieve it, is the want of money, which is "the essential anxiety that governs [...] the tension between personal independence and taking one's place within the broader socioeconomic landscape of capitalism and modernity."[12] The same formulation occurs in the persons of Lucien de Rubempré, Pip, Stephen Dedalus, Harry Ormond, Imogen St. Dorval, and Thurston's Max/Maxine.

Each of these novels is set in and depends upon the relationship between its protagonist and the socioeconomic landscape of a cosmopolitan city. In *The Atlas of the European Novel 1800–1900* Franco Moretti argues that the *Bildungsroman* is fundamentally a product of the great capital cities and their socioeconomic development.[13] Indeed, Moretti declares that "*without a certain kind of space, a certain kind of story is simply impossible*. Without the Latin Quarter, I mean, and its tension with the rest of Paris, we wouldn't have the wonder of the French *Bildungsroman*."[14] This fundamental morphological connection between the literary tradition of the *Bildungsroman* and the city emphasizes the significant connection between the development of the individual and his or her ability to participate within the social and economic material realities of the city. As Patsey's claim makes clear, an individual in want of money is an individual in want of a life of his or her own making.

The Habit of Repression is Not Easily Broken: The Patriarchal Space of Ireland

The development of, and the underlying material force behind, this urban practitionership are the overarching concerns of Somerville and Ross's 1928 novel. *French Leave* follows two young Irish runaways who escape the patriarchal and policed space of rural Ireland in order to pursue their dreams of becoming artists in *fin-de-siècle* Paris. The novel's bifurcated focus on its two protagonists, Patsey Kirwen and Young George Lester, explicitly introduces two extraordinarily important and complex social distinctions that mediate and affect the individual's relationship to, and ability to participate in, the metropolitan landscape: gender and class. Patsey, the daughter of "Sir Ingram Kirwen, Bart., M. F. H., D. L., J. P., last year High Sheriff for the County, not, in short, a person to be trifled with, or to suffer easily what he disliked," comes from the world of the Anglo-Irish Protestant Ascendancy.[15] Vera Kreilkamp argues these Anglo-Irish families, occupying "property confiscated from native Catholic families in the sixteenth and seventeenth centuries," "signalled division, not community."[16] The emphasis on Sir Ingram's status as a "pillar of the State" through his long litany of titles and positions reinforces Kreilkamp's point that the Ascendancy "was increasingly imagining itself as the modern version of the imperial Roman state."[17] Inherent to this self-identification with an imperial order of the State is the expression of "not just the typical disparities of class and wealth between landlords and tenants, but also difference of political allegiance, ethnicity, religion and language."[18] Patsey cannot be divorced from the socioeconomic position in which she was born, even when she finds herself on the train to Paris: indeed, Somerville claims that "at this stage of her career, it was unthinkable that she could travel by any other class" than first-class.[19] Nor can she be divorced from the social construct of her gender and the ways in which both Irish and French society respond to and treat her as a woman.

Patsey exhibits an almost schizophrenic identity that highlights her membership of this Anglo-Irish sociopolitical elite and her contrasting urge to achieve the alternative identity of an independent and professional artist; this manifests itself in a manner remarkably redolent of a persistent trend in New Woman writing of the *fin de siècle*, but also in several Irish New Woman writers' novels, including Sarah Grand's *The Heavenly Twins* (1893). Both her parents, Sir Ingram and Lady Kirwen, recognize Patsey's similarities with her father. After "watch[ing] Patricia swing in long strides along the garden path, as Sir Ingram had swung and stridden a few minutes before," Lady Kirwen cannot deny "how alike they were in how many things."[20] Sir Ingram silently praises Patsey for having "taken after his side of the house."[21] Her parents' observations suggest a certain masculine quality about their daughter's physical appearance. As Tina O'Toole has demonstrated and, as the next chapter will explain in greater detail, the use of the split-self, especially between a masculine and feminine embodiment of selfhood, enabled New Woman writers to "escape from surveillance, access to the public world, or the *demi-monde* by night; in other words, it provided a chance to be 'advanced' and outrageous."[22] Patsey's gender-bending not only grants her the ability to slip out of the constraints of femininity, she also inherits some of the authority that is so clearly associated with her father. In this way, she highlights the constructed nature not just of gender but, more broadly, of the patriarchal order.

Patsey becomes increasingly associated with the socioeconomic interests of the Ascendancy through her rebellious entrance into masculine spheres of business and property. At one point, Sir Ingram orders his daughter, whom he calls "Pat," to "go and put on [her] hat and take Corran up over Slieveroe" to hunt, while he must "meet Casey at the office."[23] Patsey becomes an able-bodied substitute for the patriarchal figure of the Anglo-Irish Landlord in what her father defines as "the masculine domain of sport," a trait that we will see again in Thurston's novel.[24] It is well-known that Somerville and Ross were both avid hunters and that hunting figures prominently in their fiction, but Sir Ingram does "not approve of Patsey's interest" and feels "it like a spur, irritating and stimulating."[25] Patsey's identification with the Anglo-Irish Ascendancy already provides a clear instance of a gendered experience of society. Although she is quite capable of participating within the hunt, this same ability earns Patsey's father's disdain because it transgresses well-established normative behavior.

On the hunt with her cousin, Jimmy Corran, Somerville and Ross redeploy Patsey as a substitute for the patriarchal authority of the Ascendancy. Before leaving for Slieveroe, Patsey heard her father's gamekeeper mention shots that suggest "the mountain [is] being poached."[26] When Patsey and her party encounter the poacher, Young George Lester, she swells "full of the pride that is no doubt felt by the special constable when he makes his first arrest."[27] This re-emphasizes Patsey's masculine qualities and her subversive identification with the masculine realm. Moreover, the comparison of Patsey to "the special constable" echoes the initial description of her father as "last year['s] High Sheriff for the county."[28] Somerville and Ross additionally identify Patsey with the economic, not just the social, interests of the Anglo-Irish gentry when "she advance[s] upon the poacher, and [says] in tones of ice: 'May I ask what you are doing here? I suppose you know this is private property.'"[29] Patsey's reinforcement of the laws of private property firmly locates her within the world of the Anglo-Irish landlord, especially in this exchange with the son of one of Sir Ingram's tenants.

This moment crystallizes the complexity of *French Leave*'s dual focus on Patsey Kirwen and Young George Lester, the presumed poacher. Because Somerville and Ross construct a *Bildungsroman* with two developing figures who embody different classes and genders, the novel necessarily directs critical attention to two simultaneous experiences of the same, or similar, spaces. Patsey enters this exchange with the authority of the Anglo-Irish upper classes behind her, a fact exhibited not only in her instantiation of the laws of private property but also in her characterization as the special constable, a figure endowed with authority from the State. George Lester does not so much enter this exchange as much as he is found trespassing in a territory not his own. His dislocation registers physically as his "pallid countenance [becomes] livid with alarm" and as he stoops "down out of sight."[30]

George clearly evinces the anxiety of someone who does not know how to operate within his current space. His discomfort marks the troubled class relations that existed within the sociopolitical environment of late nineteenth-century Ireland. His membership in the Irish Protestant bourgeoisie mediates his experience of Ireland.

Patsey's "increasing satisfaction" with the hope that "she was going to equal her father in the slaughter of this shameless poacher" exhibits a subtler but nonetheless important anxiety that is embedded within her identification with the Ascendancy.[31] The reference to her father's response to the transgression of his property brings to the fore Sir Ingram's contentious relationship with "these damned Land Commissioners cutting down rents every five minutes."[32] As Somerville and Ross's contemporary George Moore wrote, "In Ireland there is nothing but the land," a characteristic of the Irish economy that tilts the weight of the socioeconomic structure decidedly against women like Patsey.[33] Post-Famine landlords, like the Kirwens, "collectively and statistically [...] constituted a rich and powerful interest; individually their economic position left a lot to be desired" because "taxation, recurrent charges, debt servicing, family encumbrances and wages were all fixed, and vulnerable to fluctuations in rents."[34] The fixed nature of landed wealth, like that which funds and maintains the Kirwen estate, contrasts problematically with the "increasing liquidity of capital freed from land, which was so central to the economic fortunes of the middle class" so that competition for access to capital increased despite an overall wealthier status.[35] For Somerville and Ross, as for other Anglo-Irish authors more generally, this economic shift separated "proprietor and tenant" and they felt this wound deeply, perceiving legislation "designed to protect tenants" as superfluous.[36] The movement away from an economy dependent upon landed estates functions broadly as a symptom of "familial and cultural collapse," especially for the patriarchal order.[37]

In conjunction with Anglo-Irish Ireland's gender politics, Sir Ingram Kirwen's economic background of the Ascendancy dramatically informs Patsey's experience of Irish, and, later, Parisian spaces.

Somerville and Ross explain that the Anglo-Irish father "did not hold that his duties to his daughters extended further than was involved in providing them with creditable husbands."[38] This dictum severely restricts Patsey's, or indeed any Anglo-Irish daughter's, ability to choose a life for herself. This is especially true when the chosen life is that of the artist, as in Patsey's case. The young daughter of the Ascendancy, Somerville and Ross explain, "had never wavered in her resolve to express herself in terms of paint [...] from the time that she was able to clutch a pencil in her infant fist and scribble over her picture-books [...] up to her present age of twenty years."[39] Her artistic impulses place her in direct opposition to the dominant social thinking about women becoming professional artists in nineteenth-century Ireland. While girls "were positively encouraged to draw and paint," they were not allowed to become professional artists because "high art implied a free floating individualism which ran counter to the modesty and willingness to divert energies to others" that defined the "central demands" of femininity in Victorian Anglo-Irish Ireland.[40] Síghle Bhreathnach-Lynch reports that in 1876 Ellen C. Clayton prophesied the fate of a woman artist who seeks to move from amateur to professional status: "[t]he moment she dares to cross that Rubicon, she forgets [...] her social position, and is henceforth barely tolerated."[41] The expression of an individualized female identity is "barely tolerated" in the Ireland of 1884 in which *French Leave* is set, which reflects Finn's claims about women's relationship with the labor market "habitually told in terms of the rise of the autonomous individual."[42] Unsurprisingly, Somerville and Ross consistently refer to their female protagonist as "the Rebel" and "the insurgent," whose opposition to the socioeconomic strictures of Ireland becomes a "mutiny."[43]

The socioeconomic structures of nineteenth-century Ireland prevent Patsey from achieving her goal of individualization, especially those that restrict women's access to capital. It is important to note here that *French Leave* is set merely two years after the passage of the Married Women's Property Act of 1882, part of a series of statutory reforms which "disrupted established legal relations" between husbands and wives, who had previously "secured their daughters' economic status upon marriage through the creation of equitable trusts," which "offered affluent wives a degree of financial security without allowing them to exert active control over the funds."[44] It is in this interstitial position of increased security, without complete self-determination, that Patsey's narrative must be situated. Sir Ingram declares that "You may tell Patsey she can put Paris, or anywhere else, out of her head [...] I've no money to waste on nonsense like that."[45] Patsey's childhood dream of becoming an artist depends upon the finances of her father because the societal norms of the Ascendancy, similar to those of the landed classes in England, largely denied women the possibility of becoming "active economic agents" and participating in the inherently masculine realm of the economic market.[46] Underpinning Patsey's struggle for autonomy is the Simmelian relationship between economics and individual liberty, which William Gallois explains as the simple fact that "there are important qualitative differences between the kinds of choices one can make which are connected to one's relation to institutional and financial power."[47] Obviously in Patsey's case, it is her gender that informs her relation to the institutional and financial powers that control her ability to choose.

George Lester experiences the relationship to those same institutional and financial powers from a different gendered and class-based perspective. Jimmy Corran, Patsey's Anglo-Irish cousin, and Gilbert Kirwen, Patsey's brother, each have been raised to expect and demand "his freedom, his strength, his money, his power to order his life as he chose," but the same cannot be said for "Young George Lester."[48] That is strictly the privilege of the sons of the Anglo-Irish Ascendancy. The Lesters, as "farmers, tenants of Sir Ingram's," are considered only a "little removed from the Tuppeny class."[49] In this strata, young men like Young George Lester cannot expect the same unimpeded command of the finances that would enable him to choose his future freely. In fact, he is decidedly not free to choose his own future. Somerville and Ross reveal the fact that he is "destined by his father for the Irish Church."[50] The use of the passive voice emphasizes his lack of choice, his forced submission to what Moretti has termed "determin[ation] from without."[51] George himself further explains that his inability to choose arises "because behind him there was an all-powerful being, armed with what George visualised as a thick stick."[52] George's representation of his father, Holy George, expresses the latter's power in an image that references religious iconography of St. George with his dragon-slaying spear. But, in a passage that echoes Simmel's claims, Somerville explains that "this was inadequate as an allegorical representation of his father, because Holy George's weapon was more potent than any stick, however thick, being the key of the money-box."[53] The authors' contention that the "key of the money-box" is more powerful than any stick emphasizes capital's foundational relationship to the achievement of independence and the articulation of an independent identity.

There is also a shift in the recognition of the socialization-formation process from that which has dominated the economic *Bildungsromane* of earlier chapters. Instead of the Edgeworthian double legitimation, *French Leave* introduces the sort of socialization-formation processes that fundamentally trouble the genre. Even the Balzacian narrative of fashionable *Bildung* that characterized the world of the Connals in *Ormond* was seen as legitimating itself because it was based on desire, both desire for a fashionable commodity and a desire to be seen as fashionable, a desire to submit to the laws of fashion. Both Sir Kirwen and Holy George are depicted as "autocratic," enforcing their will with a "weapon," if necessary.[54] This overt rhetoric and the imagery of violence demonstrate new difficulties in containing "a turbulent segment of life," one of the "three great symbolic tasks" of the nineteenth-century *Bildungsroman*.[55] For Moretti, this crisis begins largely with Joseph Conrad's *Youth* (1898) and Thomas Mann's *Tonio Kröger* (1903), in the same *fin-de-siècle* period in which *French Leave* is set. Instead of the former narrative structure that was capable of "[c]onvincing the subject that what he must do is also symbolically right," Somerville and Ross present a pseudo-Society of the Tower that exerts its influence through "sheer coercion [....] arbitrary and unfair punishments."[56] What these violent attempts at socialization mean for the *Bildungsroman* is a radical shift away from the previous goal of the genre. Previously, the individual sought to achieve a sense of unity, admittedly only a fleeting unity in the fashionable and Balzacian *Bildungsroman*, but now "youth looks for its meaning within itself: gravitating further and further away from adult age."[57] *French Leave* captures this rebellion against the authoritarian forces that seek to impose socialization-formation on the youthful protagonist, the crisis of the European *Bildungsroman*.

The different ways in which these two protagonists achieve their initial financial independence further reveals their different relations to financial institutions. Since the Kirwens' economy is founded in their land and tenants' rents, Patsey's lack of access to liquid capital complicates her escape to Paris. She turns to her cousin Jimmy Corran, who has previously offered, since "it's only rotten money that's stopping you—I've got money to burn—honour bright I have! Let me lend you what'll see you through."[58] Here, as in the case of the Lesters, there is a male figure with the "key of the money-box."[59] Additionally, in a moment that follows almost directly from Somerville's own experience, Patsey finds a small yet significant store of capital from female sources. As mentioned above, the historical date of 1884 provides an important opening for women to begin to participate in the modern capitalist marketplace since it follows the passage of the Married Women's Property Act of 1882, which empowered women "to hold and dispose of property in their own right."[60] As such, Patsey receives her grandmother's "forty pounds a year," which the young Irishwoman conceives as "quite a lot, and heaps of people have told [her] one can live in Paris on half-nothing," as well as the money raised when Lady Kirwen decides that "she might sell some of Aunt Austin's pearls."[61] Patsey's £40 a year, however, seems to pale in comparison with Jimmy's offer to "make the cheque a hundred."[62] The contrast between Jimmy's ready access to large sums of liquid capital and women's difficulties in raising commensurate amounts demonstrates the difficult straits in which Irish women, even of the Ascendancy, find themselves in their struggle for self-determination.

Lady Kirwen's intervention provides greater insight into the biographical background of the novel. In her biography of Edith Somerville, Gifford Lewis recounts that Somerville's mother, Adelaide, "in all the fraught discussion about funding Edith's art training, [...] volunteered to give to Edith the £100 left to her by her sister Florence."[63] According to Lewis, this intervention "marks a quite critical point of acceptance by her parents that she was to aim at being a professional artist."[64] But, as Síghle Bhreathnach-Lynch claims, "Somerville's family did not oppose the idea of her becoming an artist and in fact encouraged her initial training, it was an entirely different matter when she announced that she wanted to go to Paris."[65] Indeed, in *Irish Memories* (1917), Somerville recounts her family's opposition to her studying in Paris:

> They said that Paris was the Scarlet Woman embodied; they also said,
> "The IDEA of letting a GIRL go to PARIS!"
> This they said incessantly in capital letters, and in "capital letters" (they were renowned for writing "capital letters"), and my mother was frightened.[66]

French Leave resonates this "capital letters" opposition to Paris in the voices of Sir Ingram Kirwen and Holy George Lester. Sir Ingram boldly declares that he "wouldn't consent for a moment of letting her go away by herself—perfectly unheard of," a pronouncement that is grounded in the power of the Anglo-Irish patriarch and in the social mores of that society.[67] Holy George refers to the French capital as "That Sink of Iniquity" and believes his son, now an inhabitant of that city, "to be yoked with unbelievers in that City of Belial [...] gone like Judas, to his own place."[68] The hyperbolically religious sanctimony clearly indicates a vitriolic distaste for *fin-de-siècle* Paris.

Just as Patsey relies upon others to achieve her escape, Young George Lester lacks a clear-cut path to his own financial independence. He fulminates as "indignation bubbled up in him again. If only he was treated as any other man of his age was treated, and given a proper allowance instead of having his bills paid for him, as if he were a baby."[69] He construes his lack of economic independence as a slight against his masculinity and compares his situation to that of "negro slaves," who were often depicted as requiring such treatment because of their supposedly infantile nature.[70] In addition to recalling the violence of an illegitimate system of socialization, this discourse reflects the growing expectation of access to capital in the *petit bourgeoisie*. Significantly, the means by which he achieves his initial independence to escape to Paris represents the *coup de grâce* in the shift from a landed economy to the money economy of modern industrial capitalism. After a fight with his father, he finds "the long blue cardboard cover of the cheque-book."[71] The checkbook symbolizes the liquid capital that is easily transferrable from one individual to another, a hallmark of Simmelian metropolitan independence because it encourages an impersonal relationship in which "any personal bondage resulting from rigidly fixed [terms] has already been thrown off."[72] In Simmel's view, this shift to a money economy, which is always located first in the city but moves outward as part of the unequal development of modern industrial capitalism, provides "a *magna charta* [sic] of personal freedom."[73] George Lester's use of this money economy reflects Simmel's claims about increased individual freedom. He proposes tearing a

> cheque entirely out of it [...]. Of course, the last one in the book would be the one to take—if one *did* take it—that way it might be months before it was to come, and no one, hardly, could be so exact to know by the numbers how many cheques were in the book [...] The signature would be no trouble at all; it was as like his own as two peas, only for the flourish, and that'd be no trouble [...] It'd likely be a month, anyhow, before the Father'd know the money was gone [...] Mr. Day at the bank would be safe to think it was all right, with term at college beginning next week [...] He could cash it in Dublin.[74]

The emphasis on not knowing and not recognizing reveals the impersonal quality of the money exchange. As long as the account held the requisite amount for the check and the signatures were similar, the bank teller would not question cashing the check and handing George his independence.

Lastly, this passage points to the increased freedom in the metropolitan sphere, a point which the remainder of *French Leave* explores. For George, the anonymity of the money economy is repeated in the urban landscape of Dublin. The freedom of movement from the rural space of Munster to the metropolitan space of Dublin anticipates the freedom of movement that characterizes the city, a movement that both reflects and is predicated upon the free exchange of capital. From a Simmelian perspective, this should not be surprising because the German sociologist declares "the metropolis has always been the seat of the money economy because of the many-sidedness and concentration of commercial activity."[75] This many-sidedness encourages the anonymity of exchange, which, as Simmel explains, further encourages the development of an independent identity free from the personal and policed relationships of the rural sphere. Conversely, the modern city "is supplied almost exclusively by production for the market, that is, for entirely unknown purchasers who never appear in the actual field of vision," a freedom to construct an individual identity beyond the panoptic realm of the small town.[76] George's comfort within the Hibernian metropolis provides a small glimpse of the sort of opportunities available to him in Paris, the capital of nineteenth-century culture.

It is necessary to keep in mind the fact that George, as a man, is able to expect access to the marketplace, while Patsey cannot expect equal access to the same metropolitan institutions. This gendered aspect of modernity fundamentally informs their divergent experiences of Paris. Even before he arrives in the French capital, George has an established economic and social network that ensures entry into the Parisian marketplace. In his preparations for escaping Ireland, George "had written to the Professor of French in his Dublin college," who "had sympathised with him in a desire to desert Dublin for Paris."[77]

M. Dupin, the Professor of French, "arranged about his passport, and had communicated with an English colleague in a Paris *Lycée*, and, between them, the way had been made comparatively straight."[78] Already Somerville and Ross construct the escape to Paris as a venture enabled by masculine privileges. Patsey has no recourse to such an assistant because of Sir Ingram's views of "this trash of Women's Colleges (just then coming into notoriety)."[79] Beyond Lady Kirwen's suggestion that "'The First Mademoiselle' [...] would be a good person to write to in Paris. Didn't she keep a *pension* for ladies only," Patsey lacks any of the material benefits M. Dupin provides for George.[80] George's access to this resource provides material benefits that enable his successful participation within the Parisian marketplace. His gendered privilege fundamentally affects the trajectory of the novel's two protagonists.

Paris at Last! The Wonderful Reward of Rebellion: Parisian Society, Metropolitan Identity, and Social Mobility

Once in Paris, M. Dupin's machinations prove essential to George's success, especially in contrast to Patsey's failure. Somerville and Ross reveal that the effects of George's benefactor "had procured for him a couple of English tuitions at night classes that sufficed to pay for his lodging, an attic, *au sixième*, in the same street as the Studio," a geography of the French capital that emphasizes the intimate relationship between the arts, the private sphere, and the economic arena.[81] He calculates that "he could exist on his store of money for nearly a year," proof of the material benefit of M. Dupin's intervention in terms of the metropolitan marketplace.[82] This calculation of finances and the subsequent ability to budget and project his future existence in the metropolitan realm is a fundamental and necessary component of urban legibility and practitionership, as we saw in terms of Owenson's *The Novice of Saint Dominick*. George's ability to acquire this skill, as we will see, radically differentiates his ability to navigate the city and its institutions from Patsey. Additionally, his ability to calculate and understand his financial position is more significant in contrast to his previous inability to manage his funds. Before forging his father's signature on the stolen check, George "*had* those few pounds in the bank, to be sure! Not many, faith! So few he had nearly forgotten them."[83] So few in fact that "how much was in [the account] he didn't know—he hadn't looked at his bank-book this long time—where the mischief was it now."[84] The fact that he has not maintained a watchful eye on his account, let alone his ledger, reveals a startling lack of economic capability. The contrast, then, between his earlier inability to maintain his checkbook and his new-found ability to earn and to budget his finances reveals the remarkable degree to which he has acquired the skills of the metropolitan marketplace. Access to capital and opportunities to earn it remain largely a masculine privilege, even in the modern metropolis.

Of course, George's tuition is merely the means by which he supports himself until his art becomes a source of income rather than a drain on his meager accounts. This occurs remarkably quickly. Before three months pass, *The London Descriptive* accepted a set of George's drawings and "paid for them a quite respectable sum [...] and had asked for more of the same vintage."[85] George uses this first payment from his art in order to repay the sum of the forged banknote. This act of reparation demonstrates George's development of the economic and mental traits of a metropolitan figure. His attitude toward the stolen check shifts as the Irish artist "was coming to look upon that five-and-twenty pounds as a loan from his father; an involuntary loan, no doubt, but one that should and would be paid off to the uttermost farthing."[86] There is a dramatic difference between theft and a loan, especially in the terms of capitalism. Where theft violates the foundational principle of private property that drives the commercial exchange, loans and the extension of credit embody the liquid capital that Simmel views as essential to the metropolitan market. George's rationalization deploys the rhetoric of capitalism, expressing the impersonal attitude that defines Simmel's metropolis and the metropolitan figure. In a relationship that is so complex that Simmel cannot discern which came first, the metropolis and its inhabitants "acquire a relentless matter-of-factness, and its rationally calculated economic egoism need not fear any divergence from its set path because of the imponderability of personal relationships."[87] George seems to disregard the personal relationship he shares with his involuntary creditor and merely views the loan as a transaction that is normal in the capitalist landscape of the Parisian metropolis.

In addition to this mental transformation, *The London Descriptive*'s check, which materially symbolizes George's capitalistic endeavors, enables his physical transformation into a metropolitan figure. He spends "some of the *Descriptive*'s next cheque on such a slouch black felt hat, and flowing black necktie, as were considered thoroughly *chic* in the *Quartier*."[88] George's check enables him to participate in Paris's marketplace where he *purchases* the hat and the necktie, exchanging money for the products that grant him access to the fashionable artistic Quartier Latin around the Sorbonne in the fifth *arrondissement*. This demonstrably makes plain the historical and narratological landscape of the French capital in the era of modern capitalism. Moretti explains this phenomenon in terms of Balzac, but it applies equally to the Paris of Somerville and Ross:

> It is really the secret shape of the city, where the indirect—triangular—nature of social relations becomes unmistakable and unavoidable. In the end, this is what "forces" Balzac to modify Propp's binary structure: he is trying to write the story of the city-as-market—where A sells to B in order to buy from C, and C sells to A in order to buy from D, or E, and so on, in the endless chain of what Marx called the "three *dramatis personae*" of the exchange process. And in order to capture this underlying structure of the city, a binary narrative configuration is not enough—it's wrong, actually: it misses the point.[89]

The simple mention of George's participation in these two moments of commercial exchange carries the weight of this limitless chain that instantiates capitalism in the urban realm. The fact that Somerville and Ross do not grant any real selfhood to the men, or women, who sell George these items reinforces the impersonal nature of the metropolitan marketplace. This enables the narrative focus to remain trained solely on George and the development of his urban literacy, demonstrating the independence that Simmel claims capitalism grants to its participants. Just as neither George nor the reader particularly cares about the identity of these merchants, they have no vested interest in his identity beyond the moment of exchange. It is this independence that marks the landscape of the metropolis, and the capitalist system that undergirds it, as the capital of the *Bildungsroman*.

George's art, in addition to providing the means of his transition into a metropolitan figure, exists in a medium that is both a cause and an effect of modern industrial capitalism in the city. The commodification of art in *French Leave* actually enables George's success, allowing him to become more enmeshed within the broader marketplace, imbricating him further into the expansion of capitalism. While Benjamin ultimately criticizes this for weakening the "aura" of the art object, George's commodified art provides him the constant access to lines of capital and credit that are both necessary for the successful navigation of the Parisian marketplace and are so clearly denied to women, especially Patsey and, as we will see, Thurston's Max/ine, in the same artistic cityscape. This chapter argues that this gendered and unequal access to the marketplace is fundamental to the experience of the *fin-de-siècle* city; alongside the analysis of Thurston's novel *Max*, it becomes clear that the Irish woman's novel at the end of the nineteenth century calls greater attention not simply to the reification of capitalism, but also to the increasing awareness of its inequality, which connects more broadly to proto-feminist and suffrage movements of the same period. Thus, it remains important to understand how George's art grants him this privileged access. His success as an artist depends upon the relationship between art and the world of the newspaper. The development of lithography, as Walter Benjamin explains, "marked a fundamentally new stage in the technology of reproduction," in which it became "possible for graphic art to market its products not only in large numbers, as previously, but in daily changing variations."[90] The ease with which newspapers and lithography could reproduce works of art in mass quantities has a real and dramatic economic effect that influences George's position within the urban marketplace. Mass production "greatly extends the sphere of commodity exchange [...] by flooding the market with countless images of figures, landscapes, and events."[91] While this makes available these representations "which had previously been available either not at all or only as pictures for individual customers," it necessarily devalues such commodities because of the increase in supply.[92] Moreover, the fact that George is able to use his art as a means of earning a living reveals the economic potential of the artist, especially in the increased commodity exchange of the newspaper. This reflects Benjamin's declaration that the artist "goes to the marketplace as a flâneur—ostensibly to look around, but in truth to find a buyer."[93]

According to Benjamin, the artist entered the market largely through the genre of panoramic literature, works that "consist of individual sketches."[94] These sketches, connected to the tradition of the "pocket-size volumes called 'physiologies,'" investigate "the human types that a person taking a look at the marketplace might encounter."[95] This is, in turn, connected with the development of urban legibility, indelibly involved with "fashion[ing] the phantasmagoria of Parisian life."[96] As Benjamin explains, these literary and artistic caricatures of Parisians included everyone "from the itinerant street vendor of the boulevards to the dandy in the opera-house foyer" in order "to give people a friendly picture of one another" because of the newness of the rapidly urbanizing experience of modernity.[97] In the end, however, these caricatures could not escape the influence of the economic exchange: "people knew one another as debtors and creditors, salesmen and customers, employers and employees, and above all as competitors," assuring the viewer and reader that he could "make out the profession, character, background, and lifestyle of passers-by."[98] While Benjamin and Baudelaire focus more explicitly on the "man of letters," the similarities between these sketches and the caricatures of George's art are significant because they both highlight the essential necessity of urban literacy, which emphasizes George's understanding of the urban socioeconomic landscape.

Thus, the project in which George is involved is that of developing a coded system of urban literacy, recognizing in individuals their socioeconomic status within the urban landscape. His art not only enables his entry into the metropolitan marketplace, but also signals his mastery of its aesthetics; he is, like Balzac and Poe, learning to read what has largely been seen as illegible. This question of urban literacy is, as Prendergast notes, central "in the history of the city throughout the nineteenth century."[99] Richard Lehan argues that, as "the city becomes more complex as a physical structure, the ways of seeing it become more difficult," which leads to "challenging systems of order and encouraging disorder and chaos."[100] Thus, as Paris has become more complex since Owenson's time, the development of urban codes and "physiologies" to help crack those codes have become more complex and more necessary. This style of art, whether in paint or print, cannot be divorced from the expansion of the urban marketplace beyond the boulevards and into the salons and art studios. George's financial success comes from his ability to integrate the pursuit of art with the pursuit of capital, and his ability to successfully read and replicate the complex socioeconomic landscape of Paris.

Somerville and Ross further reveal the instantiation of the capitalist system in the relationships between George and his fellow artists. When he receives his first check from the London newspaper, George's fellow artists consider him "with respect, even with some apprehension as a caricaturist of quality."[101] The unease embedded in the term "apprehension" conveys this significant sense of competition that reflects the pressures of the market.[102] As Benjamin and Simmel claim, the metropolitan economy governs metropolitan relationships, imbuing them with their characteristic impersonal disregard. Benjamin notes that people saw each other not in terms of individuals but as economic entities and "above all as competitors," reflecting the forces of the labor market that determined one's employment status.[103] The marketplace's influence on personal relations, even in the Parisian art schools, reveals the degree to which artists and individual urban citizens participate in the continual re-edification of modern and metropolitan capitalism.

George's entry into and success in the marketplace provides him greater freedom of movement across the disparate capitalist spaces of Paris. After purchasing a Parisian outfit with his second check from *The Descriptive*, he asks one of the female art students who studies with Patsey "to do him the honour of lunching with him on the following Sunday" at "the *Paradis des bons Cochers*, [...] the fellows in the *Atelier* tell me it's a good place."[104] Firstly, he feels "himself so supported by the hat and tie" that the check has procured, a statement that demonstrates the development of a metropolitan identity, grounded in his participation within the urban marketplace as both an agent of consumption and of production.[105] It is important to note the work that the fashionable commodities seem to perform here. These clothes truly make the man, and make him something he had not previously been, providing him so much support that he was able to command enough courage to ask "Miss le Mont in the *cour* of the Studio" to join him for the extravagant luncheon he had planned.[106] These fashionable objects, having imparted to their new owner their sense of fashionability, enable him to reach for a higher desire, to want more, which is the aim of the capitalist metropolis. Secondly, the dinner at the *Paradis des bons Cochers* contrasts so sharply with earlier representations of Parisian cafés that Somerville and Ross reveal a socioeconomic geography of the French capital. Mercy Le Mont, one of the female artists whom George has invited to lunch, believes the *Paradis des bons Cochers* to be "much too grand for poor painters like us."[107] George's lunch proves very grand indeed as he had "taken a private room" and "Monsieur, the *Chef* of the *Paradis*, had done him well, and the student appetites of the guests responded to his skill."[108] The emphasis placed on both the privacy and the culinary skill of the luncheon suggests that George must have spent a huge amount of money. The space in which this event takes place contrasts starkly with the two earlier representations of cafés, providing greater evidence of how George's money opens spaces previously unattainable for these students.

On Patsey's first day in Paris, her fellow *pensionnaires* and soon-to-be fellow artists take her to "the *Crémerie* in the Rue Bréa, where most of the studio crowd go" in order to introduce her to both the people and socio-geographic space she will occupy as an impoverished art student.[109] Immediately Miss Le Mont warns Patsey, "You won't mind if it's not quite Meurice," which suggests that the *Crémerie* falls short of the high-class cafés of the broad boulevards like the Champs Elysées.[110] Implicit in Miss Le Mont's statement is that this particular café is located in a specific elsewhere from the *Meurice* in the socio-economic geography of the city. The *Meurice* is located in the Quartier Palais-Royal on the Rue de Rivoli alongside the Jardin des Tuileries in the first *arrondissement*, while the *Crémerie* is located in the Quartier Latin on the other side of the Seine near the Sorbonne and the Jardin du Luxembourg. Although Somerville and Ross do not provide the *Paradis des bons Cochers* a specific location on the map, the private room, the wine, and the chef all suggest a radically different social space than the world of the Quartier Latin and the *Crémerie*. In the cafés of the Latin Quarter, Patsey finds none of the luxurious privacy of the *Paradis*; instead, she finds "a long narrow room, with bare sanded floor, and rows of small tables up either wall, leaving a very limited central passage."[111] In the place of the celebrated chef, "a hurried and harried waiting maid" staffs the *Crémerie*, darting "to and fro, between, the clients and the hidden source of supplies at the end of the room, chaffed, scolded, reproached, cajoled, her short full skirts snatched at as she flew by."[112] Clearly these two distinct locations, no more than three kilometers apart, occupy two different worlds in the Paris of Somerville and Ross.

Separated by the Seine, the remarkable differences between these two worlds demonstrate George's economic and social success, and his ability to maneuver and navigate between these two social spheres. This is the fundamental development of his urban legibility. Moretti has written extensively about the literary geography of Paris in Balzac's *Comédie humaine*; his criticism has divided the socioeconomic geography of the French capital into "five, six major spaces, whose borders are crossed and re-crossed in the full light of day [...] a true mosaic of worlds, where the social division of labor seems to have literally stamped itself upon the urban surface."[113] This narratological landscape, embodied in the works of Balzac and Zola, depends upon the different spaces that populate the metropolitan map. Each space provides the specific material and economic realities that determine who can and cannot be admitted, creating disparate worlds that exert the narrative tensions that largely govern the nineteenth-century French novel. Thus, when Mercy Le Mont explains that the *Crémerie* is not the *Meurice*, she is essentially introducing this urban geography to Patsey; when George earns his second check from the newspaper, he is able to buy access to the worlds beyond the Quartier Latin.

His income, of course, enables this transgression across the socioeconomic landscape, but Moretti argues that his very movement must be understood in terms of the material development of his occupation. While George is indeed an artist, it is through the newspapers that he earns his living. Moretti discusses this role of journalism in terms of Balzac's Lucien de Rubempré, a provincial poet who moves to Paris in order to publish and become a literary celebrity. However, he soon leaves behind the world of the Quartier Latin and his dreams of poetry in order to become a journalist. Journalism, Moretti argues, constitutes a "fluid space [...] disseminated a bit everywhere: and rightly so, because journalism here embodies *mobility*—spatial, mental, social mobility."[114] All of these manifestations of mobility can be seen in the development of George Lester's urban legibility. His luncheon at the *Paradis* reveals his spatial mobility, across the river into the world of the first *arrondissement*; his reconceptualization of the stolen check as a loan demonstrates his mental mobility; lastly, his emphasis on the *chic* dress of the *quartier* encapsulates his social mobility as it suggests an affinity with the fashion of the Parisian dandy. Similar to the performative way in which Connal employed commodities to affect a Parisian identity, George's association with the dandy recalls similar problematics of a commodified sense of self that is necessarily fluid in order to integrate itself into the landscape of the metropolis.

A Shock for Which She Was Quite Unprepared: The Gendered Experience of Metropolitan *Bildung*

Somerville and Ross maintain their bifurcated focus on Young George Lester and Patsey Kirwen. George, as we have seen, successfully navigates Paris's metropolitan landscape, earning his living in the marketplace of journalism as an artist. His prospect, the authors insist, holds "a brighter promise for the future than Patricia could look forward to."[115] It becomes imperative to understand Patsey's prospects, as well as the material and sociocultural reasons for their lackluster quality. Patsey's berth to France depended upon an external source of funding; additionally, she travelled without any of the readily established network that prepared George's arrival in the French capital. This lack of economic potential has long-lasting and dramatic effects on Patsey's ability to navigate and participate within the metropolitan marketplace. A foundational quality of capital, as has been seen above, is its need to "grow, and change form, and *never stop*," but because Patsey acquires capital in a one-off fashion she is unable to return it to the circulating stream of the metropolitan economy and, as a result, cannot start that process of change to which capital is subject.[116] As George has exhibited, the metropolis, which "has always been the seat of the money economy," becomes a site for liberation if one is able to participate in its indifferent marketplace.[117] This is because Marx's *dramatis personae* construct a system in which "the person is actually excluded from the product and the demands no longer extend to him."[118] This indifference enables the individual to cultivate an identity independent of the demands of others. Patsey's inability to participate in this endless exchange of commodities means that she cannot shed the identity of the daughter of the Anglo-Irish Ascendancy. Unlike George, she cannot take advantage of spatial, mental, and social mobility to create a new and independent metropolitan self.

As with George, the development of this metropolitan identity depends upon the individual's ability to cultivate the skill-set of urban literacy. Throughout her three months in Paris, Patsey decidedly cannot cultivate this literacy. The novel continuously applies a Romantic and often naïve tone to Patsey's observations of the Parisian cityscape. On her first foray into Paris with her new fellow *pensionnaires*, the young Anglo-Irish woman finds herself "in a mental condition bordering on delirium."[119] In this state of delirium, the other young women become "enchantresses, who were putting the gilded roof on it all, feeling as though she were walking in the streets of the New Jerusalem."[120] While the sense of delirium corresponds to the Simmelian notion of metropolitan splendor, which itself provides the need to create the distinction between an internal emotional existence and an external intellectualistic existence, Patsey's perceptions of the Quartier Latin as gilded streets of "the New Jerusalem" seem excessively bewildered.[121] The Romantic qualities of her engagement with Paris reveal a startling lack of urban literacy, as Somerville and Ross present the alternative, realist landscape through which Patsey and her colleagues are walking. Instead of a New Jerusalem, the Parisian street narrates its own identity in a fashion that dramatically contradicts Patsey's version of the cityscape:

> The humble Rue Vavin, through which she was being led, narrow, rough, and unclean, as in those days it was, cherished no pretensions about itself, and would never have suggested that it was made of pure gold, or even of transparent glass.[122]

The street's recognition of its own humble and dirty status explicitly contrasts the self-awareness of the city with Patsey's delirium in a more realist narrative that is redolent of the naturalist writings of the *fin de siècle*. The focus on glass that is not even "transparent" recalls "the transparent yet opaque" urban landscape that characterizes broader trends of anxiety in the nineteenth century that result from the expansion of commodity culture.[123] Andrew Miller argues that these windows "radically transfigured the experience of walking through commercial sections" of the city, while stimulating "elaborate fantasies of consumption, sensuous experiences of imagined acquisition."[124] Such fantasies both characterize Patsey's initial foray into the Parisian metropolis and undercut the sense of access to the goods behind the glass. The degree to which the glass remains distinct from "transparent glass," then, emphasizes the distance between the fantasizing Patsey and the goods; more than the transparent glass separates Patsey from her Parisian fantasies.

Somerville and Ross continue to exacerbate this contrast, repeatedly emphasizing realist details of the urban environment of which Patsey remains blissfully ignorant. For example, "this entranced enchantress" recasts "the sour, vinous smells of the frequent *cabarets*, the whiffs of luscious cookery that issued from the open doors of small restaurants, the mingled odours, all-pervading as the ether, of garlic and strange tobacco" as "airs of Paradise."[125] Patsey strips this urban landscape of all its material reality in favor of a Romantic and idealized vision, omitting the sensorial experience that otherwise bombards the text. This erasure highlights her lack of economic awareness because she forgets, or at least does not recognize, that these "airs of Paradise" are in fact evidence of pervasive economic exchange, which is precisely the way in which *fin-de-siècle* capitalism was intended to function. The use of "Paradise" specifically recalls Émile Zola's *Au Bonheur des dames* (1883), one of whose English titles is *The Ladies' Paradise*. The story of Octave Mouret and his store preys upon "the irrational desires created and enhanced in a consumerised society."[126] Moreover, as Gallois explains, Mouret's Paradise "delineates the gendered structure of capitalist development in France" since the store's profits depend on women being "seduced by the surface glamour of the mode of production."[127] Patsey's Parisian seduction begins with the smells of "the frequent *cabarets*, the whiffs of luscious cookery" and the "strange tobacco," all of which are evidence of the expanding marketplace; however, she remains unaware even of the "sight of blue-bloused masons, hard at work, on the white walls of a house, regardless of the fact that it was the day of rest."[128] That she is unaware of the workers highlights the fact that "the surface glamour" has done its job.[129]

As such, she cannot recognize, let alone participate in, the metropolitan economy. Patsey again exhibits this Romantic misperception of the Parisian landscape in Pianelli's *Atelier des Dames*, the art studio at which she enrolls. When she first meets her fellow artists at the *pension*, Miss Henriette von Kapff, otherwise known as Hans, explains the *atelier* to Patsey in terms that, she is sure, will sour the young Anglo-Irishwoman. Pianelli's studio "iss not clean. English ladies do not often stay there. Zey come, and zen zay go. It is *l'académie* for all day there. It is too serious for zem."¹³⁰ Hans's emphasis on Pianelli's uncleanliness echoes the representation of the Rue Vavin, maintaining a focus on the material and sensorial reality of Paris. She elaborates on this *leitmotif* of grittiness, declaring the studio to be "as good as any other—better than some—cheaper than any of them—and, dirtier! It's knee-deep in charcoal and bread-crumbs, but you won't mind that."¹³¹ The tone of Hans's description of Pianelli's creates the sense more of a warning than a welcome, attempting to prepare the newest addition for the grime and work of which she seems ignorant. Hans's preparation does not in fact work; instead, Patsey again recasts the reality of the studio in the Romantic terms of a fairytale. Reemploying the language of delirium, Somerville and Ross state that Patsey "felt as if she were walking in a dream" as she first entered the *atelier*.¹³² Disregarding Hans's earlier warnings of urban squalor, Patsey portrays the studio as "a forest of tall wooden easels, and lesser groves of rush-bottomed stools of varying height, all ranged in serried half-circles."¹³³ Comparing the easels and the stools to rural images, Patsey creates the sense of a fairy-tale forest, a world stripped of the material reality of work. In Oona Frawley's formulation, the adaptation of "a traditional pastoral nostalgia within Irish culture corresponds, unsurprisingly, to the development of an urban society."¹³⁴ These urban-based sentiments about landscape and nature ignore "natural realities."¹³⁵ There is a parallel between Irish pastoralism and Patsey's fairy-tale depictions of the Parisian art studio in that both "consciously ignor[e] the realities of an emerging urban society."¹³⁶ According to Raymond Williams, the ideological project of pastoralism defends "certain kinds of order, certain social hierarchies and moral stabilities" that the fluidity of social and economic forms within the modern metropolis has rendered obsolete.¹³⁷ In Patsey's continued representation of the French capital as a romanticized space, there is a subtle acknowledgment of her refusal or inability to adapt to the socioeconomic landscape of Paris. The consistent usage of this Romantic rhetoric signals a dramatic distinction between George's economic maturation and Patsey's rather provincial and anti-modern engagement with the metropolis.

Patsey, however, cannot maintain this conception of Pianelli's as a Romantic idyll. She turns "crimson, and wished that the studio floor, grimy though it indubitably was, might swallow her up" when she realizes that M. Pianelli "had been arranging the pose of an entirely naked female model."[138] The blatant emphasis on the model's corporeality and M. Pianelli's indifferent treatment of her shocks Patsey to the core. The model, instead of being treated as a human, is treated more like a commodity, an object. This trope of the woman as model "became a pervasive and provocative cultural image in the late nineteenth century," highlighted explicitly through Zola's *L'Œuvre* (1886), which "showcased the seedy underworld of Parisian artists and their models."[139] For women in *fin-de-siècle* Paris, modelling, selling the body as an object, "was not just a rite of passage for would-be artists but was also a serious profession."[140] "Arranging" the model as one would a piece of furniture calls attention to the degree that this body has become commodified, fetishized. These models, as Rose explains, displayed themselves throughout the city at specific "model markets" in any area of the city that was frequented by artists; here, they would drape "themselves around the fountain dressed up in brightly coloured rags as nymphs, cherubs, and Greek Gods," calling to mind both the commodification and the performativity of the body.[141] Much like Mouret's fashionable displays in the windows, Patsey's response to the body of the model is the "consequence of the seductive psychology of the *nouveauté*," which is "an unplanned for over-identification with commodities."[142] Patsey seems both seduced and repulsed by the attempt to seduce her with the fetishized female body.

While Patsey does not seem to register this economic treatment, she is still shocked, more at the sexuality of the body. The adverb "entirely" conveys her astonishment at her first confrontation with a naked body. This jarring experience reveals the degree to which she cannot shed the social mores of Ascendancy Ireland in favor of a metropolitan and Parisian sensibility. In an aside, the omniscient narrator explains that Victorian Ireland "was a country that, at that time, prided itself upon its extreme delicacy of feeling and regard for the conventions" of "protracted and intensive decorum."[143] "Taking these facts [...] into consideration," the narrator claims, will enable the reader to better understand Patsey's reaction to the model's nakedness.[144] This narratorial aside not only seeks to explain nineteenth-century Ireland to an early twentieth-century and largely English audience, but distinguishes Ireland from the sexualized and seducing commodity culture of *fin-de-siècle* Paris, reiterating the complaint and critique that Somerville's own memoirs recall. Moreover, this is not the only example of Patsey's revulsion at the corporeality of her artistic training. She had "almost come to the conclusion that she had made the mistake of her life in believing that Art was her vocation" because, in addition to the morning's model, "the afternoon study, a very ugly old man, attired in a loin-cloth and a long white beard, had revolted her."[145] The human body, for Patsey, poses a fundamental challenge to art; it is not a subject of beauty, but a cause of disgust. For readers of nineteenth-century French literature, this critique of the disgusting nature of the human body will recall Zola's preface to the second edition of *Thérèse Raquin* (1867). After being accused of exhibiting an "unhealthy preoccupation with lust, corpses, and decay," Zola responded that he "set out to study, not characters, but temperaments," "individuals existing under the sovereign dominion of their nerves and their blood, devoid of free will," individuals who are "human animals, nothing more."[146] Zola's animalistic representation of the human body, of the human individual, reflects a similar dehumanization and created a similar discomfort amongst the French public as Pianelli's handling of the model creates in Patsey, based on a Victorian notion of femininity that is diametrically opposed to the culture of *fin-de-siècle* Paris.

Patsey's aversion to the artistic representation of the naked body becomes even more striking in comparison with the first piece of George Lester's art described in *French Leave*. This is "a rough drawing in charcoal on grey paper touched up with coloured chalks. It showed two naked men fighting, their weapons gigantic paint brushes, with palettes borne as shields."[147] The fact that the men's nakedness passes without comment demonstrates the degree to which George is already able to assimilate to the taste and the culture of *fin-de-siècle* Paris, whereas Patsey can hardly stand the very concept, let alone the finished object. His comfort could not contrast more starkly with Patsey's revulsion. If George's success as an artist is founded upon being able to read and to represent the sociology of the city in its presentation of the different types of its citizens, then Patsey's inability or refusal to encounter the gritty reality of those citizens and those spaces evinces her inability to develop the urban geography requisite for navigating the metropolitan environment. She remains, instead, sidelined in a fantastic and circumscribed Paris, while George can and must roam the entirety of the city.

Patsey's lack of urban literacy reflects significant gendered qualities of the modern metropolis that privilege men's interactions with its socioeconomic institutions. Where George's involvement with journalism opens a multitude of Parisian spaces, Patsey's Paris becomes increasingly circumscribed in the space of the Quartier Latin that lies between Mademoiselle Leroux's *pension* and M. Pianelli's *Atelier des Dames*. The text applies to both of these spaces a specifically feminine quality. Somerville and Ross explain that the *pensionnaires* "were all of what has been called 'the more plentiful sex,'" confirming Lady Kirwen's memories that Leroux maintained "a *pension* for ladies only."[148] As Julie Johnson notes, this gendered space, even in the world of art, reflects two contradictory historical trends. The intersection of "crisis, pleasure, and spectacle actually coalesced at the end of the nineteenth century and created a space in which Parisians, particularly women, could strike out in new and creative ways."[149] During this period, women artists "received artistic training and education and possessed an 'optimism' about their potential for careers as artists," despite the fact that they were not permitted to join "the most traditional and institutionalized levels of art education."[150] Because of this institutional bar, women artists emerged "through a considerable, and ever-increasing number of ateliers and academies," which also functioned as "venues through which artists could gain important professional exposure."[151] This social gendering of space extends beyond the walls of the *pension* into the realm of art itself, reflected in the name of M. Pianelli's studio: *Atelier des Dames*. As Síghle Bhreathnach-Lynch argues, this gendered experience of the French capital emerges from the "professional gendering of space in [Somerville's] account of her training in Paris."[152] Somerville's recollections of her own experiences in the studio of Filippo Colarossi, where she first studied, recall another young artist whose "home chanced to be the house next but one to the Studio [...] none the less, a *bonne* came daily at 12 o'clock to escort her home for *déjeuner*."[153] The memory of a young woman who could not venture down the street without a proper chaperone mirrors the way in which Patsey's gender constricts her experience of the city, denying her the freedom that characterizes George's metropolitan life. The novel never depicts Patsey moving about the Parisian streets without the accompaniment of her fellow *pensionnaires* or, in one rather scandalous instance, George Lester. Thus, even while women find alternative modes of education and development, they remain segregated in gender-specific *ateliers*; similarly, their access to urban space remains segregated and unequal.

Patsey's constrained movement contributes to her lack of urban literacy, which continues to deny her the opportunity to participate in the broader metropolitan marketplace. Just as the *atelier* reveals the gendering of professional space and Mademoiselle Leroux's *pension* reveals a gendered social space, Patsey's limited movements through Paris reveal the gendered nature of the broader Parisian cityscape. Since the *atelier* commands the vast majority of her time, Patsey finds herself with little time "for aught save housekeeping, and its attendant marketings" during her excursions into the city.[154] The fact that her everyday engagement with the metropolitan marketplace does not extend beyond "shopping together [with Hans] on their way home from the Studio, buying for the pot at the little shops of the quarter" means that her experience of the French capital is largely an extension of the domestic sphere.¹⁵⁵ She finds excitement in "sampl[ing] a new *Crémerie*, and there to receive six stewed prunes for the same price that *Le Père* Fusco charged for four; to buy a small gobbet of raw meat, and with it to wing her way home."¹⁵⁶ Instead of the earlier metropolitan opulence of a New Jerusalem, Patsey's Paris is an entirely domestic realm, separate from the shops of the Boulevards and the theaters of the Quartier Latin. While George roams freely throughout the disparate Parisian realms, Patsey's Paris is inseparable from the two feminine poles of the *atelier* and the women's *pension*. There is a remarkable contrast to the way in which she dominates the physical space of the Anglo-Irish demesne in her first encounter with George, reinforcing the uncomfortable nature of her position within the modern and cosmopolitan world of the metropolis.

This daily engagement with metropolitan commodity exchange, however, suggests the potential development of an economic mindset similar to George's. Patsey learns from "Hans [who] was an economist, skilled and subtle" and how to "shop in *sous*, and to keep account of her weekly expenditure for food (which, it may not be out of place to say, came, all told, to little over three francs a week)."¹⁵⁷ That Patsey is able to replicate Hans's financial management introduces a similar sensation to the freedom that George's first few paychecks provided. There is a remarkable parallel between the two moments of economy. Where George was able to provide a lavish meal at the *Meurice*, Patsey delights in a more meager and economical meal, "completing her repast with what was known as a resurrection omelette."¹⁵⁸ On even rarer occasions, she takes particular delight in "join[ing] with *ces dames* in a dinner to a studio friend, when Hans would give a demonstration of her *hauslich* skill in a series of masterpieces, produced for the sum of fifteen *sous* a head."¹⁵⁹ These decidedly *hauslich*, or domestic, "minor joys" reinforce the distinction between Patsey's and George's economic and social mobility.¹⁶⁰ George's paycheck enables a public display of his new-found economic wealth, while Patsey's economy reinscribes her within the domestic space of the *pension*. Depicting Patsey and the other young women engaging in attempts to stretch their limited funds by means of parsimony, the text tantalizingly introduces this image of Patsey as an urban practitioner, able to negotiate the Parisian socioeconomic landscape.

Fundamentally lacking from Patsey's potential development as an urban practitioner, however, is any opportunity for her to increase her accumulated capital. In the *dramatis personae* of Marx's commercial exchange, Patsey is never allowed to occupy the stage as any character other than a consumer. She is never allowed to take on the role of producer or merchant who then is able to become another consumer in the endless chain of commerce. Thus Patsey must continue to measure her economic participation in Paris's marketplace in terms of, and against, "one of Aunt Austin's pearls."¹⁶¹ Patsey's income remains bound not only to a finite number of pearls but, more importantly, to a source that is not her own.¹⁶² As such, her finances always occupy a precarious position within the text. An inquiry into these limited funds gives her "a shock for which she was quite unprepared," which leads her to ask: "How had the money gone? When had it gone? Where had it gone?"¹⁶³ The shock of her inquiry, in conjunction with this string of fundamental questions, reveals a complete lack of understanding about her own finances, reinforcing the degree to which she has not developed the economic skills that enable successful navigation of the metropolitan marketplace. Whereas George, because of his income in addition to his personal parsimony, can project his finances into the future with relative accuracy, Patsey believes "herself to have budgeted for a year 'or thereabouts'—a period of time that is practically endless when one is twenty."¹⁶⁴ These two conceptions of time are radically different: for George, time is measured and measurable; for Patsey, time is much less fixed and much more existential. A similar attitude manifests itself in the two Irish runaways' treatment of their finances. Again, George's income is the budgetary means by which he occupies the city, allowing him to determine the requirements for his continued residency in Paris. Conversely, Patsey's income "was melting faster. Impossible to say how it went; whenever she examined her resources they had mysteriously dwindled."[165] Somerville and Ross continue to attribute to Patsey the language of a fairy tale; her finances remain mysterious, contrasting sharply with the systematic and intellectualistic approach that characterizes both Simmel's and George's experience of the modern metropolis.

Patsey applies this sort of fairy-tale rhetoric to her ultimate decision to return to Ireland. She attributes her failure to "the Fates [who] had turned down their beastly thumbs," recognizing only the fact that "*Soit!* Her career was to be cut short."[166] This conceptualization of her departure from Paris relies upon imagery from Ancient Greek mythology. The reference to the Fates recalls Sennett's claims about the lack of understanding that characterized nineteenth-century conceptions of the marketplace. While Sennett described this in terms of the game of chance and Moretti uses the metaphor of the roulette table, the centralizing thread is the role of an external force, whether that is luck, chance, or these beastly Fates. The use of the Fates, as an external, governing force, recalls a passage from Edgeworth's *Ormond*, in which Lady Annaly remonstrates Ormond for his use of a similar phrase that blames divine intervention.[167] She declares that fate problematically "leads us to imagine that we are *fated* or doomed to certain fortunes or misfortunes in life," while, in reality, "it appears to me that far the greater part of our happiness or misery in life depends upon ourselves."[168] Lady Annaly understands the common use of fate as a means of denying personal responsibility for the events that shape an individual's life, which is exactly what Patsey's invocation attempts to do. Placing herself in the position of the acted-upon object of the sentence, Patsey construes the Fates as the active agents while she remains passive in a metropolitan environment that demands activity and cultivates agency from its individual citizens.

Far from contributing to the dominant critical conception of Anglo-Irish women's literature as firmly entrenched behind the walls of Ascendancy demesnes, *French Leave* points to a much more complicated and significant literary tradition. Somerville and Ross's novel highlights the fundamental relationship between the city and modern capitalism, while questioning the ability of individuals from different classes and genders to navigate the shifting terrain of the modern metropolis. The value of analyzing Irish women's literature, both before and after Somerville and Ross, in terms of this relationship to the geographic space of the European city and the concomitant development of modern financial and consumer capitalism, lies in its ability to recover undocumented and individualized experiences of modernity. *French Leave* interrogates Irish women's literature within an ideological framework that expands its geographic scope, engaging the lens of capitalist development and European literary systems.

CHAPTER FOUR

First Life—and then Fame
Gendered *Fin-de-Siècle* Cityscapes in *Max*

> It was well said of a certain German book that "er lasst sich nicht lesen"—it does not permit itself to be read. There are some secrets which do not permit themselves to be told.
>
> —Edgar Allen Poe, "The Man of the Crowd"

Originally published in 1840, seventy years before Katherine Cecil Thurston's *Max*, Edgar Allen Poe's "The Man of the Crowd" highlights the anxieties that emerge around the illegibility of the modern city, which nightly presents "the hideousness of mysteries which will not *suffer themselves* to be revealed."[1] The menacing figure of Poe's tale embodies the modern cityscape by refusing to be revealed, by withholding permission to be read. While Poe's tale sets out a recognizably Gothic vision of London's heterogeneous and thronging crowd, Julie Abraham argues that Honoré de Balzac's *La Fille aux yeux d'or* (*The Girl with the Golden Eyes*, 1835) establishes the terms that will dominate attempts to read the nature of the modern metropolitan landscape. In his attempt to lay out the "cadaverous physiognomy" of Paris, Balzac turns to "[a] few remarks on the Parisian" that depict the French capital in hellish terms which recall Dante's Inferno.[2] Just as Poe relates his attempt to read the modern cityscape to the act of reading its citizens, Balzac connects the landscape of Paris, where "smoke billows, fires roar, everything flashes, boils, burns, and evaporates, everything is extinguished and rekindled, everything sparkles, glitters, and is itself consumed," to an attempt to read the infernal physiognomy of the Parisians themselves and their "twisted, contorted faces [which] exude from every pore the thoughts, desires, and poisons which bloat their minds."[3] Indeed, Poe's narrative ends because physiognomy fails to provide an accurate reading of the metropolitan figure; similarly, Balzac's narrator admits that the faces he is attempting to read "are not faces but masks, masks of weakness or strength, masks of misery, joy, or hypocrisy, each one drained and marked with the indelible signs of breathless greed."[4] Balzac's emphasis on masks undermines the very attempt of "physiological terms" to render this infernal cityscape as legible, calling attention instead to the city as "a universe of secrets, founded in careful efforts to manage knowledge, and [...] revealing only avidity itself."[5] The city, then, remains a place where "secrets [...] do not permit themselves to be told."[6] Even to the all-knowing male gaze of nineteenth-century realism, the streets of London and, especially, of Paris remain illegible, providing an unique opportunity for New Woman writers to exploit this illegibility.

Central to the argument that this study has been making is the claim that urban literacy is a fundamental component of the skills conveyed in Irish women's capitalist *Bildungsromane* like *The Novice of Saint Dominick*, *Ormond*, and *French Leave*. All of these novels suggest that the cityscape can itself be read, that it is fundamentally legible. Katherine Cecil Thurston's New Woman novel *Max* challenges this notion of urban literacy by problematizing attempts to read the city. Instead of an overarching realist legibility, *Max* provides competing gendered modes of reading *fin-de-siècle* Paris that correspond to and complicate the novel's critical relationship to the project of New Woman fiction.

While *Max* initially attempts to articulate a space for women in the modern metropolitan landscape, the gendered modes of reading the city ultimately confirm that a decisive movement of women into the urban sphere severely disrupts its heteronormative structures. This is figured throughout the novel in twinned gendered and literary norms because of the novel's representation of a young woman who performs masculinity in *fin-de-siècle* Paris. *Max* utilizes the masculine adventure narrative and *Bildungsroman*, on the one hand, and the feminine romance narrative and the *Künstlerroman* on the other, before finally reasserting a heteronormative urban space and articulation of literary selfhood through the problematic resolution that typifies the inability to resolve the competing desires of independence and social stability in the female *Bildungsroman* of the nineteenth century.

Thurston's *Max* is the narrative of a young boy who arrives in Paris from St. Petersburg in Russia in order to become a painter, wanting "more than pleasure [...] more than money [...] I want first life—and then fame," but who ends up revealing his true gender identity as a woman to Blake, the Irishman who plays the love-interest, as the novel restores a heteronormative conclusion to what might have been a remarkably subversive representation of gender fluidity and performativity.[7] That this revelation of Max/ine's cis-gender identity follows a portrait of his female self reinforces the novel's initial appearance as a straightforward *Künstlerroman*, similar to Balzac's *Illusions perdues* or Joyce's *A Portrait of the Artist as a Young Man*, in which the young protagonist struggles to articulate his aesthetic and artistic vision of the world as an outlet for his frustrations with the social order. Gerardine Meaney argues that, as *French Leave* demonstrates, the "woman artist, or potential artist, was an important figure in the increasingly self-reflexive fiction which these women produced."[8] The increased prominence of women artists in *fin-de-siècle* literature mirrors the fact that "the woman artist expanded what had been a feminine accomplishment, sketching, into an art and a profession," epitomizing "the new century of possibility" as well as the New Woman.[9] This has clear echoes of Somerville and Ross's *French Leave*; and, as in that novel, this genre and its formation of selfhood continue to recognize structural elements that inhibit women's ability to inhabit this form. This is why George Lester achieves his artistic selfhood and Patsey Kirwen returns to Ireland defeated, blaming fate for the socioeconomic conditions that cause her failure. I will discuss the critical debate regarding gendered iterations of the *Bildungsroman* and the *Künstlerroman* below. *Max* complicates this relationship from the very outset by playing with constructions of gender since the protagonist is performing as a boy for the majority of the novel in what Gerardine Meaney would describe as "an act of self-invention that would surely have impressed Wilde."[10] This "figure of a boy" named Max is in reality a young woman named Maxine, who left Russia on the eve of a second marriage which "was to be the same as" her emotionally abusive and cruel first marriage.[11] *Max* attempts to present gender as what Judith Butler has identified as "an artificial effect [...] performative—that is, constituting the identity it is purported to be."[12] Following Butler, Max appears to subvert gendered essentialism, or the "metaphysics of substance," because he is "doing" masculinity and "gender is always a doing."[13] Moreover, in the latter third of the novel, he moves fluidly between the identities of Max and Maxine, reinforcing this initial claim that gender is fluid.[14]

In her seminal study of the Irish New Woman, Tina O'Toole points out that the figure of the boy in New Woman fiction intentionally plays with this sense of fluidity in order to make a critical point regarding the constructed nature of gendered spheres. Although adding grist to the mill for anti-New Woman press, many of these novels utilize "[t]he figure of the Boy, or the attribute of 'boyishness,'" as "one avenue through which they could access male privilege, at least temporarily."[15] While many New Woman texts depict the New Girl as a sort of tomboy "to demonstrate the ways in which such girls are then contained within the private sphere as they grow older," novels like *Max*, which carry the figure of the Boy into adulthood via a "female-to-male transvestite," provide New Woman writers and their characters the chance to "escape from surveillance, and access to the public world," especially the public world of the city.[16] Despite the fact that the space of the modern city is an important one for New Woman writers of the *fin de siècle*, the recourse to figures like the Boy and female-to-male transvestites fundamentally recognizes the masculine privilege invested in the public sphere of the metropolis.

By venturing into the urban sphere, the middle-class New Woman was in fact venturing onto the territory of the prostitute. As Ledger notes, the New Woman "wanted the streets of the metropolis to herself, free of the constraints imposed by the impropriety associated with the appearance of unaccompanied women in the public cities."[17] The fundamental proximity between "public woman" and "streetwalker" reflects both the anxiety over the figure of the New Woman and the "radical instability of the New Woman as a category."[18] This, in turn, reminds us of the omnipresence of the male gaze throughout the city at the *fin de siècle*; moreover, it recalls the fact that, despite the gains of the New Woman campaigners, this urban and modern landscape remains notably the province of its male citizens. The issue of access to urban space is at the heart of Thurston's novel, which, despite its attempts to expand the realm of the feminine into the heart of the modern metropolis, calls attention to the ongoing inequality of the modern metropolitan experience. In addition to calling attention to the privileged access of men to metropolitan space, *Max* encodes this experience of the urban in terms that are fundamental to this study. They recall Gallois's claim, cited above, that modernity is a place of increased choices, but which are always already constrained by one's relationship to institutional and financial powers; moreover, the novel embeds this spatial element in literary terms, connecting the ability to inhabit the modern metropolis to one's ability to read it, which I have described as "urban literacy." Surprisingly for a work of New Woman's fiction, urban literacy in *Max* remains as gendered as the access to metropolitan space itself. While urban space obscures its own meaning through illegibility in Poe and Balzac, in Thurston's novel, Paris becomes a gendered space for gendered readers, all of whom necessarily perform a gendered self.

The Masculine Urban Adventure

As Max disembarks from the overnight train that has brought him from Saint Petersburg to the Gare du Nord in the tenth *arrondissement* of Paris, the narrator establishes what will be the gendered binary that dominates the modes of reading and inhabiting the city, as well as the potential subversion that this novel proffers. Explaining that "journeys end in lovers' meeting," the narrator positions Max's journey in a literary tradition that extends from Daniel Defoe to Shakespeare.[19] Quoting from Act II of Shakespeare's *Twelfth Night*, the narrator declares that the idea of a journey

> conjures a picture. The court-yard of some inn, glowing ripe in the tints of the setting sun—open doors—an ancient coach disgorging its passengers! This—or, perhaps, some quay alive with sound and movement—cries of command in varying tongues—crowded gangways—rigging massed against the sky—all the paraphernalia of romance and travel. But the real journey—the journey of adventure itself—is frequently another matter: often gray, often loverless, often demanding from the secret soul of the adventurer spirit and inspiration, lest the blood turn cold in sick dismay, and the brain cloud under its weight of nostalgia.[20]

This bifurcated form of experiential reading falls along two dominant lines: the lines of adventure and the lines of romance, the former associated with a "gray, often loverless" realism.[21] Before moving on, however, it is important to note that this bifurcation between a feminine romance narrative and a masculine adventure narrative is not common in *fin-de-siècle* literature. Indeed, as LeeAnne Richardson has argued, these two subgenres "both revolve around one another, affected by the other's gravitational pull," but that "New Woman novels are generally character-driven and colonial adventure novels are typically incident driven," which broadly associates the New Woman novel with realism and the masculine adventure narrative with romance.²² Thus, while it might seem more natural that the generic debates within *Max* should be characterized as a masculine romance and a feminized realism, the novel's entry into Paris clearly destabilizes these categories. Instead, following from Shakespeare's *Twelfth Night*, these categories seem to become inverted.

So, we must look to a different gendered distinction for these genres; I argue that we can see Thurston's novel reflecting a much earlier definition, one which "expect[s] adventures and intrigues."²³ The novel confirms this association of a masculine expectation of adventure through the initial introduction on the train, in which the narrator describes the masculine-identified Max as "that free fascinating creature, the born adventurer—high of courage, prodigal of emotion, capturer of the world's loot," which explicitly evokes the rakish masculinity of the late eighteenth- and early nineteenth-century novel like Henry Fielding's *The History of Tom Jones: A Foundling* (1749) or, especially important for *fin-de-siècle* writers of adventure narratives, Daniel Defoe's *Robinson Crusoe* (1719).²⁴ The significance of Defoe for late Victorian adventure narratives cannot be overstated; Richard Phillips has demonstrated Defoe's significance in the Victorian period, arguing that *Robinson Crusoe* "was canonised as the archetypal modern adventure story [...] in the nineteenth century when the story took its place among the foundational myths of British culture."²⁵ We can see echoes of the *Crusoe* narrative in the passage quoted above. The maritime and naval imagery is obvious in the evocation of Shakespeare's *Twelfth Night*, which famously begins with a shipwreck on the shores of Illyria; moreover, the connection to "some quay alive with sound and movement [...] crowded gangways—rigging massed against the sky" evokes the iconography of the British naval vessel.²⁶ But, more importantly, in the contrast with this romanticized imagery of some ship, we can see Robinson Crusoe's archetypal isolation in the narrator's emphasis on the adventurer's isolation and the celebration of "spirit and inspiration."²⁷ Each of these celebrates the characteristics of empire building through the traditional colonial story of exploration, adventure, self-reliance, and a recognizably imperial form of masculinity.

In this emphasis on isolation and self-reliance, it is important to note that this dominant and masculine imagery's emphasis on isolation also echoes the urban criticism of Georg Simmel, whose writings repeatedly stress the loneliness of the modern metropolitan experience. Simmel's "Metropolis and Mental Life," as explained above, stresses the ambivalent freedom available to the modern urban dweller, one of increased choices but also of increased anonymity and isolation. The connection between the representation of the city and this narrative of adventure is significant not just because it highlights the mode of transportation that brings Max to Paris, nor because it introduces the novel's primary characters, but because both these spaces function as emblems of a problematic modernity, a site of anxiety, a site of surveillance, and a site of adventure. Of course, Max does not arrive in Paris via a Crusoe-esque shipwreck, with its rigging against the sky, but aboard the modern vehicle of exploration and imperial expansion: the railroad.

The association of the railroad and the space of empire is well documented; it is implicitly related to the colonial geography of the *fin-de-siècle* adventure narrative. Eric Hobsbawm, for example, called it a "synonym for ultra-modernity."[28] As Marian Aguiar notes, the railroad originally occupied a "part of a national economic space" in the British popular imagination; its speed and the goods it carried helped "make the colony appear more proximate."[29] Ultimately, this increased movement of people, of goods, and of ideas fostered "a distinctive kind of 'railway imperialism' that could integrate and annex territories" to the imperial center, making the railroads in India "nothing more than an extension of their own line from Manchester to Liverpool."[30] Thus, while the narrator declares the possibility of viewing the city and the journey as either one "of romance" or "of adventure," this framework is established firstly in terms of the railroad, suggesting that the two spaces of the city and the train can and should be read each as an extension of the other as they historically were.[31] The train's "night journey," the narrator explains, is essentially a thing of possibilities. To those who count it as mere transit, mere linking of experiences, it is, of course, a commonplace; but to the imaginative, who by gift divine see a picture in every cloud, a story behind every shadow, it suggests romance—romance in the very making.[32]

Again, these two competing forms of experiential reading recapitulate a romantic and a realist mode, the one concerned with art and the imagination, the other solely with the lived and physical experience. The connection between romance and art, as I will discuss below, highlights both a connection to the *Künstlerroman* and the more problematic question of the female *Bildungsroman*; in contradistinction to the "imaginative" passengers, who experience the train as "romance in the very making," the narrator describes these others as the train's "varying human freight—stolid Teutons, hard-headed Scandinavians, Slavs whom expediency or caprice had forced to descend upon Paris across the sea of ice."[33] In the realist mode, then, the train is connected to an important network of expanding modernity through the expansion of the capitalist marketplace, the transnational movement of people and commodities, and people-as-commodities, and ultimately the articulation of national spaces. In this way, Thurston's novel explicitly recognizes an expansive process of industrialization and commodification that extends outward from the redesigned *grands boulevards* and the Bon Marché to the Gare du Nord, the Gare de l'Est, the Gare Montparnasse, and the Gare Saint-Lazare, ultimately across Europe, all of which were built to aid the circulation of goods into and within the city. This realist mode encapsulates a public, masculine space of metropolitan capitalism, which is intimately bound up with the train, the symbol *par excellence* of modernity as William Gallois has described it. According to Gallois, the train demonstrates both "how structures of life and forms of power and behaviour are naturalised in modernity," while simultaneously "offering an account of the arrival of new forms of alienation in modernity, descriptions of the individual's loss of mastery and safety in the world, [and ultimately] of the impossibility of reading the world."[34] This sense of alienation, which is bound up intimately with the railroad, extends well beyond the Gare du Nord into the streets of Paris. And only the hyper-rational men in the novel seem able to achieve what Gallois has described as impossible and read this modern world.

The masculinity associated with this realist mode of viewing and engaging the modern landscape is first revealed on the train as a disciplinary male gaze that seeks to fit and to read the individual, which then is translated more broadly into the Parisian cityscape through the figure of the Irishman Blake. As the train thunders toward the capital of modernity, its electric lights, "worldly wise and watchful," see "the individuality—the inevitable story—behind the drowsy units who sat or lay or lounged unguarded beneath them."[35] This, of course, depends upon and indeed reveals an individual's relationship to the Foucauldian order of surveillance and institutional power, which dominates within the modern metropolis. Those who enjoy "a place of power (the property of a proper)" are able to make use of *strategies* in order to "control and 'include' [...] by reading a space."[36] While the cityscape enables such "erotics of knowledge," de Certeau also describes the space of the train as a "bubble of panoptic and classifying power, a module of imprisonment that makes possible the production of an order," which classifies the railroad and the railcar as a space that functions in terms of this strategy.[37] In this space, the traveler is "pigeonholed, numbered, and regulated," which undeniably recalls the panoptic order that informs the de Certeauian space of the strategist.[38] These lights, then, recall the panoptic order that characterizes de Certeau's description of the train; indeed, that the lights treat the passengers as "units" reinforces this sense of surveillance and an eroticized, disciplinary knowledge.

The disciplinary mechanism becomes embodied and manifest with the entrance of the novel's cis-male protagonist, Blake, and the other male passengers return from playing cards. As they re-enter the carriage, they stare at Max, "frankly curious. When they had left the compartment he had been a huddled figure demanding no attention; now he was awake and an individual, and human nature prompted interest."[39] The male gaze, here personified and given a masculine body, is immediately associated with a disciplinary impulse that is characterized in terms of curiosity and interest, especially before "an individual." These men "[e]ach in turn looked at [Max], and at each new glance his coldness of demeanor deepened," establishing an oppositional relationship between the two parties: a surveillance mechanism and an individual who seeks to slip through the very disciplinary gaze.[40] This relationship quite clearly anticipates and participates in the system of disciplinary observation that Michel de Certeau describes in his *The Practice of Everyday Life*. According to de Certeau, who has described the act of walking through the city as a "pedestrian speech act," the modern urban-dweller "actualizes only a few of the possibilities fixed by the constructed order [and] increases the number of possibilities" available in the spatial order.[41] This, of course, depends upon and indeed reveals an individual's relationship to the Foucauldian order of surveillance and institutional power, which dominates within the modern metropolis. Blake and the other card players, the cis-men, are able to replicate this attempt to control and include Max through their curious gaze at the figure of the boy. The potential for control becomes even more obvious through the revelation of the three men's individual jobs and characters: the elder of the three, "a tall, spare American," declares "'We're well on time, Blake,' [...] drawing out his watch [...] with the loving interest of one to whom time is a sacred thing."[42] This first gentleman confirms the disciplinary mechanism of the railroad through the standardization of time, as well as the more obvious understanding of a capitalization of time through which time does indeed become sacred. The railroad, then, becomes a masculine space of business, demonstrating the expansion of capitalism into the very experience of time. The youngest of the three, an Englishman who "open[s] a large bundle of illustrated papers—French, German, and English," is revealed to be a diplomat, declaring "[i]n diplomacy nothing's too insignificant to notice."[43] While the American recognizes the expansion of discipline into time, this Englishman demonstrates the expansion of the disciplinary mechanism of the state, blending the field of international relations through his diplomacy with the field of journalism through the close analysis of his weekly papers. Instead of registering a sort of cosmopolitanism, as the inclusion of English, French, and German papers might suggest, the state's policing of actions becomes the dominant take-away and threat through his reference to "this Petersburg affair [...] [t]he disappearance of the Princess Davorska," anticipating the revelation of Max/ine's actual identity in Russia before she escaped the second of what she assumed would be an abusive marriage.[43] This demonstrates not only the threat the male disciplinary gaze poses to Max/ine as an individual, but also the broader threat it poses to any tactician who attempts to subvert the dominant and heteronormative order embodied in this group of cis-gendered men and the modernity they represent.

The last of the three men whose gaze unsettles Max is the Irishman, Blake. While the previous two embody specific forms of discipline, the capitalization of time and the expansion of the state apparatus, Blake is described as "a man who knew his world the globe over, and in his bearing lurked the toleration, the kindly scepticism that such knowledge breeds."[45] In this initial description, it is difficult to pinpoint a specific embodiment of any disciplinary mechanism; instead, Blake's characterization as a global citizen, at home everywhere, recalls the Baudelairean figure of the *flâneur* who speaks to a more diffuse and gendered modernity, who is both above and apart from the emerging urban disciplinary mechanism that constitutes and constructs the modern urban landscape in the second half of the nineteenth century.[46] While Blake's toleration seems to undercut a connection to a disciplinary regime, the first words he speaks in the novel are censorious, ordering Max not to do something. Speaking "easily and pleasantly," he commands, "Don't do that! [...] Don't do that—if you want the air."[47] Despite the tone, the actions here clearly embody the disciplinary position of a strategist, capable of controlling and including, as de Certeau says. The authoritative speaking position clearly falls to a cis-gendered man whose ability to feel at home everywhere allows him the expectation of a sense of authority.

This expectation of authority recalls Richardson's characterization of the Victorian adventure novel as being "written from the perspective of the authoritarian, culturally dominant male, often justifies the subaltern's subordinated status."[48] Collapsing the *flâneur* into the adventure narrative, Blake becomes both the symbol of *fin-de-siècle* masculinity and the vehicle through which the novel most obviously associates the metropolis with the adventure narrative of *Crusoe*, who was himself at home not in the crowd but in the geography of adventure.

Feminist critics have long identified the masculine privilege that undergirds Baudelaire's description of this "prince who everywhere rejoices in his incognito," who is able to "feel [himself] everywhere at home; to see the world to be at the centre of the world."[49] And it is a critical commonplace to note that Baudelaire's "perfect *flâneur*" is a man precisely because the gendered dynamic of the modern city and of the modernity which he embodies: the freedom of movement, the right to occupy urban space, the characteristics that define de Certeau's strategist. Thus, the *flâneur* expresses a comfort in the type of cosmopolitanism that the narrator attributes to Blake; the fact that his "manner was the most indifferent, his temper the most unruffled" bespeaks an expectation not only of authority but of ease, a complete right to privilege.[50] This relationship to the Baudelairean figure, however, becomes more significant for the literary geography of the novel once the train arrives at the Gare du Nord because it demonstrates the emergence of a Simmelian metropolitan mentality. As they disembark, Blake alone remembers the young Russian and inquires, "'Look here! you aren't alone in Paris?' [...] in the easy, impersonal way that spoke his nationality."[51] His question, beginning with an imperative phrase, is premised again on an unacknowledged masculine right to speak and to discipline. But, more importantly, the question flags the issue of metropolitan isolation, which is fundamental to the experience of the modern city; its very impersonality recognizes that this space is in fact one characterized by anonymity and the metropolitan blasé that Simmel has described.

For the rest of the novel, this anonymity reinforces and is premised upon the masculine privilege of access to urban space, characterizing the modern metropolitan landscape as one in which men are de Certeauian strategists and women are tacticians. The initial foray into the streets of Paris on the Rue de Dunkerque provides an early instance of this gendering of the urban landscape, demonstrating the degree to which the French capital restricts access to certain spaces. At this moment of introduction to the cityscape, the Englishman from the train reasserts the disciplinary mechanism of the male gaze, complaining that "Paris on a wet day is like a woman with draggled skirts."[52] While the city itself is a feminized landscape, the right to surveil and critique remains a masculine remit, privileging the position of the observer. The identification of Paris with "a woman with draggled skirts" does not so much reclaim the cityscape for women as it reasserts men's dominance. Both the negative tone of the description and its replication of the hierarchizing male gaze suggest the metropolitan binary opposition that Janet Wolff identifies. Because of the association of urban space with a hierarchizing male gaze, Wolff argues that it is "impossible to identify a female *flâneuse*" since the modernity that Baudelaire discusses is predicated on "public/private (masculine/feminine) binary opposition."[53] Moreover, the class connotations of "draggled" create the specter of the prostitute or streetwalker. Where else would her skirts have collected their debris, if not wandering the Parisian streets? Thus, underlying this male privilege of urban space lies a significant obscuring, if not outright denial, of women in the cityscape.

This reflects contemporary ambivalence between the New Woman and the metropolitan space. While New Women and feminist campaigners were "emerging more and more into the public spaces of the city," these women had to contend with "the figure of the prostitute."[54] This potential confusion, or at least association, undermines the free movement of women into the metropolitan spaces that the male *flâneur* was able to enjoy. The novel echoes this concern for the crowd's threat to women through its description of the crowd's physicality, "the jostling of elbows" that characterizes "that odd medley of men and women, unadorned, jaded, careless."55 The focus on the physical competition that "jostling" connotes suggests a corporeality and violence that reinforces the gendered characterization of the city as masculine; it is a space fit for the adventurous, self-reliant man of the *fin de siècle* who is able to colonize and conquer, not the woman who converts. The novel continues this association through the Simmelian emphasis on the city's indifference to the individual; instead of welcoming these arrivals into some New Jerusalem, as Patsey Kirwen hoped, "nothing could be less inviting than the Glimpse of Paris" as Max "fare[s] forth into the gloom."56 Obviously refuting any romantic notions of the City of Light, this initial representation casts a Gothic, foreign, almost Balzacian pall over the streetscape. It is important that this Paris recalls Balzac, especially the preface to *The Girl with the Golden Eyes*, because, as I suggested, this novel sets the terms for Max's later experience of the city in a way that reinforces a masculine representation of modernity. As such, it should be no surprise that the protagonist commits to the identity of Max, instead of the cis-female identity of Maxine, for the vast majority of this urban novel. More importantly, this first encounter with the Parisian landscape is heavily coded in language reminiscent of the adventure narratives that dominated the *fin de siècle*.

Indeed, despite the "darkness and chill and the listless misery of a winter dawn [... the] face of such dejection," "the soul of the adventurer" keeps Max "undaunted."57 The repetition of adventurer recalls the generic and gendered debate I am attempting to highlight, clearly associating both the protagonist with a masculinity common in the literature of the *fin de siècle* and the landscape of the metropolis with the geography of adventure. Just as *Crusoe*, Stevenson's *Treasure Island* (1883), H. Rider Haggard's *King Solomon's Mines* (1885), or Joseph Conrad's *Heart of Darkness* (1899) venture into the unmapped territories of foreign lands in an attempt to create a disciplinary map, so too does Max venture into the urban, "moving onward with the excitement that is born of absolute uncertainty," before he arrives in the "Rue de Dunkerque! It conveyed nothing to his mind. But was he not seeking the unknown."⁵⁸ The boy, explicitly invoking the colonial and unmapped territory of the adventure novel, positions himself as the disciplinary figure of imperial expansion. He inserts himself into the youthful and masculine tradition of Defoe's Crusoe, Stevenson's Jim Hawkins, and Haggard's Allan Quartermain by mapping a territory and "possessing it, in the same way that British explorers [...] possessed what they saw."⁵⁹ This combination of exploration and possession uniquely suits the young boy to success. As the narrator claims, "[o]nly a creature infinitely young could have held firm in face of such dejection," but Max "looked at it all with a certain steadfastness that seemed to say, 'Yes, I see you! You are hideous, slatternly, unfriendly; but through all the disguise I recognize you. You are Paris!'"⁶⁰ This passage contains the germ of this argument: masculinity is required in order to read and decode the city. Max is able to see "through all the disguise" and, as such, is able to take his place within the implacable and unfriendly landscape of Paris. The act of surveying and mastering, a trope of Victorian "discovery rhetoric," produces a significant connection between the act of spatial possession and literacy; indeed, Max is only able to participate in this urban space because he is able to see through the disguise and because, "peering up through the misty light he read the legend, 'rue de Dunkerque.'"⁶¹ That his mastery is a consequence of his ability to decipher the "legend," and then to read the map of the streetscape, reinforces the connection between masculine mastery of space and what I have articulated as urban literacy, the ability to read the space of the city. This is, of course, not new; in many ways, it recalls the disciplinary knowledge of Foucault and de Certeau's rhetorics of walking, but it is a term with a significant claim. While architects have often discussed the legibility of urban spaces, the idea of an urban practitionership that depends not upon the ability of the space to be read, but of the urban citizen to read the space, accurately highlights the fact that these spaces are arranged in order to obscure their own politics and power dynamics.

Only the masculine urban practitioner who is, like Max, able to see "[t]hrough the mask" is able to navigate these disparate urban spaces, especially in what Moretti describes as the "mosaic of little worlds."⁶² Moretti uses this term to describe the "'demographic plan' of the *Comédie Humaine*":

> Paris has five, six major spaces, whose borders are crossed and recrossed in the full light of day. It is Robert Park's plural city: a true mosaic of worlds, where the social division of labor seems to have literally stamped itself upon the urban space: trade near Les Halles, entertainment on the Boulevards, publishing around the Cité, education at the Sorbonne ... But the movement between these worlds, on the other hand, is probably less "quick and easy" than Park had in mind. [...] A city where movement cannot be taken for granted.⁶³

If, as Moretti suggests, the movement between and across these "worlds" is not quick and easy, it suggests instead an imbricated, intersectional nature: that only certain people of certain classes are able to navigate these spaces freely. For Thurston in *Max*, those people are the bohemians, the cosmopolitans who, like Blake, are men "who knew his world the globe over, and in his bearing lurked the toleration, the kindly scepticism that such knowledge brings."⁶⁴ This connection to the "little worlds" of Paris is fundamental to the novel's argument not only because of Max's desire to plunge into the unknown spaces of Paris, but also because of the sheer number of spaces that he and Blake end up exploring. It is worth quoting Moretti in full precisely because of the number of spaces shared by the map of the *Comédie* and *Max*. As Max ventures into Paris on his second full day in the city, he is confronted with the debris of this "mosaic" and its social division of labor. In the neighborhood surrounding the Gare du Nord, it is unsurprising that his second major sighting of the city should be varied and heterogeneous:

> The majority of passers-by at this morning hour were workers—work-girls out upon their errands, businessmen

going to or from the *cafés*; but here and there was to be seen an artisan, unconsciously picturesque in his coarse working clothes; here and there a well-dressed woman, sunning herself in the cold bright air like a bird of gay plumage. It was the world in miniature, and it stirred and piqued his interest.[65]

The replication of Lefebvre's rhythmanalysis shows the rhythms of capital, the people in the street reflect the change in shifts; this demonstrates the degree to which this urban landscape is already implicated in and reifying the capitalist project. But the recognition and cataloguing of such a diverse representation of social classes, laborers, artisans, presumably *petit bourgeois* women "sunning" themselves in an attitude of leisure, demonstrates a mapping of this capitalist landscape, a project that echoes of Balzac's *Comédie* as an attempt to understand the multifaceted landscape of the French capital. However, the privileged position of observer, like the disembodied and all-knowing narrator of Balzac's survey of Paris, is a masculine figure, the boy, reinforcing the privilege of the male gaze within the urban scene.

Following this foray into the neighborhood surrounding the Gare du Nord, Max makes "his way through the wider spaces of the Place Lafayette and the Square Montholon into the long, busy rue Lafayette" in the northern ninth *arrondissement* and down "the rue Halévy he went and on into the Place de l'Opéra."[66] This geography is important, especially regarding the novel's interest in cosmopolitan art, but also for its use of urban space as it moves from the winding streets near the Gare du Nord down through the *grands boulevards* of Baron Haussmann, whose project of urban renovation is irrevocably connected to urban control. As it moves through the ninth *arrondissement* past the Rue Halévy, the novel implicitly participates in the artistic landscape of *fin-de-siècle* Paris since Gustave Caillebotte famously captured the streetscape in his impressionist rendering *Rue Halévy, Seen from the Sixth Floor* (1888). While the connection to impressionism might seem merely an interesting aside, the perspective of Caillebotte's spectator reinforces my overarching argument. Surveying the street from the height of a sixth-floor apartment,[67] the painting seems to obtain a disciplinary ability to map the chaotic streetscape by escaping the street-level perspective. From the elevated distance of Caillebotte's sixth floor, the cityscape "is immobilized before the eyes" in the type of panorama that enables Paris "to be taken in 'at a single view', to be seen, and comprehended, as a totality."[68] Simply by being "lifted out of the city's grasp," the viewer's elevation "transfigures him into a voyeur" and "allows one to read [the city], to be a solar Eye, looking down like a god."[69] De Certeau's identification of this god-like vision of the city with a form of disciplinary knowledge that recalls Pratt's concept of "mastery between the seer and the seen" implies that the viewer "has the power if not to possess, at least to evaluate this scene."[70] The problematic voyeurism of this position fundamentally reinforces the masculine privilege associated with the city, but specifically with certain places in the city.

This pictorial representation of a disciplinary gaze recalls de Certeau's argument regarding the ability to read the city. However, de Certeau's argument finds a literary predecessor in Émile Zola's *Rougon-Macquart* cycle. For Christopher Prendergast, Zola's Aristide Saccard, the banker protagonist of both *La Curée* (1871) and *L'Argent* (1891), returns "obsessively to the steps of the Sacré-Cœur" in order "to dramatize the projections of the acquisitive gaze."[71] Standing before the Sacré-Cœur with "Paris slashed with sabre cuts, its veins opened," "cutting through the air" with his hands along the lines of the newly emerging boulevards and neighborhoods below, Saccard's mastering gaze "seeks to hold the objects of the urban environment in a safe relation to the subject's desires."[72] According to Prendergast, this "fixating and fetishizing" gaze grants to the surveying speculator the masculine trait of authoring and creating meaning.[73] These connections highlight the masculinity of Moretti's movement across the Parisian cityscape. Clearly, here, Max is able to move freely down to the Place de l'Opéra through the ninth *arrondissement* into "the Place de Rivoli, where Joan of Arc sat astride her golden horse," and then across "the rue de Rivoli and, passing through the garden of the Tuileries, emerg[ing] upon the Place de la Concorde" in the first *arrondissement*.⁷⁴ It is, unsurprisingly, here in the Place de la Concorde and in the Tuileries that Max coincidentally runs into Blake during a military parade. I say unsurprisingly for two reasons: firstly, because Moretti points out that it is typical of the nineteenth-century *Bildungsroman* that young men meet and "are drawn towards those unknown yet congenial faces seen in the gardens, or at the theater," those monumental and public spaces of "secondary socialization" like the Place de la Concorde.⁷⁵ These public and "monumental" spaces participate in Moretti's project of socialization, according to Henri Lefebvre, because they offer "each member of a society an image of that membership," functioning more as a "collective mirror" that produces "a 'recognition effect.'"⁷⁶ Secondly, the role of the Tuileries fits uniquely into the model of reading the city that I am proposing. As Prendergast makes clear, the center of "the ideologico-institutional apparatuses of *haute* surveillance" occupies the *pavillon central des Tuileries*, which "was not a politically neutral space or innocent point of vision; it betokened the centralizing gaze of power, the perspective of the ruler over the ruled."⁷⁷ Replicating the discourse of vision and masculine mastery that Pratt identifies in colonial narratives, these public spaces in Paris belong to both homosocial relationships of young men, of chance meetings that spark the plots of friendship that form the narratological framework of these novels—as we have seen in Edgeworth's *Ormond*—and, equally, the hierarchical vision that enables and demands a masculine association with the public urban sphere. And here, in *Max*, this world of the chance encounter with congenial faces is underlined as belonging to the world of men through the "inevitably thrilling" presence of "a regiment of infantry marching down the Cours la Reine and defiling out upon the Place de la Concorde toward the rue de Rivoli."⁷⁸ That a regiment "stir[s] the fancy" recalls both the military exploits of the Third Empire that populate Zola's novels of Paris, but also, and more importantly, the colonial adventure narratives so popular with men and boys in the *fin de siècle*. Thus it is that Max's reunion with Blake, who addresses him "in an easy, familiar voice, as one friend might address another," begins in a hypermasculine environment, deeply reminiscent of both the homosocialism of Balzacian *Bildung* and the adventure novels that encourage and construct a specific type of masculinity.[79]

The masculine privilege embedded in this encounter is palpable. While Max "[u]nconsciously made a picture," there is "one pair of eyes in the little crowd [to whom] it seemed better worth watching than the passing soldiers," a passage with an undeniable tone of homoeroticism, adding to the queer potential of the novel.[80] That Max is unconsciously an object observed by an at-first disembodied, and thus clearly masculine, figure highlights the privileged position that we saw in Caillebotte's painting, de Certeau's analysis of the cityscape, and especially in Zola's dissection of the city from Montmartre, a space to which we will return below. The pair, "stimulated by the crisp summons of the flutes and the martial rattle of the drums," start across the Place de la Concorde toward a "large building and read the legend, '*Société de Peintres et Sculpteurs Français* [emphasis in original],'" indicating the Salon du Champ de Mars, or the Salon de la Société Nationale des Beaux-Arts.[81] This complex intertwining of generic forms highlights the interrelated debates in which the novel is engaged: it is clear that the friendship begins in the mode of the adventure narrative, receiving its stimulation from "flutes and martial rattle of the drums," but it equally becomes a recognizable *Bildungsroman* and, also, a *Künstlerroman*, in the style of Balzac's *Illusions perdues* through the collapse of mentorship and the world of artistic expression. Indeed, when Blake asks the young man what it is he seeks in Paris, Max answers, "I want first life—and then fame," a word which "trembled and hung upon the air—that brief word 'fame.'"[82] The parallels to Vautrin's recognition of *parvenir* after Rastignac's first visit to the vaulted world of Parisian society are near-unmissable; in *Père Goriot*, when the young Frenchman returns, Balzac's criminal-in-disguise declares, "That day you came back with a word marked on your forehead, and one I could read easily enough: *Succeed!* succeed at any price. Bravo!"[83] This key moment, in the section entitled "Entry on the Social Scene," initiates Rastignac into both the urban realm and its new desire for ambition, teaching him that, in Paris, "it's every man for himself."[84] As a result of this connection to *Père Goriot*, it is undeniable that this access to urban space, indeed the very attempt to succeed within it, is premised upon the privilege of male access to the urban through the omnipresence of the gaze; characterizing the urban space as masculine reinforces Pratt's "relation of *mastery* predicated between the seer and the seen" which undergirds the imperial nature of *fin-de-siècle* adventure literature.[85] This initial kindling of a homosocial relationship establishes a masculine privilege the underlines the generic traits of the adventure narrative for Max's and Blake's exploration of the city.

After their initial trip to the Société Nationale des Beaux Arts, Blake leads Max back across the Seine into the mêlée of the Left Bank. Here, the "note of contrast that is bound into the very atmosphere of Paris" reveals to the Russian *arriviste* that "Parisian life [...] is as restless as the sea, as uncontrollable, as possessed of hidden currents."[86] The repetition of this nautical imagery reinforces the adventure narrative, associating the city even more with tales of exploration and mastery, as well as with a masculine literary tradition that is based upon and inculcates a certain privileged masculine gaze. Nowhere is this association of adventure and masculinity more evident than in the representation of Montmartre and its cabarets in the outskirts of the Right Bank. The social and cultural history of Montmartre makes it unsurprising that this neighborhood in the eighteenth *arrondissement* should be treated as a site that combines urban and adventure novels. As a sociocultural site, Montmartre has "always occupied a privileged position in the geography of Parisian pleasure," often leading to a Bakhtinian and carnivalesque mixture that runs "between different classes, between respectability and criminality, between Parisians and incomers [...], between 'slummers' from other fashionable districts and beyond."[87] This motley mixture of Parisians, as Nicholas Hewitt argues, stems from the "transformation of Lower Montmartre into the entertainment centre of Paris in the 1880s, through the cabarets and the music halls."[88] While the association of Montmartre with pleasure dates to the late eighteenth century construction of the Mur des Fermiers généraux and the imposition of "a severe tax on products, especially alcohol" that helped to create "a flourishing entertainment industry [...] just on the other side of the *barriers*, where cheap wine and alcohol could still be dispensed, often in dance halls," the establishment of *Le Chat Noir* in 1881 permanently changed the sociocultural landscape of the neighborhood.[89] The significance of this club is that "it offered—or so it claimed—an opportunity to mingle with genuine bohemians, artists, the demi-monde, and even the criminal classes."[90] As seen in novels like Oscar Wilde's *The Picture of Dorian Gray* (1890), this "explor[ation] of realms of hidden or forbidden knowledge," like the opium dens of south London, are typical of urban novels of the *fin de siècle*, while also recalling the "dangerous travel into the untamed jungle" of contemporary adventure novels.[91] For Richardson, this brings the dandy into a close alliance "with the colonial adventurer" through similar narratives of exploration and through the novels' exclusively masculine or homosocial nature.[92] These two genres, the decadent urban novel and the adventure narrative, both highlight a "purely masculine company and have little regard for women's political action, which is typically denigrated as 'ugly.'"[93] Thus, by prioritizing the urban space of Montmartre, *Max* participates in this collapsing of the urban and the adventure narrative through its representation of a sexualizing and dominant masculine gaze that surveys and maps the people and space of the urban jungle.

From the very beginning, Montmartre is associated with the idea of adventure. Blake derides Max's initial suggestion that he live in "[f]ashionable Paris"; he insists, instead, that "[f]or us it must be the highways and the byways," the space both of the adventurer and of the eighteenth-century rake.[94] This description usually represents, as Bakhtin tells us, "the spatial and temporal paths of the most varied people—representatives of all social classes, estates, religions, nationalities, ages [... p]eople who are normally kept separate by social and spatial distance."[95] While Moretti, via Bakhtin, argues that the road in novels with colonial geographies differ from those in picaresque and urban novels insofar as these latter roads are characterized by a "space where strangers are never entirely strangers," Max's ultimate decision to move into a studio in the Rue Müller, lying in the shadow of the Sacré-Cœur, earns from Blake the praise that "You're a fine adventurer! You have the right spirit."[96] The association of Montmartre, especially the area surrounding the Sacré-Cœur, with adventure reinforces Pratt's claim about mastery, precisely because it functions as a site of surveillance not only for Max but for literature throughout the nineteenth century. Max declares that if he is "to know Paris [he] will know her from here—study her, love her from here," staring out from "the wooden paling that fronts the Sacré-Cœur, his elbows resting upon it, his face between his hands, his eyes held by the glitter of Paris lying below him."[97] Recalling the mastering surveillance of de Certeau and Pratt, this scene re-enacts the power dynamic of disciplinary attempts to map and read the city, which is exacerbated through the feminine characterization of the urban landscape. That Max makes his declaration from this specific geographic location is important because it combines the type of mastering gaze that Prendergast associates with the heights of Montmartre and that Pratt associates with the masculinity of adventure narratives. Indeed, as Prendergast makes clear, Montmartre was specifically associated with the surveillance of the Parisian landscape in the novels of Zola and his contemporaries: Zola "return[ed] obsessively to the steps of the Sacré-Cœur" especially in order to "dramatize the projections of the acquisitive gaze directed towards the city."[98] Prendergast's characterization of Zola's narratological gaze as "acquisitive" is of special significance, particularly in view of Max's need to acquire so many things: the apartment, the city, life, and fame. Even in Max's desire to "to know Paris [... to] study her, love her," there is an echo of the acquisitive drive that dominates Zola's gaze. Max's adventure and his attempts to possess the city begin from a site at the heart of a masculine disciplinary regime.

This adventure, then, begins from a position associated with the masculine urban gaze and, unsurprisingly, immediately moves into the sexualized landscape in which this gaze functions as a dominant and disciplinary force: the cabarets of Montmartre. In this, Max and Blake both follow the model of the urban adventure that Richardson identifies in *Dorian Gray* and other *fin-de-siècle* novels by diving into Montmartre's theaters. With its "altar to Bacchus," the *Bal Tabarin* "seemed in very truth the gay world" and women "formed the definite interest of the picture."[99] Max and the narrator survey these women in great detail, almost cataloguing the various types, some of whom:

> were fair, some brown, a few red-haired, but the vast majority belonged to the type that was to become familiar to Max as the true *Montmartroise*—the girl possessed of the dead white face, the red sensual lips, the imperfectly chiseled nose, attractive in its very imperfection and the eyes—black, brown, or gray— that see in a single glance to the bottom of a man's soul.[100]

This survey of the types of women, focused especially on the various colors of eyes and hair, evokes the encyclopedic quality of Balzac's *Comédie humaine* while also creating an uncanny sexualization through the suggestion of women's power to "see in a single glance to the bottom of a man's soul." This almost vampiric characteristic of these decadent and sexualized women encapsulates the complicated ambivalence that surrounds the representation of women's sexuality in the *fin de siècle*. While they safely remain sexualized objects subject to the male gaze, their very sexuality undermines the authority of the masculine disciplinary regime. In addition, this obviously sexualized landscape becomes increasingly associated with the geography of adventure through its very heterogeneity. The Spanish women who dance a can-can are "dressed in their national costume, stood preening themselves like vain birds, tossing their heads."[101] The aesthetic exoticism of the avian imagery, coupled with a foreign national costume, recalls the exact type of imperial adventure novels, an association strengthened through the narrator's description of Blake's behavior as "imperiously reckless."[102] This replicates the "decisively gendered" trope that Pratt describes as the "[e]xplorer-man paints/possesses newly unveiled landscape-woman" through its explicit identification of the women with a foreign, animalistic landscape.[103] The novel replays and enhances this colonial and racialized encounter in another Montmartre club. The *Rat Mort* intensifies the sexualization of this colonizing adventure through its representation of the only non-Westerners in the novel. "A negro and a negress—properties of the place, as were the glasses and the table linen" dance to "the barbaric" and "wild *Ztigane* music of the stringed orchestra."[104] Described as possessing a "pliant suppleness, the conscious sensuality of their race," this couple embodies all the traits of the colonial discourse that constructs, reifies, and participates within the empire building of colonial adventure novels of the *fin de siècle*. A racial essentialism, paired with the effeminizing modifiers "suppleness" and "sensuality," produce a clear racial hierarchy that is even more clear through the matter-of-fact acknowledgement that they are possessions of the club, just as the glasses and table linens.

While this racialized scene in Montmartre clearly participates in the critical recognition, most clearly articulated in Edward Said's *Culture and Imperialism*, that the British adventure novel discursively participates in the imperialist project, the representation of these black dancers more clearly reinforces the supremacy of the disciplinary male gaze, connected to the intertwined lines of surveillance, reading, and aesthetics that I have been exploring throughout this chapter. After Blake asks him what he thinks, Max describes the dance as "repulsive—like figures in a nightmare," which Blake immediately associates with their first adventure to the Salon of the Société de Peintres et Sculpteurs Français.[105] In a scene that echoes Zola's famous Preface to the second edition of *Thérèse Raquin*, described in Chapter 3, Max condemns Blake's use of "filth" to describe a

> picture curiously repulsive, yet curiously binding in its realism of conception. It was a large canvas that formed one of a group of five or six studies by a particular artist. The details

of the picture scarcely held the mind, for the imagination of the beholder was instantly caught and enchained by the central figure—the figure of a great ape, painted with cruel and extraordinary truth. The animal was squatting upon the ground, devouring a luscious fruit; its small and greedy eyes were alight with gluttony; in its unbridled appetite, its hairy fingers crushed the fruit against its sharp teeth, while the juice dripped from its mouth.[106]

I quote the entire passage because it not only provides greater context for the racialized and aesthetic discourse of the association of the black dancers with the painting of the ape, but also intimately unites the privileged position of surveyor with that of an imperial and masculine figure. As Pratt argues, in nineteenth-century "discovery rhetoric," the imperial viewer is "there to judge and appreciate" the aestheticization of the landscape and, in so doing, "produces it for others."[107] In this interaction between aesthetics and ideology, "the esthetic qualities of the landscape constitute the social and material value of the discovery to the explorers' home culture, at the same time as its esthetic deficiencies suggest a need for social and material intervention."[108] Thus, the animal and racial imagery that associates the black dancers with the bestial ape establishes the value of differentiation, separating and demarcating the lines of the animal and the human through the device and the reification of the imperial male gaze. The privileged position of observer, of reader, and of critic is premised upon the viewer's Western masculinity. The same masculinity that underlies the colonial and imperial encounters of *fin-de-siècle* adventure narratives has been transferred to the hegemonic masculinity that populates the urban landscape of *fin-de-siècle* Paris, rendering the cityscape an inescapable site of gendered readings.

The Feminine Romantic City

If the city in *Max* presents a masculine realm associated with the adventure narrative, the novel's bifurcation between gendered selves also reveals a feminine representation of the city that is most clearly associated with the romance genre. As mentioned above, the association of *fin-de-siècle* women's writing with romance upends recent critical opinions, but, borrowing from Sharon Murphy's definition of romance, this generic definition becomes more apposite and helps to explain precisely why Paris remains an ambiguous site in Thurston's novel. For Murphy, the genre of romance depends upon "imagination and improbability" as well as an inability to read the landscape so that the protagonist commits the error of "supposing that 'romances were Pictures of Life,'" a definition that ultimately recalls the cautionary tale of *The Female Quixote* (1752), in which Arabella commits this seminal error of misreading fiction for real life.[109] That Murphy's definition associates romance with both an opposition to realism and a deceptive form of fiction undergirds the fundamental narratological framework of Thurston's novel by providing two gendered models of reading and inhabiting the urban landscape. The novel, as mentioned above, divides between "the real journey—the journey of adventure itself" from the "paraphernalia of romance and travel."[110] Instead of returning to this division, it is important to highlight the ways in which this distinction functions to increase the ambivalence of the cityscape in this novel.

This chapter explores a division in Thurston's representation of Paris that echoes a broader trend in *fin-de-siècle* criticism. Julie Johnson and Jean-Pierre Bernard describe this approach as revealing "*les deux Paris* [emphasis in original]," two cities separated by "two inseparable dimensions [...] its materiality, walls, life, and organs, and its immateriality, its symbolic charge, and aura" that lead to "a sizeable body of literature that frequently characterizes the city's history as 'beleaguered' or 'belle.'"[111] The terms of this debate are necessarily intertwined with the sexualized rhetoric of "*dégénérescence* [emphasis in original]," "a state of disrepair [...] a moral and intellectual decline" that was inextricably connected to the increased emergence of women into the public sphere.[112] As Nicholas Daly argues, *fin-de-siècle* British fiction was obsessed with counteracting the "unmanliness" of degenerative French fiction in order to prevent the "decline of the true British racial stock."[113] This unmanning of the British Victorian population is part and parcel of broader attitudes toward and anxiety resulting from the erosion of distinctions "between male and female, natural and unnatural, civilized and degenerate."[114] No one more clearly embodied this anxiety over the instability of gender than the New Woman; Maxine, in her masquerade of masculinity, fundamentally participates in this cultural anxiety, calling attention not only to the ways in which gender is itself performative but also the degree to which the emergence of the New Woman in the *fin-de-siècle* city highlights the ambivalence of women's experience of the urban. The degeneracy of the nation is associated with an increasingly sexualized and public femininity that crystallizes the ways in which "fin-de-siècle Paris was a contested city, one fraught with challenges for women living [there]," a space in which the "mingling of danger and pleasure, crisis and belle époque culture" makes the cityscape confusing and ambiguous for women and, especially, for Thurston's Max.[115] On the one hand, Maxine is always the author and creator of her art and able to navigate the cityscape; however, the degree to which this creation and navigation depends upon her masculine performance raises fundamental questions about her access to the city.

The relationship between women and the *fin-de-siècle* city is complex. Critics like Sally Ledger, Elizabeth Wilson, and Rita Felski argue in favor of a positive representation of the urban sphere in New Woman writing, expanding the realms of femininity beyond the domestic. According to Sally Ledger, the emergence of women in the modern city "threatened the patriarchal construction of the Victorian metropolis as masculine public space" through the establishment of important urban institutions like "music halls, along with the theater, department stores, museums, libraries, and public transport."[116] In Émile Zola's *Au Bonheur des dames*, the female protagonist, Denise

Baudu, embodies this typical New Woman movement from the premodern to the modern by means of her successful navigation of the capitalist landscape of a fictionalized version of Aristide Boucicault's *Le Bon Marché*. The department store, as Ledger demonstrates, constitutes a "half-public, half-private social space which women were able to inhabit comfortably," enabling women of a certain class "to look, socialise and simply to stroll, to become, albeit in a somewhat confined sense, *flâneuses*."[117] However, Ledger's qualification that women's potential to become *flâneuses* was limited—"in a somewhat confined sense"—underlines the precarious relationship of the New Woman to this metropolitan landscape.[118] Just as Denise must ultimately marry Saccard in *Au Bonheur des dames*, so too must the New Woman in general, and Max/ine in particular, negotiate an urban landscape that remains fundamentally the preserve of men.

This is why critics like Janet Wolff have argued that the modern cityscape is antithetical, if not hostile, to the New Woman. Drawing on the writings of Walter Benjamin, Georg Simmel, and Marshall Berman, Wolff argues that the gendered divisions that governed the city in the nineteenth century prevented the deconstruction of the separate spheres dichotomy.[119] Undergirding Wolff's critique of life in the modern city is Charles Baudelaire's figure of the *flâneur*, the "prince who everywhere rejoices in his incognito," who "become[s] one flesh with the crowd," and "set[s] up house in the heart of the multitude, amid the ebb and flow of movement, in the midst of the fugitive and the infinite."[120] The use of "prince" here is indicative of the gender dynamics that feminist critics have long identified in Baudelaire's definitive figure of modernity. Moreover, as Ledger points out, the intimate relationship between the Baudelairean *flâneur* and the crowd becomes increasingly problematic for women precisely because of the connotations associated with the prostitute who already "inhabited the modern metropolis—and who was by no means 'new' there."[121] This problematic relationship to the *fin-de-siècle* cityscape means that women operate in a foreign territory, a landscape in which they must function as de Certeauian tacticians.

While the New Woman can hardly be said to depend upon a de Certeauian "guileful ruse," she certainly occupies the space of the other and her gender performance points out the "cracks that particular conjunctions open in the surveillance of the proprietary powers."[122] But Max, quite clearly, employs de Certeau's "guileful ruse" in order to take up residence in the masculine cityscape more fully. Max's use of these tactics begins on the train, where he seems not to fit within this order, despite or perhaps because of the panoptic presence of the train's lighting system. The lights recognize "the figure of a boy [...] who had as yet scarce passed the barrier of manhood, for the skin of the face was clean and smooth, and the limbs, seen vaguely under a rough overcoat, had the freedom and supple grace that belongs to early youth."[123] While it becomes clear that this "figure of a boy" is more a specter or a figuration, the fact that this body is indeterminate, both as a mere "figure" and as a liminal individual in that in-between-state of boyhood and manhood, demonstrates a lack of fixedness. The description of Max's figure suggests that this body is somehow not fully surveilled, but guessed at; his supposed age reinforces this sense of illegibility even in the panoptic bubble. This disruption of the normative, this slipping through the barriers of the surveillance mechanism becomes all the more apparent when the narrative attempts to reassert its heteronormativity because it becomes obvious how Max exploits this indeterminacy. Significantly, Thurston's novel recognizes this sense of being "where one is least expected" when the narrator describes Max as being "subconsciously aware that, deserted though the compartment was, it yet exhaled an alien suggestion, embodied in the rugs, the coats, the hand-baggage of the card-playing travellers, which was heaped upon the seat opposite."[124] While these rugs, coats, and hand-baggage hardly seem threatening, the fact remains that they create, even subconsciously, an "alien suggestion," which necessarily raises questions about their very difference. Indeed, this alien suggestion becomes clear only through the constrained and contested interaction that occurs between Max and the bags' owners, who re-assert that very disciplinary regime that Max has frustrated.

When they re-enter the carriage, "each in turn looked at him, and at each new glance his coldness of demeanor deepened."[125] This odd mutual interaction of recognizing and attempting to withdraw from that very recognition suggests an Althusserian mode of discipline, the gaze of which obviously burdens and threatens Max. The discomfort in the face of masculinity that is described as "frankly curious" recalls both the eroticized knowledge upon which de Certeau's panoptic order depends and the performative and dislocated nature of Max's tactics.[126] It is in this light of tactical performativity that de Certeau's phrase "a guileful ruse" seems remarkably appropriate for the protagonist of this New Woman novel as he attempts to slip through the boundaries.

Throughout the remainder of the novel the titular character experiences this same sense of alienation and disempowerment in the urban landscape, especially when interacting with the cityscape after being revealed as a woman. Max reveals to Blake his masterpiece, which is a portrait of a beautiful young woman. Blake insists that he meet the subject of the painting. Following this, Max persuades Blake that the woman in the painting is his sister and that she has fled from France forever. The subsequent row between them results in a severing of their relationship. During this period, Max, alone and isolated, suffers through "[t]he saddest human experience [which] is to view through other eyes—to walk solitary where one has walked in company."[127] In order to escape the "walls of the *appartement* [which] seemed to close in about him, stifling—suffocating him," Max "haunt[s] the galleries and attend[s] classes like any art student; by night, he range[s] the streets and *cafés*, seeking inspiration, returning to his lonely room to lie wakeful, fighting his ghosts, or else to sob himself to sleep."[128] While this lonely wandering might recall the *flânerie* of Baudelaire's prince of modernity, the intense isolation and despondence clearly marks these urban wanderings as those of the tactician, one displaced, experiencing instead the negative freedom that characterizes Simmel's modern metropolis. The threatening rhetoric of "stifling—suffocating" demonstrates the degree to which this urban landscape is antithetical to his very existence, recalling the prominence of suicide amongst women artists in *fin-de-siècle* Paris.[129] The "suicide problem" that occupied many writers in the late nineteenth century "was an increasing problem for Parisian women in particular, one they described as an 'epidemic.'"[130]

This threat of suicide amongst urban women highlights the Balzacian representation of the cityscape that ultimately emphasizes the masculinity of the metropolis. Seeing Paris "bereft of the glamour of romance" for the first time, Max's once-beloved city quickly becomes a nightmarish landscape "of unpleasant sights, unpleasant sounds," while its citizens possess a "morbid realism in the forbidding dinginess of their appearance."[131] Even though this representation might suggest that Max is now seeing Paris as it truly is thanks to the loss of romance, the specific use of "nightmare" recalls the representation of the same city in Balzac's *La Fille aux yeux d'or*; Balzac's nightmarish Paris becomes "[o]ne of life's most terrifying spectacles," in which the population is "a people ghastly to behold, gaunt, jaundiced, and leathery," a "living dead."[132] At the beginning of this chapter, I argued that Balzac's *La Fille aux yeux d'or*, like Poe's "The Man of the Crowd," emerges out of a desire to read the city through a largely realist, if Gothicized, lens. Despite the nightmarish landscape of Balzac's Gothic Paris, the privileged position of the omniscient narrator always is completely confident in his capacity to decode the cityscape; he is omniscient because he is able to interpret the nightmare, rather than succumb to it. As we have seen throughout the analysis of *Max*, the masculine adventure narrative is largely based on the same desire to read the cityscape through an equally realist lens, most clearly embedded in the distinction between the competing modes of understanding the world, "romance" or "the real journey."[133] If the masculine adventure narrative is largely associated with this ability to read the cityscape and the development of Max's relationship with Blake as an artist is based on learning how to read the city from the heights of Montmartre, this feminine narrative line reflects Max's inability to read the city accurately; it emphasizes the degree to which he is involved in the fashioning of a fiction that blinds him to the realist and capitalist landscape in which he must operate. And while this darker representation of Paris does in fact begin when he views the city "bereft of the glamour of romance," which might seem to undermine the claims I am trying to make regarding the inability to understand the cityscape, this representational shift equally results from the lack of "Blake's wise and penetrating gaze [with which] he had seen it in true perspective; but to-night there was no sane interpreter to temper vision."[134] The masculine gaze, associated with wisdom, also becomes the *sine qua non* of urban literacy. As a result, Max "swung with grievous suddenness to the opposing pole of thought," away from the rational interpretation of Blake's wisdom.[135] As with Somerville and Ross's Patsey Kirwen, this inability to read the urban landscape presages the ultimate restoration of the conservative gender norms that characterize the modern metropolis as a masculine realm.

For Max, however, this issue of urban literacy and proper interpretation of the urban landscape is intimately tied up with the performance of gender in the city. Indeed, the very performance of Max might best be summarized in his declaration that "I am my own romance," a declaration that highlights the false and fanciful nature of this identity.[136] That he repeats this phrase after Blake attributes the trait to him not only highlights the degree to which his identity is a masculine creation, but also reinforces the gendered division I have been attempting to elucidate; perhaps even more significantly, if we follow Murphy's notion that the genre of romance is characterized by an inability to distinguish fiction from real life, Max's acceptance of this idea of being his own romance emphasizes the degree to which he succumbs to the very problem Murphy describes: Max seems to convince himself that he can, in fact, author his own self, regardless of his cis-gendered body. From the beginning of the novel, even before he arrives in Paris, this boy is associated with the idea of fiction. His very journey is "a thing of possibilities," which suggests "a story behind every shadow [...] romance in the very making."[137] Even inside the uniquely modern environment of the train carriage, there remains an awareness of "the inevitable story" behind the passengers.[138] The repeated rhetoric of fiction and storytelling signals the degree to which the novel is about these competing generic distinctions, but, more importantly, it also signals the way in which this gendered body must suffer through the very type of interpretation that is later associated with the idea of masculinity. He is always already subject to the disciplinary gaze that he seeks to escape and deny. This inescapability becomes even clearer through the representation of Max as artist. He attempts both to author a masculine identity as artist and to erase a feminine identity through the aesthetic authority of the male gaze.

While the position of women in *fin-de-siècle* Paris has received renewed scholarly attention especially with the resurgence of interest in the New Woman, these women often arrived in Paris, like Thurston's Max or Somerville and Ross's Patsey Kirwen, with a desire to achieve fame through art. We have already seen Max express this desire for "first life—and then fame."[139] As Julie Johnson has demonstrated, this fictional community of women artists reflects the historical situation of women in Paris at the end of the nineteenth century, a period which has often been described as "the 'glory days' for women artists in France, who received artistic training and education and possessed an 'optimism' about their potential for careers as artists."[140] There was a burgeoning community of "ateliers and academies, such as the Académie Julian," as well as women's art associations like the Union des Femmes Peintres et Sculpteurs.[141] These, however, stand in contrast to the most traditional of artistic institutions like the École des Beaux-Arts, which barred women from membership until 1897. To help women enjoy the same privileges as their male counterparts, there were organizations that explicitly recognized the unequal economic difficulties of metropolitan life for women. The Association des Femmes Artistes de Paris, "a cooperative organization created in 1894 by women painters, sculptors, engravers, writers, and musicians," explicitly set itself up as a community of "working professionals who relied on their artistic livelihoods for financial support and economic survival."[142] That these women depended upon a type of union dues to support those who were "absolutely, but temporarily" unable to support themselves demonstrates the degree to which women artists in the city "suffered from depression, illness, and financial uncertainty."[143] Their precarious economic condition results in a compromised position for women artists that was remarkably common. As women artists struggled to make ends meet solely on the profits of their art, they often sat for male artists as models.[144] Having to exist as both creators of art and the objects of an artistic male gaze, these women essentially had to "act as muses for other, usually male, artists," an historical fact that undermines New Woman claims to the urban landscape because this economic access reinforces the privileged hierarchy of the masculine gaze.[145]

Unsurprisingly these "model markets" emerged with particular fervor in Montmartre. This geo-social landscape, already associated with the male artistic and sexual gaze, becomes doubly implicated in the complicated representation of the ambiguous position of the woman artist-as-model in *Max*. As Max pursues fame and art, he writes to Blake that "[m]y idea—the true idea—has come to me" and locks himself in his studio in the heart of Montmartre.[146] The "great work" that Max presents to Blake is

> the portrait of a woman seated at a mirror—a portrait in which the delicate reflected face looked out from its shadowing hair with a curious questioning intentness, a fascinating challenge at once elusive and vital.[147]

Blake insists that this feminine representation is "the living image of you—but you with such a difference."[148] Of course, the difference between Max and the subject of the painting is that the latter reveals the true, cis-gendered identity of the painter as a woman; however, "[i]n a sudden panic" of a "fear [that] assailed him," Max declares the subject to be "my sister—Maxine."[149] The combined use of panic and fear at revealing his "living image" fundamentally recognizes the ambivalent and fraught position of women artists specifically, and women more broadly, in the *fin-de-siècle* city. Earlier, Thurston's narration highlights this same tension between the revelation of the true self and the performative external self in the moment at which Max is finally revealed to be a woman in disguise. Sitting in front of a mirror and holding a lock of her hair:

> The boy with his bravery of ignorance, his frankly arrogant egoism was effaced as might be the writing from a slate, and in his place was a sexless creature, rarely beautiful, with parted, tremulous lips and wide eyes in which subtle, crowding thoughts struggled for expression.[150]

This passage presages the latter one in so far as the tension between man and woman threatens to undo the masculine act of creation; by revealing the feminine self, Maxine effaces the very person of the boy just as "the writing from a slate" might be erased. By undoing the boy's existence, the emergence of the feminine reaffirms both the masculine privilege of art and the threat posed by women to that privilege, which has been identified by feminist critics as far back as Gilbert and Gubar.[151] More importantly, Max's anxiety over his true image highlights and reinscribes the hierarchical nature of the masculine gaze that underlies Johnson's representation of the woman artist-as-model trope. It suggests that women cannot be the authors or creators of art, only ever its subject.

This inability to create, or at least the need to mask creation in the authority of masculinity, reflects the paradox of the female *Bildungsroman*, especially as it overlaps with the *Künstlerroman* of the late nineteenth century. While recent criticism has queried the efficacy or even the validity of the type of growth allowed to women in a female *Bildungsroman*, Marianne Hirsch suggests that this contradictory experience of development actually mirrors a pattern of development in the *Künstlerroman*. These (almost always) male protagonists are "[s]imilarly dissatisfied and led to withdraw into the inner life," yet these men are able to "find a solution that saves them from the heroines' death, the solution of art which is virtually unavailable to women in the nineteenth-century novel."[152] Hirsch continues, explaining that "female spiritual *Bildung* is the story of the potential artist who fails to make it," a claim that proves true for both *French Leave* and *Max*, especially the latter, in which Max is able to demonstrate his ability to produce "the great work" that would assure him fame, but is forced into the ineluctable decision to achieve fame and professional fulfilment as a man, or settle for domestic fulfilment as a woman.[153] Upon initially being discovered to be a woman, Max declares to her neighbor, Jacqueline, that "the thought came to me—the mad thought, that I had, perhaps, lost something—that I had, perhaps, put something from me" and that she "wished to see the woman in me—and to dismiss her."[154] The desire to dismiss "the evil spirit" of her femininity in order to recommit herself to her artistic endeavor demonstrates this fundamental opposition: art cannot provide a solution to the female Maxine, but its salvific power remains available to her male counterpart, Max.[155] Thus, we can begin to read the "great work," the portrait of the true feminine self, in a manner similar to Dorian Gray's portrait; it functions as an attempt to be "killed into a 'perfect' image," "to 'kill' *herself* into art."[156] As Jacqueline reveals to her the true picture of her feminine self, Max declares her intention to "destroy [the feminine] utterly. [...] If a spirit—no matter how evil—could be materialized, it would cease to affect the imagination. I shall materialize mine. [...] I shall render my evil spirit powerless by materializing it."[157] The associations between the feminine and the "evil spirit" highlight the problematic way in which this novel figures the feminine body, especially in terms of its relationship to the city. Her materiality, her very embodiedness must be separated from the individual in order to achieve both access to the urban and, especially, access to the higher world of art; that is to say, the woman must become objectified, even as, or especially if, she seeks to become the creator of the art object.

The woman artist-as-model reinforces Hirsch's argument. Art attempts to provide a solution to the contradictions of and dissatisfactions available within female *Bildungsromane* by offering women the potential to participate in the world of art, but ultimately always only reminds them of their dependence upon the sexualized male gaze to gain access to that world of creation. More importantly, Max participates in this very tension, which he describes in bellicose language. The conflict between the masculine and the feminine is "a relentless, eternal war; for one nature must conquer, and one must fail."[158] The inability for these twinned natures to coexist within the individual ultimately reinforces masculine privilege not only in art and the cityscape, but in modern selfhood as embodied in the *Bildungsroman* of the long nineteenth century. If this central genre of the nineteenth century depends upon the achievement of maturity, that "double 'I do' of the wedding ritual," "that 'pact' between the individual and the world," then for Max the marriage cannot be an act of individual self-actualization.[159] Instead, the marriage must be between a distinct man and a distinct woman. When Blake demands the story of Max's secret sister, the novel shifts more clearly into a conventional romance plot that, as Tina O'Toole describes it, "'rescues' the novel and [its] protagonist in the last from accusations of inversion, or the possibility that Max is in fact a transgender figure of a homosexual man."[160] However, in this rescuing of the plot from accusations of more overt homosexuality, Thurston exposes the intractability of the female *Bildungsroman*, especially of the female *Künstlerroman*. In the revelation of Maxine's history emerges a central critique of the metaphor of marriage that Moretti uses to define the selfhood upon which the *Bildungsroman* is premised. Describing Maxine's earlier marriage, Max explains to Blake that "[t]he man did what every man does [...] when a woman lies down beneath his feet—he spurned her away [...] dragging her with him—step by step, step by step—down the sickening road of disillusionment."[161] Obviously, the echoes of Flaubert's *Madame Bovary* (1856) and Tolstoy's *Anna Karenina* (1875–77) are rife; but what is central to this critique is that marriage in the nineteenth-century novel rarely provides the achievement of selfhood for women that Moretti argues it provides for its male protagonists.

This marriage, Max continues to explain, barred Maxine from turning to art:

> Art, like nature, exacts—and she had already given! She was too frightened—too hurt to meddle with great things. She dried her tears before they had time to fall; she hardened her heart, and went back to the world that gives nothing and exacts nothing. [...] She went back to the world—and the world poured oil on her wounds, and soothed her fears and taught her its smiling, shallow ways.[162]

If Goethe's Wilhelm Meister achieves his completed self through the act of marriage, it is clear that Maxine's marriage provided no such sense of completion. Moreover, as Hirsch's analysis and this passage demonstrates, "the solution of art [...] is virtually unavailable to the young women in the nineteenth-century novel."[163] Crying that Max is "tarnishing the picture" of his sister by relating this history, Blake demonstrates again the relationship between women and fiction that characterizes the aesthetic authority of the male artist: the ideal is not woman as she is, but woman as he wishes her, woman "killed into a 'perfect' image" of herself.[164] But, as demonstrated above, Max's painting has already perfected this process of killing his female self into an art object, removing the blemishes of the feminine from the body by placing it within the framework of the canvas. Maxine has already been denied the autonomy and authority of the artist thanks to the sociocultural landscape of the *fin-de-siècle* city in which she attempted to carve out her career.

The novel's ultimate rescuing, the restoration of the heteronormative marriage plot, occurs in the same public space in which Blake's and Max's relationship truly began: the Place de la Concorde. This landscape, instead of being marked by the masculine presence of the military regiment, becomes feminized in the repetition of its celestial beauty. Almost echoing Wordsworth's "Composed Upon Westminster Bridge," Paris becomes "gilded" and "rapture tremble[s] on the air like vibrations of a chord struck from some celestial harp."[165] This is an urban landscape aestheticized to the point of being hardly urban. The "divine gift" of the "first autumnal frost" emphasizes a natural landscape that has largely been absent in earlier representations of the city, a natural and romantic landscape that mirrors an increased emphasis on Max's emotional state. Upon seeing Blake, the "fierce excitement, the melting tenderness of her moods warred until emotion ran riot," enhancing the effeminate nature of this landscape, further shifting the dominant terms of the representation of the cityscape from a masculine legibility to a feminine emotionalism to the point where Max must make sure "[i]t is not a dream."[166] This is one of the few times, it is important to note, that Max is depicted in the cityscape as a woman; as such, it is unsurprisingly paired with the romanticized language of dreams, emphasizing the fantastic element that characterized Patsey Kirwen's engagement with the same *fin-de-siècle* metropolis. Moreover, the shift toward a more natural and pastoral representation of Paris in this passage dominates the remainder of the novel, signaling the end of Max's attempts to inhabit a masculine urban selfhood. In the final chapters of the novel, Max and Blake eschew the cabarets and theaters of Montmartre for "fruitful oasis of the Bois [du Boulogne]," on the western edge of the sixteenth *arrondissement*, enveloping the lovers in "the illusion of Arcadia."[167] This shift away from a recognizably urban representation of the cityscape toward pastoral gardens mirrors the final moments of the novel in which Max and Blake achieve the ultimate heteronormative ending of an engagement. This passage shows the degree to which their marriage begins with a rejection of the urban in favor of a pastoral and natural landscape:

> Ardent and eager—yet restrained, as befitted a woman aware of her high place—she left the room and passed down the Escalier de Sainte-Marie. A rush of cool air came to her across the plantation, kissing her hot cheeks, the holly bushes whispered their secrets—which were her secrets as well, the eyes of the stars looked down, smiling into her eyes. She observed

no face in the thronging faces that passed her; she made her steadfast way to the one point in the universe that was her goal by right divine. Even in the hallway of Blake's house she did not stop to question, but mounted the stairs and knocked upon his door, regardless of the stormy beating of her heart, the faintness of anticipation that encompassed her.[168]

The intimacy of Max's relationship with nature here is striking; the holly bushes' secrets are "her secrets as well"; the eyes of the stars are able to smile "into her eyes."[169] Just as the crowds disappear, nature takes an oddly prominent role in this most modern of cities. That the increased presence of nature immediately follows Max's "unburden[ing] herself of her boy's garments" underscores the relationship between the pastoral and the feminine, as well as the urban and the masculine.[170]

Ultimately, this New Woman novel cannot seem to provide the space for a woman artist within the landscape of *fin-de-siècle* Paris. Through Max's own inability to read the city accurately, through the omnipresence of the masculine gaze, through the ambivalent position of the woman artist, Thurston's *Max* presents a frustrating cityscape. However, central to these frustrations remain the same anxieties and contradictions that have characterized Irish women's representations of Paris since the Act of Union. Max shares the struggle for social, sexual, and economic autonomy with Imogen St. Dorval, Madame de Connal, and Patsey Kirwen. As in *The Novice of Saint Dominick* and *French Leave*, *Max* ultimately ends with a retreat from the urban to the pastoral, suggesting that, despite the movement of the New Woman into the space of the metropolis, Irish women's literature can only occupy Paris temporarily, fleetingly. It will take another forty-eight years for Kate O'Brien's Clare Halvey to return permanently to Paris and the Place de la Concorde in order to make a living. But for the moment, Thurston's novel means that Irish women writers must be content to surveil Paris as quickly as they can from the heights of Montmartre, while they steal whatever time they can from the European metropolis.

A City She Must Postpone:
A Conclusion

Kate O'Brien describes her 1962 travelogue, *My Ireland*, as "an invitation to travel."[1] Her novels turn out to be more an invitation to travel than an invitation to stay at home. Rome and Roman locations seem to appear more often than anywhere else in O'Brien's Europe-based, non-historical novels. Rome is mentioned in *Without My Cloak* (1931), *Mary Lavelle* (1936), *The Flower of May* (1953), and *As Music and Splendour* (1958) nearly 100 times; Paris is mentioned nearly 75 times; while Dublin and London are mentioned 35 and 33 times respectively. These novels thus invite us to relocate them to a European context, or at least into a European landscape and a European map.

Without My Cloak is one of only two Kate O'Brien novels to feature a male protagonist; the other, of course, is *Pray for the Wanderer* (1938), which itself needs critical attention. This gendered aspect is worth noting, not least because the *Bildungsroman* is often considered to be an exclusively male genre, or at least one which privileges male development. *Without My Cloak* is also the novel that appears to adhere most closely to Moretti's model of the classical *Bildungsroman*; it also embodies what Moretti has described as the "crisis of the European *Bildungsroman*."[2] The 1931 James Tait Black Prize-winning novel is a voluminous history of the Considine family as they rise through the ranks of Mellick society from a mere horse thief to a family that runs an international business that stretches across Continental Europe and across the Atlantic; it becomes a *Bildungsroman* through its focus on Denis Considine, the heir apparent of the Considine estate. Denis, from a young child, is the great hope of the Considine clan and he appears to achieve maturity when he accedes to the Goethean position of married bliss in his family's stately home. As we will see momentarily, this is hardly an Irish *Wilhelm Meister*. Denis celebrates his eighteenth birthday in Antwerp as part of "a long business tour [that includes] London, Paris, Bordeaux, Marseilles, Paris again, then Antwerp and Amsterdam and Haarlem, then Hamburg and Copenhagen, then Brussels, then Antwerp again, then London, then home."[3] A conversation in London just before returning to Mellick makes clear the significant role played by Paris in this inaugural journey of self-discovery. Denis's Uncle Eddy, perhaps the first queer character in O'Brien's œuvre, asks the young man how he liked Paris. This seemingly innocuous question reveals the machinations of an already ongoing *Bildung*. Denis pauses because, the narrator explains:

> A tempest of words and emotions swept over Denis—for in Paris he knew that he had found himself—found his own ghost, his own projection of himself, his own future, his own unchained, unchallenged, unclaimed personality—waiting for him, as a dream-self waits for every imaginative egoist in Paris. [...] He had been fantastically, obliviously happy. He had felt at home. How to explain that?[4]

Denis's reverie reveals rather little about how Paris contributes specifically to his *Bildung*; instead, it suggests that Paris performs an alternative role. The repeated use of the singular possessive "his own" combined with the string of "unchained, unchallenged, unclaimed personality" signals just how controlled, chained, and challenged his identity is, marking Paris as an exceptional space that enables this sort of self-discovery. This is essentially the crux of Moretti's argument regarding the crisis of the *Bildungsroman*, which he dates from Joseph Conrad through Joyce and into Kafka. Essentially, the *Bildungsroman* had previously functioned by means of a legitimate process of socialization, what Moretti has defined as the "beautiful symmetry [...] between the individual and the world, that reciprocal 'consent.'"[5] However, Denis's *Bildung* only achieves that beneficence by a rather contorted *deus ex machina* ending; instead, his socialization is recognized as externally imposed by the persistent use of metaphors of threat, "weapon," and "prison."[6] For Moretti, this "neglects the subjective side of the process: the legitimation *of* the social system."[7] When asked about his future life as the head of the Considines' family business, Denis views this prospect like "a dungeon into which he had just been flung," a clear instance of coerced development that is typical of the *Bildungsroman* in its crisis phase.[8]

But Paris clearly functions as a separate space in which Denis is free from these threats, a place where he is able to develop and explore his own personality. So where in Paris does this *Bildung* occur? O'Brien's novel mentions only two specific places during this Paris interlude: the Champs Elysées, where Denis and Anthony have dinner, and, crucially, the Petit Trianon, a small *château* built for the Louis XIV's mistress, Madame de Pompadour within the grounds of the Palace of Versailles. But Denis is not interested in the palace or even the *château*; his focus is planted squarely on the gardens. This is extremely important for the Parisian *Bildungsroman*. As Moretti explains, "[i]t is the public space of the [gardens] and the Champs Elysées, with its oblique gazes and ephemeral meetings" that is fundamental to the definitive characteristic of daydreams and grand projects, the very essence of egoistic self-expression and rebellion against the provincialism of the elsewhere.[9] In this, O'Brien captures the secondary socialization, the social division of labor that seems at the heart of Denis's rejection of his own overdetermined career path into the family business. The garden is a space of leisure, a space where one entertains such flights of fancy that are antithetical to the regulated and profit-driven world of business.

And yet despite its associations with leisure and self-indulgence, this garden cannot be extricated from its association with the state, most specifically with Louis XIV, Louis XV, and Louis XVI. Indeed, it is Louis XIV, who purportedly said "L'État c'est moi," who moved the French court to Versailles in 1682. In this collision of self-determination and autocratic authority, le Petit Trianon seems the perfect embodiment of the complicated and contradictory *Bildung* that inaugurates O'Brien's œuvre.

Jumping, then, to the *Bildungsroman* that concludes O'Brien's career, we find another novel that seems to embody the problematic and conflicting pattern of development that defines the crises of the *Bildungsroman*. Paris in *As Music and Splendour* is a deeply complicated location. It is the site of Rose's and Clare's initial exile, the beginning of their "transcendental homelessness," their unasked-for and enforced initiation into the world of opera; it is where they cease being young girls and become "Irish investments."[10] This depersonalization is crucial to the underlying economics of the novel, but it is also crucial for the sense of crisis that pervades Clare's, if not always Rose's, experience of *Bildung*. But does the geography of Paris in this novel contribute or frame this experience of crisis?

Paris, at the beginning of *As Music and Splendour*, involves movement from the ninth *arrondissement*, the then site of the Conservatoire de Musique, to the "ugly streets about the Place du Roi de Rome" in the western sixteenth *arrondissement* near the Palais de Chaillot and the Trocadero.[11] O'Brien meticulously maps the girls' walk home from the Conservatoire. Under the guidance of Frau Sturz:

> the chosen young ladies of Rue des Lauriers [...] crossed the river by the Pont de la Concorde, they followed the Quai d'Orsay to the Champ de Mars, re-crossed the Seine at Pont d'Iena into the Quai de Passy, and shortly, through dull and solemn streets, reached the ugly Rue des Lauriers.[12]

This early representation is significant not only for its transitoriness, but also for its concentration on space. In following the route home, O'Brien's novel implicitly aligns the arts with the economy since the path through the ninth and eighth *arrondissements* threads between the Palais Garnier, the site of the Paris Opéra, and the Bourse de Paris, which registers the economic gamble that governs the novel's internal logic. In this route, we see none of the public spaces that defined Denis's earlier moment of *Bildung* and that re-emerge later when Clare returns, having reached maturity and acceptance of her life in the opera. The last sentences of the novel place O'Brien's protagonist on the Rue Royale in the eighth *arrondissement* as the "Place de la Concorde [strikes] exaggeratedly against the sad quiet of her heart."[13] This location seems to embody the contradiction at the heart of Clare's *Bildung*: lying in the epicenter of the metropolitan world of fashion and consumption, the Place de la Concorde leads, at one end, to the Champs Elysées; yet, at the other end of the Place, the Rue Royale leads to the Place de la Madeleine, site of a Catholic church of the same name. This geographical nexus highlights the tension that defines Clare's struggle between the world of fashion and the pull of the sacred songs she longs to sing, which, as she is told so often, are not economically viable. The Place de la Concorde, like the gardens of Versailles or the theaters where she sings, functions as a space of leisure. For Clare, this public contest is truly a trial; hence, the significant use of 'struck' in the final sentence, signifying an antipathetic relationship between Clare and this metropolitan proving ground.

Perhaps the most interesting use of Paris is in the under-studied *The Flower of May*, a novel which focuses on the development of Fanny Morrow of Mespil Road, Dublin. *The Flower of May* contains two significant Parisian moments: one at the beginning of Fanny's development and the other set in the future. The initial mention of Paris is remarkably similar to that of *As Music and Splendour* in that it reflects the transcendental homelessness of O'Brien's *Bildungshelden*. Before beginning the grand tour of Milan and Venice, Fanny and the de Mellins pause in Paris. The brief description of Fanny's experience in the French capital is worth quoting in full:

> Paris, where the luxuriously travelling de Mellin party had paused for two days and nights, had indeed been an encounter she would reflect upon very much—when she had time for reflection. But, confused though she was in Paris, she did fumblingly apprehend that it was a city that she must postpone; certainly she had wit enough to know that in two days and from the foyer of the Meurice she could only be confounded by the place. Almost deliberately, certainly in a strong mood of self-defence, she let its first impact run over her like water. Paris was for the adult, and she looked about it eagerly, and understood that in French terms she was not adult. She would become adult, and would return to Paris. But she was relieved that she need spend no more than two extremely silly tourists' days there now.[14]

In this representation, Paris is a place deferred. Its confusion, its sense of threat, and its overwhelming nature forces Fanny into "a strong mood of self-defence," where she plays a silly tourist.[15] The geography of this initial foray into the metropolitan landscape is important: it is "from the foyer of the Meurice" that Fanny begins to apprehend the cosmopolitan confusion.[16] Located on the Rue de Rivoli at the heart of the first *arrondissement*, the Meurice faces the northern edge of the Jardin des Tuileries, which separates the Place de la Concorde and the Louvre. The Meurice symbolizes the luxury of the Right Bank, enhancing the sense of grandeur of the Louvre and the Tuileries. It is decidedly not the Paris that Fanny wishes to experience; indeed, this sense of luxury is the exact opposite of the Paris of Fanny's future.

Following the inheritance of the family estate in Glasalla, Fanny is, as her confidante Lucille de Mellin says, "free [… to] go off to Paris or wherever."[17] It is, indeed, to Paris that Fanny intends to travel. Fanny and Lucille plot to "go to Paris and cram for the *bachot* whilst provisionally taking university lectures" at the Sorbonne, where they plan to "begin."[18] This is, like *Mary Lavelle*, a *Bildung* that is not complete; it is a *Bildungsroman* that ends with the beginning. How natural that this development begins in Paris, but an entirely different part of Paris than we have seen in any other Kate O'Brien novel. The Sorbonne, going back to the medieval university, looms large throughout nineteenth-century *Bildungsromane* set in the French capital. Indeed, according to Moretti, all of Balzac's *Bildungshelden* make their start "in a handful of streets around the Sorbonne," leading the critic to designate this region of Paris in the fifth *arrondissement* "*the world of youth* [emphasis in original]."[19] Emphasizing the significance of this district, Moretti declares that "[w]ithout the Latin Quarter [...] and its tension with the rest of Paris, we wouldn't have the wonder of the French *Bildungsroman*, nor that image of youth—hungry, dreamy, ambitious—that has been its greatest invention."[20] We can see, already, that the Sorbonne sits outside of the broad geography that dominates O'Brien's map, signaling a new kind of development in this *Bildungsroman*. New for O'Brien, but a form that belongs, as I have demonstrated, to a tradition much, much older.

Moretti's celebration of the nineteenth-century French tradition emphasizes its representation of youth because it is "hungry, dreamy, ambitious."[21] With perhaps the exception of Clare in *As Music and Splendour*, these characteristics apply to O'Brien's youthful protagonists. And yet, as this concluding chapter has demonstrated, the other *Bildungshelden* struggle in order to achieve the happiness that legitimates the classical and Goethean tradition; instead, Denis and Clare depict the *Bildungsroman* in crisis. So, for Fanny, we find a different space that inaugurates a different story. The Sorbonne and the Rive Gauche, along with her inheritance, allow her to fulfill her earlier prophecy that she "would return to Paris."[22] So, in the end, for O'Brien's representation of Paris, we must invert Moretti's claim; with a certain kind of space, a certain kind of story becomes possible.

Notes

Notes to *Parvenir*: An Introduction

1. Balzac, *Père Goriot*, 263.
2. Balzac, *Père Goriot*, 263.
3. Harvey, *Paris*, 24.
4. As Christopher Prendergast explains, "[b]y 'capital of the nineteenth century', Benjamin meant that in the developing urban forms of life exemplified by Paris we see some of the distinctive features of 'modernity' in general and its complex, unsettling effects on both society and the psyche" (Prendergast, *Paris and the Nineteenth Century*, 5).
5. Moretti, *Way*, 166.
6. Moretti, *Atlas*, 100–01.
7. Bakhtin, "The *Bildungsroman*," 19.
8. O'Toole, "Going West," 111.
9. Deane, *Strange Country*, 8; O'Toole, "Going West," 111.
10. Norris, "The Big House," 107–08.
11. Deane, "Production," 119–20.
12. Wright, *Representing*, xvii.
13. Corkery, "The Peasant," 105.
14. Corkery, "On Anglo-Irish Literature," 113, 112.
15. Corkery, "On Anglo-Irish Literature," 116–17.
16. Deane, "Production," 123, 124.
17. Deane, "General Introduction," xxii.
18. Deane, *Strange Country*, 7.
19. Deane, *Strange Country*, 7.

20 Deane, *Strange Country*, 11.
21 Prendergast, *Paris*, 2.
22 Prendergast, *Paris*, 3.
23 Baudelaire, *Painter*, 795.
24 Buckley, *Season of Youth*, 11, 20.
25 Fraiman, *Unbecoming Women*, x.
26 Pratt, *Archetypal Patterns*, 36.
27 Fraiman, *Unbecoming Women*, 5.
28 Fraiman, *Unbecoming Women*, 6.
29 In Moretti's formulation of the classical *Bildungsroman*, choice and coercion are not separate categories; an individual chooses the path laid out for him by the coercive institution of the Society of the Tower. Michael Bell argues that the machinery behind Goethe's *Bildung* calls attention to "the kind of power and knowledge ascribed to, or assumed by, some of the mentor figures" (Bell, *Open Secrets*, 91).
30 Gallois, *Zola*, 87.
31 Both *Au Bonheur des dames* (1883) and *The Belly of Paris* (1873) depict women whose lives are altered by the transitions of capitalist society.
32 Copeland, *Women Writing*, 4.
33 Russell, "Faro's Daughters," 844–45.
34 Russell, "Faro's Daughters," 845.
35 Copeland, *Women Writing*, 61.
36 Foley, "Public Sphere," 35.
37 Moretti, "Useless Longing," 43.
38 Simmel, "Metropolis," 335.
39 Bakhtin, "The *Bildungsroman*," 19; emphasis added.
40 Moretti, *Way*, 16; emphasis in original.
41 Moretti, *Way*, 21.
42 Bell, *Open Secrets*, 90, 91–92.
43 Moretti, *Way*, 21.
44 Moretti, *Way*, 21.
45 Moretti, *Way*, 26.
46 Simmel, "Metropolis," 342.
47 Moretti, *Way*, 27.
48 Simmel, "Metropolis," 341.
49 Mandel, *Late Capitalism*, 120.
50 Moretti, *Way*, 26.
51 Moretti, *Way*, 26.
52 Simmel, "Metropolis," 335–36.
53 Moretti, *Way*, 21.
54 Edgeworth, *Ormond*, 116.
55 Goethe, *Wilhelm Meister's Apprenticeship*, 418.

56 Between the years 1789 and 1815, Moretti argues that "[a]n entirely new narrative form takes [the *Bildungsroman*'s] place," one that necessarily contends with the "great world" (Moretti, *Way*, 75).
57 Moretti, *Way*, 75.
58 Harvey, *Paris*, 25.
59 Simmel, "Metropolis," 338.
60 Moretti, *Way*, 131.
61 Baudelaire, "Painter," 796.
62 Simmel, "Fashion," 214.
63 Moretti, *Way*, 132.
64 Bell, *Models*, 112.
65 Moretti, *Way*, 26; emphasis added.
66 Edgeworth, *Ormond*, 117.
67 As an emblem of modern and metropolitan selfhood, Connal's conversation bears more than a passing resemblance to Mephistopheles's wager with Faust, which depends upon the man's "headlong striving [...] his never-to-be-sated craving" (Goethe, *Faust Part I*, 1859–64).
68 Marx, *Capital vol. I*, 165.
69 Moretti, *Way*, 172.
70 Moretti, *Way*, 131.
71 Moretti, *Way*, 177; emphasis original.
72 Nash, "Remapping," 236, 237.
73 Julia Anne Miller is using "union" here to refer both to the union of marriage between "English or Anglo-Irish suitor and an Irish heroine" and the Act of Union, "the legislative annexing of England to Ireland in 1800" (Miller, "Acts of Union," 13).
74 Miller, "Acts of Union," 13, 15.
75 Ferris, *Romantic National Tale*, 11.
76 Miller, "Acts of Union," 16; Tracy, "The Mild Irish Girl," 83.
77 Nash, "Remapping," 237, 236.
78 Ina Ferris argues that Owenson's handling of the national tale "unhinges if it does not overturn notions of agency, belonging, and history underwritten by emergent middle-class constructs of gender and the nation," providing a more proto-feminist reading of the tradition (*Romantic National Tale*, 75). But, as Chapter 1 will demonstrate, the surprisingly Goethean conclusion of *The Novice* shuts down the potential for an economically independent woman, reinscribing her within the patriarchal norms of marriage and economic dependence.
79 Simmel, "Metropolis," 343.
80 Gallois, *Zola*, 87.
81 While they are all set in the past, arguably only *The Novice of Saint Dominick* and *As Music and Splendour* achieve what Lukács understands to be the hallmark of the historical novel, the "derivation of the individuality

of characters from the historical particularity of their age" (*The Historical Novel*, 19). Even *The Novice*, although set in the sixteenth century, reflects more contemporary than historical concerns, looking back to a period in which religious strife was overcome. This might explain why Owenson admired Henry IV of France so much. Additionally, according to Moretti, historical novels "flourish only *away from the center*," but these novels, even when set in the sixteenth century, exhibit a persistent movement toward the cosmopolitan center (*Atlas*, 33; emphasis in original).

82 See alternatives such as Kate O'Brien's *Without My Cloak* (1931), *The Flower of May* (1953), and *As Music and Splendour* (1958), Elizabeth Bowen's *The House in Paris* (1935), and Julia O'Faolain's *Adam Gould* (2009).
83 Whelan, "Foreword: Writing Ireland," ix.
84 Weekes, *Irish Women Writers*, 20.
85 Edgeworth, *Ormond*, 265.
86 McCormack, "Introduction," xii.
87 In this bifurcated focus, *French Leave* recalls the gendered experience of metropolitan selfhood that forms a significant theme in Edgeworth's *Ormond*, specifically the contrasting narratives of Dora Connal and Harry Ormond.
88 Moretti, *Atlas*, 109.
89 O'Toole, *Irish New Woman*, 110–11.

Notes to Chapter 1: The Novice in the City: Sydney Owenson and the *Bildung* of Metropolitan Economics

1 Campbell-Ross, "Mapping Ireland in Early Fiction," 1–2.
2 Moretti, *Novel, vol. I.*, x; Moretti, *Atlas*, 13.
3 Moretti, *Atlas*, 13.
4 Moretti, *Atlas*, 13.
5 Moretti, *Way*, 205.
6 Muir, "The Novice of Saint Dominick," 99.
7 Muir, "The Novice of Saint Dominick," 99.
8 Muir, "The Novice of Saint Dominick," 99.
9 Owenson, *Novice I*, 69.
10 Ellis, *Appearing to Diminish*, 16.
11 Ellis, *Appearing to Diminish*, 18–19.
12 Ellis, *Appearing to Diminish*, 18, 19.
13 Moretti, *Way*, 16, 22; emphasis in original.
14 Greengrass, *France in the Age of Henri IV*, 4.
15 Moretti, *Way*, 18–19.

16 Moretti, "A Useless Longing," 44, 45.
17 Moretti, "A Useless Longing," 45.
18 Owenson, *Novice I*, 205.
19 Bell, *Models*, 112.
20 Bell, *Models*, 112.
21 This term moves away from the recent critical focus in urban studies on the city's ability to be read—urban legibility or de Certeau's "spatial stories"—to the individual's ability to read and navigate the city. Kevin Lynch's *The Image of the City* (1960) was key in prioritizing urban legibility.
22 Marx, *Grundrisse*, 145.
23 Chakrabarty, "Universalism and Belonging," 655.
24 Owenson, *Novice I*, 206.
25 Finn, *Character of Credit*, 31.
26 Cheah, "Introduction Part II," 24.
27 Cheah, "Introduction Part II," 23.
28 Owenson, *Novice I*, 269.
29 Owenson, *Novice I*, 268.
30 Owenson, *Novice I*, 268.
31 Owenson, *Novice I*, 271.
32 Owenson, *Novice I*, 273–74.
33 Moretti, *Atlas*, 68.
34 Moretti, *Atlas*, 68.
35 Owenson, *Novice I*, 273; Jones, *Paris*, 107.
36 Owenson, *Novice I*, 275.
37 Simmel, "Metropolis," 341.
38 Simmel, "Metropolis," 345, 342.
39 Gallois, *Zola*, 87.
40 Owenson, *Novice I*, 275.
41 Owenson, *Novice I*, 276.
42 Owenson, *Novice I*, 287.
43 Owenson, *Novice I*, 292.
44 Moretti, *Atlas*, 109.
45 Owenson, *Novice III*, 212.
46 Moretti, *Atlas*, 65.
47 Owenson, *Novice III*, 325–26.
48 Owenson, *Novice III*, 326.
49 Owenson, *Novice III*, 327.
50 Milne, "Introduction," 11–12.
51 Milne, "Introduction," 11, 12.
52 Jones, *Paris*, 141.
53 Jones, *Paris*, 141.
54 Owenson, *Novice III*, 326, 365.
55 Jones, *Paris*, 141.

56 Jones, *Paris*, 107.
57 Owenson, *Novice III*, 338, 339.
58 Owenson, *Novice III*, 365.
59 Owenson, *Novice III*, 328; emphasis added.
60 Descamps, *Psychologie*, 15, 16, 207, 208.
61 Owenson, *Novice III*, 329.
62 Owenson, *Novice III*, 329.
63 Burke, *Reflections*, 79.
64 Owenson, *Novice III*, 329–30.
65 Simmel, "Fashion," 214.
66 Edgeworth, *The Absentee*, 5, 12, 13; emphasis in original.
67 Edgeworth, *The Absentee*, 36.
68 Owenson, *Novice III*, 328.
69 Bell, *Models*, 67.
70 See Bell's *Models of Power*. See also Wasserman, "Financial Fictions," 193–214; Gallois, *Zola*, 89–117; Ali, "Literature and Market Realism," 140–45; Moretti, *The Way of the World*, 135–39.
71 Benjamin, *The Arcades Project*, 220.
72 Owenson, *Novice III*, 337.
73 Owenson, *Novice III*, 338.
74 Owenson, *Novice III*, 339.
75 Jones, *Paris*, 110, 142.
76 Jones, *Paris*, 110.
77 Jones, *Paris*, 139, 133.
78 Jones, *Paris*, 141.
79 Jones, *Paris*, 143.
80 Owenson, *Novice III*, 342; emphasis in original.
81 Bell, *Models*, 112.
82 Owenson, *Novice IV*, 6.
83 Moretti, *Way*, 135.
84 Owenson, *Novice IV*, 6.
85 Owenson, *Novice IV*, 7.
86 Owenson, *Novice III*, 342.
87 Finn, *Character of Credit*, 28.
88 Owenson, *Novice IV*, 7.
89 Owenson, *Novice IV*, 7–8.
90 Bourdieu, *Outline of a Theory of Practice*, 192.
91 Finn, *Character of Credit*, 28.
92 Finn, *Character of Credit*, 35, 36.
93 Owenson, *Novice III*, 339.
94 Owenson, *Novice III*, 339.
95 Sennett, *Fall of Pubic Man*, 138–39.
96 Moretti, *Signs*, 121.

97 Owenson, *Novice IV*, 92.
98 Moretti, *Signs*, 122.
99 Owenson, *Novice IV*, 92.
100 Owenson, *Novice IV*, 93–94.
101 Finn, *The Character of Credit*, 9–11.
102 Owenson, *Novice IV*, 94.
103 Bourdieu, *Outline of a Theory of Practice*, 126.
104 Owenson, *Novice IV*, 104.
105 Owenson, *Novice IV*, 114.
106 Owenson, *Novice IV*, 114–15.
107 Simmel, "Metropolis," 337.
108 Finn, *Character of Credit*, 37.
109 Owenson, *Novice IV*, 187–89.
110 Owenson, *Novice IV*, 226.
111 Owenson, *Novice IV*, 229.
112 Owenson, *Novice IV*, 248.
113 Owenson, *Novice IV*, 247.
114 Owenson, *Novice IV*, 247.
115 Owenson, *Novice IV*, 271–72.
116 Owenson, *Novice IV*, 272.
117 Owenson, *Novice IV*, 267, 269.
118 Owenson, *Novice III*, 212–13.
119 Owenson, *Novice IV*, 245–46; emphasis added.
120 Wright, "The Nation Begins to Form," 939–57.
121 Owenson, *O'Briens*, 45.
122 Jones, *Paris*, 183.
123 Jones, *Paris*, 183.
124 Jones, *Paris*, 55.
125 I say "unsurprisingly" because Edgeworth has represented the opera house as a site of social mobility, albeit in a negative manner, in both *The Absentee* and *Ormond*. For further discussion, see my chapter "He Should Go to the Théâtre François" in *Travelling Irishness in the Long Nineteenth Century* (Palgrave 2017).
126 Owenson, *O'Briens*, 526.
127 Wright, *O'Briens*, 526.
128 Johnson, *Listening in Paris*, 165–66.
129 Simeone, *Paris*, 204.
130 Johnson, *Listening in Paris*, 102.
131 Johnson, *Listening in Paris*, 104.
132 Johnson, *Listening in Paris*, 104–05.
133 Owenson, *O'Briens*, 534.
134 Owenson, *O'Briens*, 534.
135 Owenson, *O'Briens*, 535.

Notes to Chapter 2:
Much More than Only *Le Bel Irlandois*:
Metropolitan Socio-Economics and Parisian
Bildung in Maria Edgeworth's *Ormond*

1   Butler, "Introduction," 26–27.
2   Butler, *Maria Edgeworth*, 306.
3   Moretti, *Way*, 20.
4   Connolly, "Introductory Note," xi.
5   Ó Gallchoir, *Maria Edgeworth*, 137.
6   Ó Gallchoir, *Maria Edgeworth*, 12.
7   Edgeworth, *Ennui*, 322.
8   Moretti, *Way*, 22.
9   Moretti, *Way*, 27; emphasis original.
10 Moretti, *Atlas*, 12.
11 McCormack, "Introduction," xii.
12 Deane, *Strange Country*, 37.
13 Deane, *Strange Country*, 37.
14 Deane, *Strange Country*, 37.
15 Edgeworth, *Ormond*, 306.
16 Moretti, *Way*, 22.
17 Simmel, "Metropolis," 337.
18 Moretti, *Way*, 26.
19 Edgeworth, *Ormond*, 59, 107.
20 Edgeworth, *Ormond*, 83.
21 In Owenson's *The O'Briens and the O'Flahertys*, however, the Abbess's ability to shift identities remains a positive trait and an expression of her metropolitan practitionership. This signals a key difference between Owenson's and Edgeworth's attitudes toward the increased Simmelian liberties and autonomy made possible by the metropolis.
22 Edgeworth, *Ormond*, 112.
23 Edgeworth, *Ormond*, 113.
24 Edgeworth, *Ormond*, 112.
25 Edgeworth, *Ormond*, 114.
26 Throughout Edgeworth's œuvre, the self-fashioned dandy and coxcomb is a repeated object of derision, pointing more broadly to one of the figurations of France that Ó Gallchoir has described (see Ó Gallchoir, *Maria Edgeworth*, 132–54).
27 Cook, "Democratic Dandyism," 2010.
28 Edgeworth, *Ormond*, 113, 114–15.
29 Edgeworth, *Ormond*, 116.
30 Poovey, *Genres of the Credit Economy*, 49.

31 Bell, *Models*, 131.
32 Bell, *Models*, 131.
33 Edgeworth, *Ormond*, 120.
34 Edgeworth, *Ormond*, 120.
35 Marx, *Capital I*, 166.
36 Marx, *Capital I*, 166.
37 Ó Gallchoir, *Maria Edgeworth*, 150.
38 Edgeworth, *Ormond*, 120.
39 Trotsky, *The History of the Russian Revolution*, 27; Moretti, *Atlas*, 65–68.
40 Moretti, *Atlas*, 68.
41 Thomson, "The Fashion Not to be an Absentee," 180.
42 Edgeworth, *Ormond*, 117.
43 Bell, *Models*, 131, 17.
44 Edgeworth, *Ormond*, 120.
45 Richard, *The Romance of Gambling*, 9.
46 Edgeworth, *Ormond*, 6.
47 For deeper analysis of the role of paper money and speculation in *Ormond*, see my article "Absurd Speculations."
48 Edgeworth, *Ormond*, 49.
49 Edgeworth, *Ormond*, 49.
50 Poovey, *Genres of the Credit Economy*, 72.
51 Rowlinson, *Real Money and Romanticism*, 74.
52 Moore, *Swift*, 134.
53 Moore, *Swift*, 134.
54 Edgeworth, *Ormond*, 120.
55 Edgeworth, *Ormond*, 243; emphasis in original.
56 Edgeworth, *Ormond*, 244–45.
57 Edgeworth, *Ormond*, 255.
58 Catani, *Evil*, 53–54.
59 Catani, *Evil*, 54.
60 Moretti, *Signs*, 122; emphasis in original.
61 Moretti, *Signs*, 121.
62 Edgeworth, *Ormond*, 255.
63 Moretti, *Signs*, 122.
64 Simmel, "Metropolis," 337.
65 Edgeworth, *Ormond*, 243.
66 Simmel, "Metropolis," 337.
67 Edgeworth, *Ormond*, 243.
68 Moretti, *Atlas*, 109.
69 Deane, *Strange Country*, 27.
70 Burke, *Reflections*, 43.
71 Burke, *Reflections*, 43.
72 Burke, *Reflections*, 47.

73 Finn, *The Character of Credit*, 19.
74 Finn, *The Character of Credit*, 19.
75 Barry, "The Suspension of Cash Payments," 261.
76 Finn, *The Character of Credit*, 9.
77 Finn, *The Character of Credit*, 19.
78 Finn, *The Character of Credit*, 20.
79 Edgeworth, *Ormond*, 243.
80 Edgeworth, *Ormond*, 243.
81 Edgeworth, *Ormond*, 113.
82 Edgeworth, *Ormond*, 120.
83 Cook, "Democratic Dandyism," 2010.
84 Descamps, *Psychologie*, 15.
85 Edgeworth, *Ormond*, 245.
86 Edgeworth, *Ormond*, 244–45.
87 Edgeworth, *Ormond*, 245; emphasis in original.
88 Moretti, *Way*, 131.
89 Edgeworth, *Ormond*, 255.
90 Reznicek, "He Should Go to the Théâtre François."
91 Reznicek, "He Should go to the Théâtre François."
92 Edgeworth, *Ormond*, 239.
93 Edgeworth, *Ormond*, 240.
94 Edgeworth, *Ormond*, 240.
95 Edgeworth, *Ormond*, 240.
96 Sennett, *The Fall of Public Man*, 113.
97 Sennett, *The Fall of Public Man*, 111.
98 Deane, *Strange Country*, 27.
99 Edgeworth, *Ormond*, 259.
100 Edgeworth, *Ormond*, 259; emphasis in original.
101 Sennett, *The Fall of Public Man*, 71.
102 Edgeworth, *Ormond*, 259.
103 Edgeworth, *Ormond*, 259.
104 Sennett, *The Fall of Public Man*, 111.
105 Edgeworth, *Ormond*, 260.
106 Diderot, "De la Poésie Dramatique," 334–35.
107 Reznicek, "He Should Go to the Théâtre François."
108 Edgeworth, *Ormond*, 259–60.
109 Edgeworth, *Ormond*, 260.
110 Edgeworth, *Ormond*, 120.
111 Moretti, *Way*, 26, 27.
112 Deane, *Strange Country*, 27.
113 Deane, *Strange Country*, 7.
114 Edgeworth, *Ormond*, 260.

115 Edgeworth's *Madame de Fleury*, although demonstrating structural and narratological parallels to the *Bildungsroman*, does not exhibit enough character development to be considered a full *Bildungsroman*; instead, this tale seems to have more in common with Edgeworth's other moral tales.
116 Cosgrove ("History and Utopia in *Ormond*," 2004) has discussed *Ormond*'s connections to Fénelon's *Les Aventures de Télémaque*, but more often discussions of the novel's intertexts are restricted to *Henry IV*, *Tom Jones*, and *Sir Charles Grandison*.
117 Charles-Louis de Sevelinges published a French translation in 1802, under the title *Alfred, ou les années d'apprentissage de Wilhelm Meister*. Marilyn Butler has demonstrated Edgeworth's adoption of aspects of the structure and plot of Goethe's *The Sorrows of Young Werther* (1774) in *Leonora* (1806) (Butler, *Maria Edgeworth*, 318).
118 Boes, "Apprenticeship of the Novel," 269.
119 Moretti, *Way*, 21.
120 Moretti, *Way*, 22.
121 Edgeworth, *Ormond*, 260.
122 Edgeworth, *Ormond*, 260.
123 Edgeworth, *Ormond*, 260, 112, 113.
124 Edgeworth, *Memoirs vol. II*, 273.
125 Edgeworth to Mary Sneyd, October 31, 1802.
126 Edgeworth, *Memoirs II*, 273.
127 Edgeworth to Henry Edgeworth, January 16, 1803.
128 Edgeworth, *Ormond*, 260; emphasis added.
129 Edgeworth to Sophy Ruxton, December 8, 1802.
130 Edgeworth, *Ormond*, 260; Descamps, *Psychologie*, 15.
131 Edgeworth, *Ormond*, 261.
132 Edgeworth, *Ormond*, 261.
133 Burke, *Reflections*, 77.
134 Simmel, "Fashion," 303.
135 Edgeworth, *Ormond*, 261.
136 Edgeworth, *Ormond*, 261.
137 Edgeworth, *Ormond*, 261.
138 Deane, *Strange Country*, 31.
139 Deane, *Strange Country*, 31.
140 Edgeworth, *Ormond*, 261.
141 Kavanagh, *Shadows of Chance*, 38.
142 Burke, *Reflections*, 76.
143 Edgeworth, *Ormond*, 265.
144 Simmel, "On Fashion," 297; Edgeworth, *Ormond*, 260.
145 Finn, *The Character of Credit*, 19–20.
146 Poovey, *Genres of the Credit Economy*, 47, 48.

147 Edgeworth, *Ormond*, 262.
148 Edgeworth, *Ormond*, 262.
149 Edgeworth, *Ormond*, 262–63.
150 Edgeworth, *Ormond*, 11, 262.
151 Edgeworth, *Ormond*, 264–65.
152 Edgeworth, *Ormond*, 263.
153 Edgeworth, *Ormond*, 263.
154 Edgeworth, *Ormond*, 263.
155 Edgeworth, *Ormond*, 263.
156 Butler, "Introduction," 7.
157 Edgeworth, *Ormond*, 260.
158 Szondi and Mendelsohn, "Tableau and Coup de Théâtre," 328.
159 Reznicek, "He Should Go to the Théâtre François."
160 Edgeworth, *Ormond*, 298.
161 Goethe, *Wilhelm Meister*, 418.
162 Edgeworth, *Ormond*, 264.
163 Edgeworth, *Ormond*, 265.
164 Edgeworth, *Ormond*, 264.
165 Edgeworth, *Ormond*, 259.
166 Edgeworth, *Ormond*, 157.
167 Richard, "Putting Hazard to a Certainty," 190.
168 Burke, *Reflections*, 233.
169 Rowlinson, *Real Money*, 13; Edgeworth, *Ormond*, 262.
170 Edgeworth, *Ormond*, 264.
171 Edgeworth, *Ormond*, 264.
172 Deane, *Strange Country*, 31.
173 Edgeworth, *Ormond*, 265.
174 Edgeworth, *Ormond*, 265, 266.
175 Edgeworth, *Ormond*, 298.

Notes to Chapter 3:
The New Jerusalem and the Rue Vavin: Urban Space, Economic Exchange, and Gendered Modernity in *French Leave*

1   Although *French Leave* was published 13 years after Violet Martin's death in 1915, Edith Somerville continued to publish under both their names.
2   Robinson, *Somerville & Ross*, 198.
3   Stevens, *The Irish Scene*, 127.
4   Bhreathnach-Lynch and Stevens, "The Irish Artist," 141; Stevens, *The Irish Scene*, 133.

5   Robinson, *Somerville & Ross*, 194, 147.
6   Oakman, "Sitting on 'The Outer Skin,'" 112.
7   Tyanan, "Irishry," 265.
8   Somerville and Ross, *The Real Charlotte*, 24.
9   Reznicek, "These Irish Investments," 197.
10 As explained in the introduction, Balzac's *Illusions perdues* (1837–43) functions as a cornerstone for the integration of capitalism in the *Bildungsroman*. *Nicholas Nickleby* (1838–39) and *Au Bonheur des dames* (1883) are key examples for the continued relationship between the development of selfhood and advanced stages of capitalism. Most of Zola's *Rougon-Macquart* cycle explicitly engages with money, but *Au Bonheur des dames* most closely adheres to the *Bildungsroman* tradition.
11 Somerville and Ross, *French Leave*, 226.
12 Reznicek, "These Irish Investments," 198.
13 Moretti, *Atlas*, 64.
14 Moretti, *Atlas*, 100; emphasis in original.
15 Somerville and Ross, *French Leave*, 16.
16 Kreilkamp, "The Novel of the Big House," 60.
17 Somerville and Ross, *French Leave*, 28; Kreilkamp, "The Novel of the Big House," 60.
18 Kreilkamp, "The Novel of the Big House," 60.
19 Somerville and Ross, *French Leave*, 125.
20 Somerville and Ross, *French Leave*, 51.
21 Somerville and Ross, *French Leave*, 30.
22 O'Toole, *The Irish New Woman*, 111.
23 Somerville and Ross, *French Leave*, 31.
24 Somerville and Ross, *French Leave*, 31.
25 Somerville and Ross, *French Leave*, 31.
26 Somerville and Ross, *French Leave*, 31.
27 Somerville and Ross, *French Leave*, 31.
28 Somerville and Ross, *French Leave*, 16.
29 Somerville and Ross, *French Leave*, 37.
30 Somerville and Ross, *French Leave*, 37.
31 Somerville and Ross, *French Leave*, 38.
32 Somerville and Ross, *French Leave*, 47.
33 Moore, *Parnell and his Island*, 6.
34 Foster, *Modern Ireland*, 377.
35 Davidoff and Hall, *Family Fortunes*, 206.
36 Kreilkamp, *The Anglo-Irish Novel*, 114.
37 Grubgeld, *Anglo-Irish Autobiography*, 40.
38 Somerville and Ross, *French Leave*, 29.
39 Somerville and Ross, *French Leave*, 62.
40 Davidoff and Hall, *Family Fortunes*, 309.

41 Bhreathnach-Lynch and Stevens, "The Irish Artist," 137.
42 Finn, *The Character of Credit*, 324.
43 Somerville and Ross, *French Leave*, 26, 33.
44 Finn, *The Character of Credit*, 265.
45 Somerville and Ross, *French Leave*, 47.
46 Davidoff and Hall, *Family Fortunes*, 272.
47 Gallois, *Zola*, 87.
48 Somerville and Ross, *French Leave*, 59, 62.
49 Somerville and Ross, *French Leave*, 119, 12.
50 Somerville and Ross, *French Leave*, 62.
51 Moretti, *Way*, 21.
52 Somerville and Ross, *French Leave*, 64.
53 Somerville and Ross, *French Leave*, 64.
54 Somerville and Ross, *French Leave*, 16, 64.
55 Moretti, "A Useless Longing," 44.
56 Moretti, "A Useless Longing," 45.
57 Moretti, "A Useless Longing," 45.
58 Somerville and Ross, *French Leave*, 61.
59 Somerville and Ross, *French Leave*, 64.
60 Finn, *The Character of Credit*, 266.
61 Somerville and Ross, *French Leave*, 27, 127.
62 Somerville and Ross, *French Leave*, 109.
63 Lewis, *Edith Somerville*, 75.
64 Lewis, *Edith Somerville*, 76.
65 Bhreathnach-Lynch and Stevens, "The Irish Artist," 139.
66 Somerville and Ross, *Irish Memories*, 110–11.
67 Somerville and Ross, *French Leave*, 47.
68 Somerville and Ross, *French Leave*, 182, 183.
69 Somerville and Ross, *French Leave*, 123.
70 Somerville and Ross, *French Leave*, 121.
71 Somerville and Ross, *French Leave*, 122.
72 Simmel, *The Philosophy of Money*, 286.
73 Simmel, *The Philosophy of Money*, 286.
74 Somerville and Ross, *French Leave*, 123.
75 Simmel, "Metropolis and Mental Life," 337.
76 Simmel, "Metropolis and Mental Life," 337.
77 Somerville and Ross, *French Leave*, 133.
78 Somerville and Ross, *French Leave*, 133.
79 Somerville and Ross, *French Leave*, 133.
80 Somerville and Ross, *French Leave*, 127.
81 Somerville and Ross, *French Leave*, 194.
82 Somerville and Ross, *French Leave*, 194.
83 Somerville and Ross, *French Leave*, 120.

84 Somerville and Ross, *French Leave*, 121.
85 Somerville and Ross, *French Leave*, 228.
86 Somerville and Ross, *French Leave*, 228.
87 Simmel, "Metropolis and Mental Life," 337.
88 Somerville and Ross, *French Leave*, 228.
89 Moretti, *Atlas*, 109.
90 Benjamin, "Work of Art," 102.
91 Benjamin, "Paris, the Capital of the Nineteenth Century," 35.
92 Benjamin, "Paris, the Capital of the Nineteenth Century," 35.
93 Benjamin, "The Paris of the Second Empire in Baudelaire," 66.
94 Benjamin, "The Paris of the Second Empire in Baudelaire," 67.
95 Benjamin, "The Paris of the Second Empire in Baudelaire," 67.
96 Benjamin, "The Paris of the Second Empire in Baudelaire," 70.
97 Benjamin, "The Paris of the Second Empire in Baudelaire," 67, 70.
98 Benjamin, "The Paris of the Second Empire in Baudelaire," 70.
99 Prendergast, *Paris*, 11.
100 Lehan, *The City in Literature*, 8.
101 Somerville and Ross, *French Leave*, 228.
102 Somerville and Ross, *French Leave*, 228.
103 Benjamin, "The Paris of the Second Empire in Baudelaire," 70.
104 Somerville and Ross, *French Leave*, 228, 229.
105 Somerville and Ross, *French Leave*, 228.
106 Somerville and Ross, *French Leave*, 228.
107 Somerville and Ross, *French Leave*, 229.
108 Somerville and Ross, *French Leave*, 229, 230.
109 Somerville and Ross, *French Leave*, 154.
110 Somerville and Ross, *French Leave*, 154.
111 Somerville and Ross, *French Leave*, 155.
112 Somerville and Ross, *French Leave*, 155.
113 Moretti, *Atlas*, 87.
114 Moretti, *Atlas*, 87.
115 Somerville and Ross, *French Leave*, 228.
116 Moretti, *Way*, 26.
117 Simmel, "Metropolis and Mental Life," 337.
118 Simmel, *The Philosophy of Money*, 285.
119 Somerville and Ross, *French Leave*, 152.
120 Somerville and Ross, *French Leave*, 152–53.
121 Somerville and Ross, *French Leave*, 153.
122 Somerville and Ross, *French Leave*, 153.
123 Miller, "Glass Before its Time," 244.
124 Miller, *Novels behind Glass*, 1.
125 Somerville and Ross, *French Leave*, 153.
126 Gallois, *Zola*, 95.

127 Gallois, *Zola*, 106.
128 Somerville and Ross, *French Leave*, 153.
129 Gallois, *Zola*, 106.
130 Somerville and Ross, *French Leave*, 150.
131 Somerville and Ross, *French Leave*, 152.
132 Somerville and Ross, *French Leave*, 160.
133 Somerville and Ross, *French Leave*, 160.
134 Frawley, *Irish Pastoral*, 53.
135 Frawley, *Irish Pastoral*, 53.
136 Frawley, *Irish Pastoral*, 53.
137 Williams, *The Country and the City*, 36.
138 Somerville and Ross, *French Leave*, 161–62.
139 Johnson, "A Contested City," 234.
140 Johnson, "A Contested City," 234.
141 Rose, *Mistress of Montmartre*, 39–41.
142 Gallois, *Zola*, 103–04.
143 Somerville and Ross, *French Leave*, 161.
144 Somerville and Ross, *French Leave*, 161.
145 Somerville and Ross, *French Leave*, 167.
146 Rothwell, "Introduction," ix; Zola, *Thérèse Raquin*, 1–2.
147 Somerville and Ross, *French Leave*, 171.
148 Somerville and Ross, *French Leave*, 149, 127.
149 Johnson, "A Contested City," 229–30.
150 Johnson, "A Contested City," 230.
151 Johnson, "A Contested City," 230.
152 Bhreathnach-Lynch and Stevens, "The Irish Artist," 140.
153 Somerville and Ross, *Irish Memories*, 113.
154 Somerville and Ross, *French Leave*, 190.
155 Somerville and Ross, *French Leave*, 191.
156 Somerville and Ross, *French Leave*, 192.
157 Somerville and Ross, *French Leave*, 189.
158 Somerville and Ross, *French Leave*, 192.
159 Somerville and Ross, *French Leave*, 192.
160 Somerville and Ross, *French Leave*, 192.
161 Somerville and Ross, *French Leave*, 191.
162 These pearls provide another instance of women receiving an important income from another woman, as in Owenson's *The Novice of Saint Dominick* and in *Castle Rackrent*, as well as in several of Kate O'Brien's novels. The significance of an independent line of credit that extends from woman to woman, especially before the series of Married Women's Property Acts in the mid- to late nineteenth century is a topic that deserves study in its own right.
163 Somerville and Ross, *French Leave*, 225.

164 Somerville and Ross, *French Leave*, 226.
165 Somerville and Ross, *French Leave*, 278.
166 Somerville and Ross, *French Leave*, 279.
167 In Edgeworth's *Ennui*, Lord Y—, who functions as the representative of the Goethean Society of the Tower for the former Lord Glenthorn, expresses a similar sentiment, declaring "I hold that we are the artificers of our own fortune" (*Ennui*, 303). But Lord Y— continues to use the metaphor of fate and connects it to "the gods" (*Ennui*, 304).
168 Edgeworth, *Ormond*, 31.

Notes to Chapter 4:
First Life—and then Fame:
Gendered *Fin-de-Siècle* Cityscapes in *Max*

1 Poe, "The Man of the Crowd," 506-07.
2 Balzac, "The Girl with the Golden Eyes," 67.
3 Balzac, "The Girl with the Golden Eyes," 67.
4 Balzac, "The Girl with the Golden Eyes," 67.
5 Abraham, *Metropolitan Lovers*, 7.
6 Poe, "The Man of the Crowd," 506.
7 Thurston, *Max*, 59.
8 Meaney, "Decadence, Degeneration and Revolting Aesthetics," 159.
9 Meaney, "Decadence, Degeneration and Revolting Aesthetics," 159.
10 Meaney, "Decadence, Degeneration and Revolting Aesthetics," 158.
11 Thurston, *Max*, 2, 205.
12 Butler, *Gender Trouble*, 33.
13 Butler, *Gender Trouble*, 33.
14 The fluidity of selfhood that characterizes *Max* seems to anticipate Woolf's *Orlando*, in which the protagonist does not so much perform gender as fluidly switch sex so that s/he is cis-gendered in each embodiment. Significantly, both Max and Orlando end in a female/feminine body, despite the fact that Woolf's novel is characterized as much more transgressive.
15 O'Toole, *The Irish New Woman*, 110.
16 O'Toole, *The Irish New Woman*, 110.
17 Ledger, *The New Woman*, 154.
18 Ledger, *The New Woman*, 154.
19 Shakespeare, *Twelfth Night*, II.III.44.
20 Thurston, *Max*, 15.
21 Thurston, *Max*, 15.
22 Richardson, *New Woman and Colonial Adventure Fiction*, 4, 16.

23 Reeve, *The Progress of Romance*, 78.
24 Thurston, *Max*, 5.
25 Phillips, *Mapping Men and Empire*, 25, 22.
26 Thurston, *Max*, 15.
27 Thurston, *Max*, 15.
28 Hobsbawm, *Industry and Empire*, 89.
29 Aguiar, *Tracking Modernity*, xiii.
30 Aguiar, *Tracking Modernity*, xiv; Headrick, *The Tools of Empire*, 182.
31 Thurston, *Max*, 15.
32 Thurston, *Max*, 1.
33 Thurston, *Max*, 1.
34 Gallois, *Zola*, 82.
35 Thurston, *Max*, 2.
36 De Certeau, *The Practice of Everyday Life*, 36.
37 De Certeau, *The Practice of Everyday Life*, 92, 111.
38 De Certeau, *The Practice of Everyday Life*, 111.
39 Thurston, *Max*, 6.
40 Thurston, *Max*, 6.
41 De Certeau, *The Practice of Everyday Life*, 98.
42 Thurston, *Max*, 7.
43 Thurston, *Max*, 7, 9.
44 Thurston, *Max*, 10.
45 Thurston, *Max*, 7.
46 Baudelaire, "The Painter of Modern Life," 795.
47 Thurston, *Max*, 6.
48 Richardson, *New Woman and Colonial Adventure Fiction*, 1.
49 Baudelaire, "The Painter of Modern Life," 795.
50 Thurston, *Max*, 16.
51 Thurston, *Max*, 17.
52 Thurston, *Max*, 16.
53 Ledger, *The New Woman*, 151.
54 Wilson, *The Sphinx in the City*, 100; Ledger, *The New Woman*, 153.
55 Thurston, *Max*, 18.
56 Thurston, *Max*, 20.
57 Thurston, *Max*, 20–21.
58 Thurston, *Max*, 21.
59 Phillips, *Mapping Men and Empire*, 40.
60 Thurston, *Max*, 21.
61 Pratt, *Imperial Eyes*, 204; Thurston, *Max*, 21.
62 Moretti, *Atlas*, 87.
63 Moretti, *Atlas*, 87–90.
64 Thurston, *Max*, 7.
65 Thurston, *Max*, 38–39.

66 Thurston, *Max*, 39.
67 The upper floors of a Parisian apartment building do not connote privilege in a sociocultural sense; in fact, they correlate to a lower-class position. However, the elevated position allows the viewer to surveil the landscape just as de Certeau argues.
68 De Certeau, *The Practice of Everyday Life*, 91; Prendergast, *Paris*, 48.
69 De Certeau, *The Practice of Everyday Life*, 92.
70 Pratt, *Imperial Eyes*, 205.
71 Prendergast, *Paris*, 49.
72 Zola, *La Curée*, 69; Prendergast, *Paris*, 41.
73 Prendergast, *Paris*, 41.
74 Thurston, *Max*, 40.
75 Moretti, *Atlas*, 65.
76 Lefebvre, *The Production of Space*, 220.
77 Prendergast, *Paris*, 47.
78 Thurston, *Max*, 40.
79 Thurston, *Max*, 41.
80 Thurston, *Max*, 41.
81 Thurston, *Max*, 44, 47.
82 Thurston, *Max*, 59, 60.
83 Balzac, *Père Goriot*, 98.
84 Balzac, *Père Goriot*, 109.
85 Pratt, *Imperial Eyes*, 204.
86 Thurston, *Max*, 54.
87 Hewitt, "Céline and Montmartre," 144.
88 Hewitt, "Céline and Montmartre," 144.
89 Hewitt, "Céline and Montmartre," 142.
90 Hewitt, "Céline and Montmartre," 146.
91 Richardson, *New Woman and Colonial Adventure Fiction*, 4.
92 Richardson, *New Woman and Colonial Adventure Fiction*, 4.
93 Richardson, *New Woman and Colonial Adventure Fiction*, 5.
94 Thurston, *Max*, 65.
95 Bakhtin, "Forms of Time and Chronotope in the Novel," 243.
96 Moretti, *Atlas*, 51; Thurston, *Max*, 65.
97 Thurston, *Max*, 72, 71.
98 Prendergast, *Paris*, 49–50.
99 Thurston, *Max*, 82.
100 Thurston, *Max*, 82–83.
101 Thurston, *Max*, 84.
102 Thurston, *Max*, 85.
103 Pratt, *Imperial Eyes*, 213.
104 Thurston, *Max*, 166.
105 Thurston, *Max*, 167.

106 Thurston, *Max*, 49–50.
107 Pratt, *Imperial Eyes*, 204–05.
108 Pratt, *Imperial Eyes*, 205.
109 Murphy, *Maria Edgeworth and Romance*, 20.
110 Thurston, *Max*, 15.
111 Johnson, "A Contested City," 229.
112 Johnson, "A Contested City," 229.
113 Daly, *Modernism, Romance and the* Fin de Siècle, 18.
114 Spencer, "Purity and Danger," 203.
115 Johnson, "A Contested City," 230.
116 Ledger, *The New Woman*, 152, 155.
117 Ledger, *The New Woman*, 155.
118 Ledger, *The New Woman*, 155.
119 It is important to note that Wolff's critical interlocutors not only are all men, but emphasize a masculine protagonist in their studies of modernity. This is most clearly seen in Felski's critiques of Berman, who celebrates Goethe's Faust, Charles Baudelaire, and Karl Marx as the heroes of modernity.
120 Baudelaire, "The Painter of Modern Life," 795.
121 Ledger, *The New Woman*, 153.
122 De Certeau, *The Practice of Everyday Life*, 37.
123 Thurston, *Max*, 2.
124 De Certeau, *The Practice of Everyday Life*, 37; Thurston, *Max*, 2–3.
125 Thurston, *Max*, 6.
126 Thurston, *Max*, 6.
127 Thurston, *Max*, 274.
128 Thurston, *Max*, 276, 275.
129 Johnson, "A Contested City," 232.
130 Johnson, "A Contested City," 232–33.
131 Thurston, *Max*, 277, 282, 278.
132 Balzac, "The Girl with the Golden Eyes," 67.
133 Thurston, *Max*, 15.
134 Thurston, *Max*, 277.
135 Thurston, *Max*, 277.
136 Thurston, *Max*, 134.
137 Thurston, *Max*, 1.
138 Thurston, *Max*, 2.
139 Thurston, *Max*, 59.
140 Johnson, "A Contested City," 230.
141 Johnson, "A Contested City," 230.
142 Johnson, "A Contested City," 231.
143 Association mutuelle des femmes, Article 2, 5; Johnson, "A Contested City," 232.

144 Johnson, "A Contested City," 233–34.
145 Johnson, "A Contested City," 234.
146 Thurston, *Max*, 189.
147 Thurston, *Max*, 193.
148 Thurston, *Max*, 196.
149 Thurston, *Max*, 196.
150 Thurston, *Max*, 178.
151 In *The Madwoman and the Attic*, Gilbert and Gubar emphasize the degree to which the very act of writing, and the realm of art more broadly, is based upon a masculine authority of authorship. The female artist, just like the female art-object, is subjected to a disciplinary and interpretive regime that undermines and calls into question her very ability to perform this artistic task.
152 Hirsch, "Spiritual *Bildung*," 28.
153 Hirsch, "Spiritual *Bildung*," 28.
154 Thurston, *Max*, 184.
155 Thurston, *Max*, 184.
156 Gilbert and Gubar, *The Madwoman in the Attic*, 15, 14.
157 Thurston, *Max*, 186.
158 Thurston, *Max*, 183.
159 Moretti, *Way*, 22.
160 O'Toole, *The Irish New Woman*, 127.
161 Thurston, *Max*, 201–02.
162 Thurston, *Max*, 203.
163 Hirsch, "Spiritual *Bildung*," 28.
164 Gilbert and Gubar, *The Madwoman in the Attic*, 15.
165 Thurston, *Max*, 286.
166 Thurston, *Max*, 286, 287.
167 Thurston, *Max*, 288, 290.
168 Thurston, *Max*, 315.
169 Thurston, *Max*, 315.
170 Thurston, *Max*, 317.

Notes to A City She Must Postpone: A Conclusion

1 O'Brien, *My Ireland*, 62.
2 Moretti, "A Useless Longing," 43.
3 O'Brien, *Without My Cloak*, 231.
4 O'Brien, *Without My Cloak*, 243.
5 Moretti, *Way*, 22.
6 O'Brien, *Without My Cloak*, 243, 239.
7 Moretti, "Useless Longing," 44; emphasis in original.

8   O'Brien, *Without My Cloak*, 242.
9   Moretti, *Atlas*, 95.
10 Lukács, *Theory of the Novel*, 41; O'Brien, *As Music and Splendour*, 14.
11 O'Brien, *As Music and Splendour*, 19.
12 O'Brien, *As Music and Splendour*, 17.
13 O'Brien, *As Music and Splendour*, 352.
14 O'Brien, *The Flower of May*, 78-79.
15 O'Brien, *The Flower of May*, 79.
16 O'Brien, *The Flower of May*, 78.
17 O'Brien, *The Flower of May*, 296-97.
18 O'Brien, *The Flower of May*, 302.
19 Moretti, *Atlas*, 95.
20 Moretti, *Atlas*, 100.
21 Moretti, *Atlas*, 100.
22 O'Brien, *The Flower of May*, 79.

Works Cited

Primary Sources

Association mutuelle des femmes artistes de Paris: Statuts. Paris: Imprimerie et librairie centrales des Chemins de fer. 1894. Dos. 700 Art, Bibliothèque Marguerite Durand, Paris.

Balzac, Honoré. "The Girl with the Golden Eyes." In *The Girls with the Golden Eyes and Other Stories*. Translated by Peter Collier. New York. Oxford University Press, 2012.

———. *Père Goriot*. Trans. A. J. Krailsheimer. New York. Oxford University Press, 2009.

Baudelaire, Charles. "The Painter of Modern Life." In *The Norton Anthology of Theory and Criticism*. Edited by Vincent B. Leitch. New York. Norton, 2001.

Bourdieu, Pierre. *Outline of a Theory of Practice*. Cambridge: Cambridge University Press, 1977.

Burke, Edmund. *Reflections on the Revolution in France*. Edited by L. G. Mitchell. New York. Oxford University Press, 2009.

Diderot, Denis. "De la poésie dramatique." In *Œuvres Complètes, vol. 10*. Edited by Jean Verloot. Paris. Herman, 1974–86.

Edgeworth, Maria. *The Absentee*. 1812. Edited by W. J. McCormack and Kim Walker. New York. Oxford University Press, 2001.

———. Letter to Henry Edgeworth. January 16, 1803. In *Maria Edgeworth in France and Switzerland: Selections from the Edgeworth Family Letters*. Edited by Christina Colvin. Oxford. Clarendon Press, 1979.

———. Letter to Mary Sneyd. October 31, 1802. In *Maria Edgeworth in France and Switzerland: Selections from the Edgeworth Family Letters*. Edited by Christina Colvin. Oxford. Clarendon Press, 1979.

———. Letter to Sophy Ruxton. December 8, 1802. In *Maria Edgeworth in France and Switzerland: Selections from the Edgeworth Family Letters*. Edited by Christina Colvin. Oxford. Clarendon Press, 1979.

———. *Ormond*. 1817. Edited by Claire Connolly. London. Penguin, 2000.

Edgeworth, R. L. *Memoirs of Richard Lovell Edgeworth, Esq. Begun by Himself and Concluded by his Daughter, Maria Edgeworth in Two Volumes*. London. R. Hunter, 1820.

von Goethe, Johann Wolfgang. *Wilhelm Meister's Apprenticeship*. Trans. Thomas Carlyle. Milton Keynes. Aegypan Press, 1917.

Moore, George. *Parnell and his Island*. 1887. Dublin. University College Dublin Press, 2004.

O'Brien, Kate. *As Music and Splendour*. 1958. New York. Penguin, 2005.

———. *My Ireland*. London. B. T. Batsford, 1962.

———. *The Flower of May*. 1953. London. William Heinemann, 1955.

———. *Without My Cloak*. 1931. London. Virago, 2001.

Owenson, Sydney. *The Novice of Saint Dominick*. London. Richard Phillips, 1806.

———. *The O'Briens and the O'Flahertys*. 1827. Edited by Julia Wright. Buffalo, NY. Broadview: 2013.

Poe, Edgar Allen. "The Man of the Crowd." In *The Collected Works of Edgar Allen Poe*. Edited by Thomas Ollive Mabbott. Cambridge, MA. Belknap Press, 1978.

Reeve, Clara. *The Progress of Romance through Times, Countries and Manners; and the History of Charoba, Queen of Aegypt*. 1785. New York. Facsimile Text Society, 1930.

Shakespeare, William. *Twelfth Night; Or, What You Will*. Edited by Roger Warren and Stanley Wells. New York. Oxford University Press, 2008.

Somerville, Edith Œ. and Martin Ross. *French Leave*. London. William Heinemann, 1928.

———. *Irish Memories*. London. Longmans, Greens, and Co., 1917.

———. *The Real Charlotte*. 1894. London. Longmans, Green, and Co., 1915.

Thurston, Katherine Cecil. *Max*. New York. Harper and Brothers Publishers, 1910.

Zola, Émile. *La Curée*. 1871. Edited by Brian Nelson. New York. Oxford University Press, 2004.

———. *Thérèse Raquin*. 1867. New York. Oxford University Press, 1998.

Secondary Sources

Abraham, Julie. *Metropolitan Lovers: The Homosexuality of Cities*. Minneapolis, MN. The University of Minnesota Press, 2009.

Aguiar, Marian. *Tracking Modernity: India's Railway and the Culture of Mobility*. Minneapolis, MN. University of Minnesota Press, 2011.

Ali, Tariq. "Literature and Market Realism." *New Left Review*. I, no. 199 (1993): 140–45.

Bakhtin, Mikhail. "The *Bildungsroman* and its Significance in the History of Realism (Toward a Historical Typology of the Novel)." In *Speech Genres & Other Late Essays*. Edited by Caryl Emerson and Michael Holquist. Austin, TX. University of Texas Press, 1986.

———. "Forms of Time and Chronotope in the Novel." In *The Dialogic Imagination: Four Essays*. Edited by Michael Holquist. Austin, TX. University of Texas Press, 1982.

Barry, Kevin. "The Suspension of Cash Payments and Ireland's Narrative Economy: The Contexts of Maria Edgeworth's 'National' Novels." In *The Empire of Credit: The Financial Revolution in the British Atlantic World, 1688–1815*. Edited by Daniel Carey and Christopher J. Finlay. Dublin. Irish Academic Press, 2011.

Bell, David. *Models of Power: Politics and Economics in Zola's Rougon-Macqaurt*. Lincoln, NE. University of Nebraska Press, 1988.

Bell, Michael. *Open Secrets: Literature, Education, and Authority from J-J. Rousseau to J. M. Coetzee*. New York. Oxford University Press, 2007.

Benjamin, Walter. "The Paris of the Second Empire in Baudelaire." In *The Writer of Modern Life: Essays on Charles Baudelaire*. Edited by Michael W. Jennings. Cambridge, MA. Belknap Press, 2006.

———. "Paris, The Capital of the Nineteenth Century." In *The Writer of Modern Life: Essays on Charles Baudelaire*. Edited by Michael W. Jennings. Cambridge, MA. Belknap Press, 2006.

———. "The Work of Art in the Age of its Reproducibility (Second Version)." In *Walter Benjamin: Selected Writings, Vol. 3: 1935–1938*. Edited by Michael W. Jennings. Cambridge, MA. Belknap Press, 2002.

Bhreathnach-Lynch, Síghle and Julie Anne Stevens. "The Irish Artist Crossing the Rubicon." In *Local/Global: Women Artists in the Nineteenth Century*. Edited by Deborah Cherry and Janice Helland. Aldershot. Ashgate Publishing, 2006.

Boes, Tobias. "Apprenticeship of the Novel: The *Bildungsroman* and the Invention of History, ca. 1770–1820." *Comparative Literature Studies*. 45, no. 3 (2008): 269–88.

Buckley, Jerome H. *Season of Youth: The* Bildungsroman *Dickens to Golding*. Cambridge, MA. Harvard University Press, 1974.

Butler, Judith. *Gender Trouble: Feminism and the Subversion of Identity.* New York. Routledge, 2007.
Butler, Marilyn. "Introduction." In *Castle Rackrent and Ennui.* Edited by Marilyn Butler. London. Penguin, 1992.
———. *Maria Edgeworth: A Literary Autobiography.* Oxford. Clarendon Press, 1972.
Campbell-Ross, Ian. "Mapping Ireland in Early Fiction." *Irish University Review: A Journal of Irish Studies.* 41, no. 1 (2011): 1–20.
Catani, Damian. *Evil: A History in Modern French Literature and Thought.* New York. Bloomsbury, 2013.
de Certeau, Michel. *The Practice of Everyday Life.* Translated by Steven Rendall. Berkeley, CA. University of California Press, 1988.
Chakrabarty, Dipesh. "Universalism and Belonging in the Logic of Capital." *Public Culture.* 12, no. 3 (2000): 653–78.
Cheah, Pheng. "Introduction Part II: The Cosmopolitical—Today." *Cosmopolitics: Thinking and Feeling Beyond the Nation.* Eds. Pheng Cheah and Bruce Robbins. London. University of Minnesota Press, 1998.
Colvin, Christina, ed. *Maria Edgeworth in France and Switzerland: Selections from the Edgeworth Family Letters.* Oxford. Clarendon Press, 1979.
Connolly, Claire. "Introductory Note." *The Novels and Selected Works of Maria Edgeworth, Vol. 8.* Edited by Claire Connolly. London. Pickering and Chatto, 1999.
Cook, Roger. "Democratic Dandyism: Aesthetics and the Political Cultivation of *Sens*." *Theory & Event.* 13, no. 4 (2010): online.
Copeland, Edward. *Women Writing about Money: Women's Fiction in England, 1790–1820.* New York. Cambridge University Press, 1995.
Corkery, Daniel. "On Anglo-Irish Literature." In *Daniel Corkery's Cultural Criticism: Selected Writings.* Edited by Heather Laird. Cork. Cork University Press, 2012.
———. "The Peasant in Literature." In *Daniel Corkery's Cultural Criticism: Selected Writings.* Edited by Heather Laird. Cork. Cork University Press, 2012.
Cosgrove, Peter. "History and Utopia in *Ormond*." *An Uncomfortable Authority: Maria Edgeworth and Her Contexts.* Edited by Heidi Kaufman and Chris Fauske. Newark: University of Delaware Press, 2004. 62–83.
Daly, Nicholas. *Modernism, Romance and the Fin de Siècle: Popular Fiction and British Culture, 1880–1914.* New York. Cambridge University Press, 2006.
Davidoff, Leonore and Catherine Hall. *Family Fortunes: Men and Women of the English Middle Class, 1780–1850.* London. Hutchinson, 1987.
Deane, Seamus. "General Introduction." In *The Field Day Anthology of Irish Writing, vol. I.* Edited by Seamus Deane, Andrew Carpenter, Jonathan Williams. Derry. Field Day, 1991.

———. "The Production of Cultural Space in Irish Writing." *Boundary* 21, no. 3 (1994): 117–44.
———. *Strange Country: Modernity and Nationhood in Irish Writing since 1790*. New York. Oxford University Press, 1998.
Descamps, Marc-Alain. *Psychosociologie de la Mode*. Paris. Presses Universitaires de France, 1979.
Ellis, Lorna. *Appearing to Diminish: Female Development and the British Bildungsroman, 1750–1850*. London. Associated University Press, 1999.
Ferris, Ina. *The Romantic National Tale and the Question of Ireland*. New York. Cambridge University Press, 2002.
Finn, Margot. *The Character of Credit: Personal Debt in English Culture, 1740–1914*. New York. Cambridge University Press, 2003.
Foley, Timothy P. "Public Sphere and Domestic Circle: Gender and Political Economy in Nineteenth-Century Ireland." In *Gender Perspectives in 19th Century Ireland: Public and Private Spheres*. Edited by Margaret Kelleher and James H. Murphy. Dublin. Irish Academic Press, 1997.
Foster, R. F. *Modern Ireland: 1600–1972*. London. Allen Lane, 1988.
Fraiman, Susan. *Unbecoming Women: British Women Writers and the Novel of Development*. New York. Columbia University Press, 1993.
Frawley, Oona. *Irish Pastoral: Nostalgia and Twentieth-Century Irish Literature*. Dublin. Irish Academic Press, 2005.
Gallois, William. *Zola: The History of Capitalism*. New York. Peter Lang, 2000.
Gilbert, Sandra M. and Susan Gubar. *The Madwoman in the Attic: The Woman Writer and the Nineteenth-Century Literary Imagination*. New Haven, CT. Yale University Press, 1979.
Greengrass, Mark. *France in the Age of Henri IV: The Struggle for Stability*. London. Longman, 1984.
Grubgeld, Elizabeth. *Anglo-Irish Autobiography: Class, Gender, and the Forms of Narrative*. Syracuse, NY. Syracuse University Press, 2004.
Harvey, David. *Paris, Capital of Modernity*. London. Routledge, 2006.
Headrick, Daniel. *The Tools of Empire: Technology and European Imperialism in the Nineteenth Century*. New York. Oxford University Press, 1981.
Hewitt, Nicholas. "Céline and Montmartre: Bohemia and the Music Hall." In *The Cambridge Companion to Paris in Literature*. Edited by Anna-Louise Milne. New York. Cambridge University Press, 2013.
Hirsch, Marianne. "Spiritual *Bildung*: The Beautiful Soul as Paradigm." In *The Voyage In: Fictions of Female Development*. Edited by Elizabeth Abel, Marianne Hirsch, and Elizabeth Langland. Hanover, NH. University Press of New England, 1983.
Hobsbawm, Eric. *Industry and Empire: The Birth of the Industrial Revolution*. New York. Penguin, 1969.
Johnson, James H. *Listening in Paris: A Cultural History*. Berkeley, CA. University of California Press, 1995.

Johnson, Julie. "A Contested City: Gwen John, Suzanne Valadon, and Women Artists in Fin-de-Siècle Paris." In *City Limits: Perspectives on the Historical European City*. Edited by Glenn Clark, Judith Owens, and Greg T. Smith. Ithaca, NY. McGill-Queen's University Press, 2010.

Jones, Collin. *Paris: Biography of a City*. New York. Penguin, 2004.

Kavanagh, Thomas M. *Enlightenment and the Shadows of Chance: The Novel and the Culture of Gambling in Eighteenth-Century France*. Baltimore. Johns Hopkins University Press, 1993.

Kreilkamp, Vera. *The Anglo-Irish Novel and the Big House*. Syracuse, NY. Syracuse University Press, 1998.

———. "The Novel of the Big House." In *The Cambridge Companion to the Irish Novel*. Edited by John Wilson Foster. New York. Cambridge University Press, 2006.

Ledger, Sally. *The New Woman: Fiction and Feminism at the* Fin de Siècle. Manchester. Manchester University Press, 1997.

Lefebvre, Henri. *The Production of Space*. Translated by Donald Nicholson-Smith. Malden, MA. Blackwell, 2000.

Lehan, Richard. *The City in Literature: An Intellectual and Cultural History*. Berkeley, CA. University of California Press, 1998.

Lewis, Gifford. *Edith Somerville: A Biography*. Dublin. Four Courts Press, 2005.

Lukács, Georg. *A Theory of the Novel: A Historico-Philosophical Essay on the Forms of the Great Epic*. Translated by Anna Bostock. London. Merlin Press, 1971.

Mandel, Ernest. *Late Capitalism*. London. Verso, 1999.

Marx, Karl. *Capital: A Critique of Political Economy, volume I*. Translated by Ben Fowkes. New York. Penguin, 1990.

———. *Grundrisse: Foundations of the Critique of Political Economy*. Trans. Martin Nicolaus. New York: Vintage Books, 1973.

McCormack, W. J. "Introduction." *Ormond*. Edited by W. J. McCormack. Gloucester. Alan Sutton, 1990.

Meaney, Gerardine. "Decadence, Degeneration and Revolting Aesthetics: The Fiction of Emily Lawless and Katherine Cecil Thurston." *Colby Quarterly*. 36, no. 2 (2000): 157–75.

Miller, Andrew H. *Novels behind Glass: Commodity Culture and Victorian Narrative*. 1995. New York. Cambridge University Press, 2008.

Miller, Julia Anne. "Acts of Union: Family Violence and National Courtship in Maria Edgeworth's *The Absentee* and Sydney Owenson's *The Wild Irish Girl*." In *Border Crossings: Irish Women Writers and National Identities*. Edited by Katheryn Kirkpatrick. Tuscaloosa, AL. University of Alabama Press, 2000.

Miller, Tyrus. "'Glass before its Time, Premature Iron': Architecture, Temporality and Dreams in Benjamin's *Arcades Project*." In *Walter Benjamin and*

The Arcades Project. Edited by Beatrice Hanssen. New York. Continuum, 2006.
Milne, Anna-Louise. "Introduction: The City as Book." In *The Cambridge Companion to the Literature of Paris*. Edited by Anna-Louise Milne. New York. Cambridge University Press, 2013.
Moore, Sean D. *Swift, the Book, and the Irish Financial Revolution: Satire and Sovereignty in Colonial Ireland*. Baltimore. The Johns Hopkins Press, 2010.
Moretti, Franco. *Atlas of the European Novel, 1800–1900*. Translated by Quintin Hoare. London. Verso, 1996.
——. *The Novel, Vol. I: History, Geography, and Culture*. Edited by Franco Moretti. Princeton. Princeton University Press, 2006.
——. *Signs Taken for Wonders: Essays in the Sociology of Literary Forms*. 2nd ed. London. Verso, 1988.
——. "'A Useless Longing for Myself': The Crisis of the European *Bildungsroman*, 1898–1914." In *Studies in Historical Change*. Edited by Ralph Cohen. Charlottesville, VA. University Press of Virginia, 1992.
——. *The Way of the World: The* Bildungsroman *in European Culture*. Trans. Albert Sbragia. London. Verso, 2000.
Muir. "'The Novice of Saint Dominick.' Rev. of The Novice of Saint Dominick, by Sydney Owenson." *Monthly Review; or, Literary Journal*. January 1807.
Murphy, Sharon. *Maria Edgeworth and Romance*. Dublin. Four Courts Press, 2004.
Nash, Catherine. "Remapping the Body/Land: New Cartographies of Identity, Gender, and Landscape in Ireland." In *Writing Women and Space: Colonial and Postcolonial Geographies*. Edited by Alison Blunt and Gillian Rose. New York. Guilford Press, 1994.
Norris, Clare. "The Big House: Space, Place, and Identity in Irish Fiction." *New Hibernia Review*. 8, no. 1 (2004): 107–21.
Ó Gallchoir, Clíona. *Maria Edgeworth: Women, Enlightenment and Nation*. Dublin. University College Dublin Press, 2005.
O'Toole, Fintan. "Going West: The Country Versus the City in Irish Writing." *The Crane Bag*. 9, no. 2 (1985): 111–16.
O'Toole, Tina. *The Irish New Woman*. New York. Palgrave Macmillan, 2013.
Oakman, Anne. "Sitting on 'The Outer Skin': Somerville and Ross's *Through Connemara in a Governess Cart* as a Coded Stratum of Linguistic/Feminist 'Union' Ideals." *Éire-Ireland*. 39, no. 1–2 (2004): 110–35.
Phillips, Richard. *Mapping Men and Empire: A Geography of Adventure*. New York. Routledge, 1997.
Poovey, Mary. *Genres of the Credit Economy: Mediating Value in Eighteenth- and Nineteenth-Century Britain*. Chicago, IL. University of Chicago Press, 2008.
Pratt, Annis. *Archetypal Patterns in Women's Fiction*. Bloomington, IN. Indiana University Press, 1981.

Pratt, Mary Louise. *Imperial Eyes: Travel Writing and Transculturation*. New York. Routledge, 2007.
Prendergast, Christopher. *Paris and the Nineteenth Century*. Cambridge, MA. Blackwell, 1995.
Reznicek, Matthew L. "Absurd Speculations: The Tragedy of Development in Maria Edgeworth's *Ormond*." *Nineteenth-Century Literature*. 71, no. 3 (2016): 291–314.
——. "He Should Go to the Théâtre François: Paris, the Theater, and Maria Edgeworth's *Ormond*." In *Travelling Irishness in the Long Nineteenth Century*. Edited by Christina Morin and Marguerite Corporaal. New York. Palgrave, Forthcoming 2017.
——. "These Irish Investments: Money as Organizing Principle in *As Music and Splendour* (1958)." *Women's Studies*. 44 (2015): 197–233.
Richard, Jessica. "'Putting Hazard to a Certainty': Lotteries and the Romance of Gambling in Eighteenth-Century England." *Studies in Eighteenth Century Culture*. 40 (2011): 179–200.
——. *The Romance of Gambling in the Eighteenth-Century British Novel*. New York. Palgrave Macmillan, 2004.
Richardson, LeeAnn M. *New Woman and Colonial Adventure Fiction in Victorian Britain: Gender, Genre, and Empire*. Gainesville, FL. University Press of Florida, 2006.
Robinson, Hillary. *Somerville & Ross: A Critical Appreciation*. Dublin. Gill and MacMillan, 1980.
Rose, June. *Mistress of Montmartre: A Life of Suzanne Valadon*. London. Richard Cohen Books, 1998.
Rothwell, Andrew. "Introduction." In *Thérèse Raquin*. New York. Oxford University Press, 1998.
Rowlinson, Matthew. *Real Money and Romanticism*. New York. Cambridge University Press, 2010.
Russell, Gillian. "Faro's Daughters: Female Gamesters, Politicians, and the Discourse of Finance in 1790s Britain." *Eighteenth-Century Studies*. 33, no. 4 (2000): 481–504.
Sennett, Richard. *The Fall of Public Man*. New York. Penguin, 1976.
Simeone, Nigel. *Paris: A Musical Gazetteer*. Ann Arbor, MI. Edwards Brothers, 2000.
Simmel, Georg. "Fashion." In *On Individuality and Social Forms*. Edited by Donald N. Levine. Chicago, IL. University of Chicago Press, 1971.
——. "The Metropolis and Mental Life." In *Reflections on Commercial Life: An Anthology of Classic Texts from Plato to the Present*. Edited by Patrick Murray. New York. Routledge, 1997.
——. *The Philosophy of Money*. Edited by David Frisby. New York. Routledge, 2011.

Spencer, Kathleen L. "Purity and Danger: Dracula, the Urban Gothic, and the Late Victorian Degeneracy Crisis." *ELH.* 59, no. 1 (1992): 197–225.
Stevens, Julie Anne. *The Irish Scene in Somerville & Ross.* Dublin. Irish Academic Press, 2007.
Szondi, Peter and Harvey Mendelsohn. "Tableau and Coup de Théatre: On the Social Psychology of Diderot's Bourgeois Tragedy." *New Literary History.* 11.2 (1980): 323–43.
Thomson, Heidi. "'The Fashion Not to be an Absentee': Fashion and Moral Authority in Edgeworth's Tales." In *An Uncomfortable Authority: Maria Edgeworth and her Contexts.* Edited by Heidi Kaufman and Chris Fauske. Newark, DE. University of Delaware Press, 2004.
Tracy, Thomas. "The Mild Irish Girl: Domesticating the National Tale." *Éire-Ireland.* 39, no. 1–2 (2004): 81–109.
Tynan, Katherine. "'Irishry' Review of *French Leave.*" *The Bookman.* August 1928: 265–66.
Wasserman, Renata R. Mautner. "Financial Fictions: Émile Zola's *L'Argent*, Frank Norris' *The Pit*, and Alfredo de Taunay's *O Encilhamento*." *Comparative Literature Studies.* 38, no. 3 (2001): 193–214.
Weekes, Ann Owens. *Irish Women Writers: An Uncharted Tradition.* Lexington, KY. University Press of Kentucky, 2009.
Whelan, Kevin. "Foreword: Writing Ireland/Reading England." *The Wild Irish Girl.* Edited by Claire Connolly and Stephen Copley. London. Pickering and Chatto, 2000.
Williams, Raymond. *The Country and the City.* 1973. New York. Oxford University Press, 1975.
Wilson, Elizabeth. *The Sphinx in the City: Urban Life, the Control of Disorder, and Women.* Berkeley, CA. University of California Press, 1992.
Wright, Julia. "'The Nation Begins to Form': Competing Nationalisms in Morgan's *The O'Brien's and the O'Flahertys*." *ELH.* 66, no. 4 (1999): 939–63.
———. *Representing the National Landscape in Irish Romanticism.* Syracuse, NY. Syracuse University Press, 2014.

Index

Abraham, Julie 139
Aguiar, Marian 146
ancien régime 11, 13, 39, 50, 67–68, 84, 91, 96, 99
Austen, Jane 11, 26, 29–30, 49, 66, 89

Bakhtin, Mikhail 3, 10, 160, 182
Balzac, Honoré 1, 2, 6, 8, 12, 27–28, 34, 36–37, 44–46, 51, 58, 60, 68, 74, 77–78, 106, 120, 123, 125–26, 139–43, 156, 163, 171, 187
    Comédie humaine 2, 15, 58, 60, 77, 125, 155–56, 163
    "Girl With the Golden Eyes" 139, 153
    Père Goriot 2, 7, 160
    see also Balzacian/fashionable *Bildung*
Balzacian/fashionable *Bildung* 12–13, 15–18, 22, 27, 45, 69, 96, 113–14, 120, 159
Barry, Kevin 80
Baudelaire, Charles 7, 15, 122, 150–52, 168, 170
Bell, David 15, 32, 45–46, 45, 48, 72, 74

Bell, Michael 8
Benjamin, Walter 2, 2n4, 6, 121–23, 168
Bhreathnach-Lynch, Síghle and Julie Ann Stevens 104, 111, 115, 134
Bildungsheld 10–11, 13–15, 17, 43, 67, 186–87
Bildungsroman
    see Balzacian/fashionable *Bildung*
    see classical/Goethean *Bildung*
    see economic *Bildung/sroman/ sromane*
    see women's *Bildung*
Bildungsromane
    see Balzacian/fashionable *Bildung*
    see classical/Goethean *Bildung*
    see economic *Bildung/sroman/ sromane*
    see women's *Bildung*
Boes, Tobias 88
Buckley, Jerome 7
Burke, Edmund 2, 5, 44, 66–68, 76, 79, 87, 91–94, 100
Butler, Judith 142
Butler, Marilyn 63, 142

Campbell-Ross, Ian 20, 24
capital
　financial 16–17, 20, 23–24, 39–40, 51, 70, 72–75, 80, 93–95, 99–101, 110–11, 113–14, 116–17, 119, 121, 123, 127, 136, 156
　social 72–73, 79–82
capitalism 3, 5–10, 12–17, 19–24, 27, 31n5, 37, 39, 41, 43, 45, 47–49, 51, 52–53, 55, 57, 60–61, 65–70, 72–77, 80, 84, 93, 95, 103, 105–06, 114, 116, 119–21, 129, 138, 140, 147, 149–50, 156, 168, 172
Catani, Damian 77
De Certeau, S.J., Michel 6, 148–52, 154, 157, 159, 162, 168–70
Chakrabarty, Dipesh 33
Cheah, Pheng 34
classical/Goethean *Bildungsroman* 10–13, 15, 19, 22, 27, 30–31, 48–49, 56, 60, 63, 65, 68–70, 82, 87–89, 94–96, 100–02, 181–82, 187
commodity/ies 13, 15, 17, 18, 20, 28, 33, 37, 39, 42–43, 45, 47–48, 53, 55, 67, 69–73, 79, 82–84, 86–87, 92, 95, 99, 122, 126–28, 131–32, 135, 147–48
　see also fashionable commodity
consciousness 71
　collective 45
　self-awareness 56
Cook, Roger 71
Copeland, Edward 8–9
Corkery, Daniel 4
Cosgrove, Peter 88

Daly, Nicholas 167
Davidoff, Leonore and Catherine Hall 111–12
Deane, Seamus 3–6, 41, 67–68, 79
debt 9, 29, 34, 36, 39–61, 80, 94, 101, 110, 122
Descamps, Marc-Alain 43–44, 81, 92
Dickens, Charles 27, 34, 36, 68, 106
Diderot, Denis 82–83, 85–86, 88, 98

economic *Bildung* 10
economic *Bildungsroman* 7, 9–10, 13, 27, 29, 40, 47, 55, 60, 66, 101, 105
economic *Bildungsromane* 7, 102, 113
economics
　women as agents and participants of economy 7–9, 18, 24, 27, 39, 41, 50–51, 57, 103, 111–12, 114, 121, 129, 136, 138, 173–74
　see also capital
　see also capitalism
　see also debt
　see also economic *Bildung*
　see also money
Edgeworth, Maria
　The Absentee 74, 45, 63, 65–66, 74, 98
　Ormond 9, 13, 15–17, 19–20, 22, 24, 63–102, 106, 113, 137, 140, 158
　Tales of Fashionable Life 56
Ellis, Lorna 29–30, 140
the Enlightenment 64–65, 67–68, 82–83, 85–89, 93, 98

fashion
　clothing and dress 12, 15, 20, 39, 43–45, 47–49, 57, 67, 71, 73, 126
　fashionable commodity 16–17, 32, 48, 73, 78, 83–84, 86–87, 113
　fashionable society 1, 18, 15, 56, 72, 74, 80, 83–84, 86
　as trend or *au courant* 50–51, 57, 68, 74, 81, 82, 85–95, 98–100, 113, 120, 131, 185
　see also Paris as fashionable
Ferris, Ina 19
Finn, Margot 34, 52, 79–80, 94, 101, 111
Foley, Timothy P. 9
Foster, R. F. 110
Fraiman, Susan 7–9
Frawley, Oona 130

Gallois, William 8–9, 23, 38, 112, 129, 143, 147–48
geography of Paris
   arrondissement(s) 58, 125–26, 144, 156, 158, 160, 179, 184–87
   Latin Quarter/Quartier Latin 2, 106, 125–26, 128, 133, 135, 187
   Left Bank 2, 26, 41–42, 56, 160
   Montmartre 159–64, 171, 174, 179–80
   Right Bank 56, 160, 186
   Seine 1–2, 41–42, 47, 57, 63, 125, 160, 184
   Sorbonne 47, 120, 125, 156, 186–87
   Versailles 71, 183–85
Gilbert, Sandra M. and Susan Gubar 175, 175n152
von Goethe, Johann Wolfgang 11, 13, 16n67, 19n78, 22, 27, 30, 34, 49, 88n117, 88–89, 95–96, 168n120, 178, 182
   see also classical/Goethean Bildung/Bildungsheld/Bildungsroman
Greengrass, Mark 31
Grubgeld, Elizabeth 110

Harvey, David 2, 14–15
Hewitt, Nicholas 161
Hirsch, Marianne 175–76, 178
Hobsbawm, Eric 146

Johnson, James H. 59
Johnson, Julie 133, 166, 173, 175
Jones, Collin 41–42

Kavanagh, Thomas M. 75, 93–94
Kreilkamp, Vera 107

labor 12–14, 27, 37–38, 42, 45, 47, 74, 112, 123, 126, 155, 183
Ledger, Sally 143, 167–68
Lefebvre, Henri 156, 158
Lehan, Richard 123

Lewis, Gifford 115
Lukács, Georg 77, 120n81

McCormack, W. J. 22, 66
Mandel, Ernest 12, 20
marketplace 7–10, 14, 16, 18, 21–24, 30, 34, 36, 38, 40, 44, 46, 54–55, 66, 68, 73, 75–78, 82, 89, 102, 114, 117–24, 127, 129, 134–37, 147
Marx, Karl 14, 17, 23, 33, 55, 73, 79
   3 dramatis personae 23, 39, 55, 79, 123, 127, 136
Meaney, Gerardine 141–42
Miller, Andrew H. 128
Miller, Julia Anne 19n73
Milne, Anna-Louise 41
money 8, 12, 14–18, 20, 30, 33, 39, 46, 52, 54, 57, 68–70, 72, 74–79, 87, 94, 99, 100, 106, 112–18, 120, 124, 127, 136, 141
   see also capital (financial)
Moore, George 110
Moore, Sean D. 76
Moretti, Franco 2–3, 6, 8–10, 12–13, 15–16, 23, 25–27, 30–31, 36–37, 40, 44, 49, 51, 63, 65–66, 68–69, 74, 78, 82, 106, 113, 120, 125–26, 137, 155, 158, 162, 177, 121–23, 186–87
Murphy, Sharon 166, 172

Norris, Clare 4

O'Brien, Kate 180–87
Ó Gallchoir, Clíona 64, 71n26, 73, 87, 90
O'Toole, Fintan 3–4
O'Toole, Tina 23–24, 108, 142, 177
Oakman, Anne 104
Owenson, Sydney 12, 17, 19, 19n78, 20n81, 21–23, 69, 103, 106, 123
   The Novice of Saint Dominick 15, 17, 20–22, 25–62, 68, 83, 118
   The O'Briens and the O'Flahertys 20–22, 24–62, 69–70

Paris
    as fashionable society 42, 56, 84, 87, 96, 98, 122, 161
    see also geography of Paris
Phillips, Richard 145
Poe, Edgar Allen 122, 139–40, 143, 171
Poovey, Mary 16, 75, 94
Pratt, Annis 8
Pratt, Mary Louise 157–58, 160, 162, 164–65
Prendergast, Christopher 2n4, 6, 77, 123, 157–58, 162

Richard, Jessica 49, 75, 101
Richardson, LeeAnn M. 144–45, 151, 161
Richardson, Samuel 50, 73
Robinson, Hillary 104
Rose, June 132
Rowlinson, Matthew 16, 100

Sennett, Richard 51–52, 83–85, 137
Shakespeare, William 144–45
Simmel, Georg 6, 9–14, 19, 27, 37–39, 47, 54, 68, 78, 83–84, 90, 112–13, 116–17, 119, 121, 123, 128, 137, 146, 151–53, 168, 170
socialization 13–15, 27, 30–31, 48, 50, 88–89, 92, 94–95, 113, 116, 158, 183
    -formation 7–11, 22–23, 63–64, 66–67, 72, 88–89, 96, 99, 113–14

society and women 8, 11, 16–17, 19–20, 38, 41, 53, 81, 83, 110–11, 114, 118, 121, 128, 132–35, 141–43, 152–53, 161, 163, 166–67, 171, 173–75, 177, 180
socioecomic(s) 5, 8, 13–14, 16, 18–19, 21–23, 32–36, 42, 44–46, 52–53, 55, 57, 60, 64, 67–68, 72–73, 79–80, 82, 87, 89, 92–95, 100, 105–08, 110–11, 123–26, 131, 133, 136, 142
    see also capitalism
Somerville, Edith Œ and Martin Ross 4, 12, 15, 17, 19–20, 23–24, 27, 72, 89, 103–38, 103n1, 141, 172, 173
Stevens, Julie Anne 104

Thurston, Katherine Cecil 12, 15, 17, 19, 23–24, 106, 108, 121, 139–80
Tynan, Katherine 104

Weekes, Ann Owens 21
Williams, Raymond 130
Wilson, Elizabeth 167
women's *Bildung* 8–10, 18, 27, 29, 31, 56, 60, 102
Wright, Julia 4, 59

Zola, Émile 6, 8–9, 12, 27, 46, 51, 58, 68, 106, 126, 129, 131–32, 157–59, 162, 164, 167

www.ingramcontent.com/pod-product-compliance
Lightning Source LLC
Chambersburg PA
CBHW021353300426
44114CB00012B/1202